The Potential of Picturebooks

FROM VISUAL LITERACY TO AESTHETIC UNDERSTANDING

BARBARA Z. KIEFER
Teachers College Columbia University

Merrill,
an imprint of Prentice Hall

Englewood Cliffs, New Jersey   *Columbus, Ohio*

Library of Congress Cataloging-in-Publication Data
Kiefer, Barbara Zulandt.
    The potential of picturebooks : from visual literacy to aesthetic
understanding / Barbara Z. Kiefer.
       p.   cm.
    Includes bibliographical references and index.
    ISBN 0-02-363535-5
    1. Picture books for children—Educational aspects. 2. School
children—Books and reading. I. Title.
LB1044.9.P49K54   1995
372.13'2—dc20

94-9782
CIP

Editor: Linda James Scharp
Production Editor: Sheryl Glicker Langner
Photo Editor: Anne Vega
Text and Cover Designer: Patti Okuno
Production Manager: Pamela D. Bennett
Electronic Text Management: Marilyn Wilson Phelps, Matthew Williams,
    Jane Lopez, Karen L. Bretz

This book was set in Galliard by Prentice Hall and was printed and bound by Von Hoffmann
Press, Inc. The cover was printed by Von Hoffmann Press, Inc.

© 1995 by Prentice-Hall, Inc.
A Simon & Schuster Company
Englewood Cliffs, New Jersey 07632

Photo credits: Photography by Scott Cunningham. Cunningham/Feinknopf photography.

Printed in the United States of America

10 9 8 7 6 5 4 3 2 1

ISBN 0-02-363535-5

Prentice-Hall International (UK) Limited, *London*
Prentice-Hall of Australia Pty. Limited, *Sydney*
Prentice-Hall Canada Inc., *Toronto*
Prentice-Hall Hispanoamericana, S.A., *Mexico*
Prentice-Hall of India Private Limited, *New Delhi*
Prentice-Hall of Japan, Inc., *Tokyo*
Simon & Schuster Asia Pte. Ltd., *Singapore*
Editora Prentice-Hall do Brasil, Ltda., *Rio de Janeiro*

PREFACE

As a child, when my head wasn't bent over a paint box it was usually buried in a book, and it seems fitting that some of my clearest memories of childhood involve art and books. I remember our district art teacher, Miss Trapann, who came each Friday with special materials and an art lesson! I recall the images in several favorite picturebooks that I would pore over in awed fascination. When I began reading novels, I loved the white space at the beginning of each chapter, an invitation to visualize the words of the author with my own un-accomplished drawings. (Librarians will be happy to know that I only drew in the books I owned and not those I borrowed.)

There was never any doubt in my mind that I wanted to be an artist, so I obtained a BA in Art Education. I loved every minute of my studio courses but was less enthusiastic about my education requirements. When I married an Air Force pilot just after graduation, however, I learned one of the first lessons of life in the arts: There weren't many jobs teaching art. Therefore, I began substituting in elementary schools and found I loved teaching. The elementary school curriculum allowed me plenty of opportunities to explore art with children and also to explore the wider world of history and science and other areas of interest. I knew I needed to read to children and share my love of books if I expected them to become readers. Therefore, I went back to school to pick up the courses necessary for certification. I taught a transitional first/second grade class in Japan, a second grade class in Ohio, and fourth and fifth grades in California. Substituting in grades K through 12 when I wasn't teaching full time gave me a wide range of experience and helped me make connections across grade levels.

When my husband was killed in an aircraft accident I had to make some serious decisions about my future instead of our future. I thought about going back to school to study interior design. I seriously considered buying an art gallery. I took more lessons in watercolor painting and sustained myself with my paint box once again. But I realized that teaching was the most exciting and fulfilling thing I had ever done, so I prepared myself to teach again, first with a master's degree and certification as a reading specialist. Then I looked for a place where I could find answers to all the questions I still had about how children learn to read and where I might combine my love for children's literature with studies in art.

I wrote to Charlotte Huck, the author of my well-thumbed children's literature text, asking whether such a place existed. She wrote back and invited me to apply to the doctoral program at Ohio State. There, with the help of Ken Marantz, then chair of the Art Education Department, and Charlotte, I was able to put together a program of studies that centered on literature, the arts, and language and literacy. My studies and my dissertation on children's responses to picturebooks grew out of my passion for art and books and my interests in children and learning. Since that time I have continued to study children and their picturebooks and to read, listen to, and explore ideas about making art and viewing art, particularly the art of the picturebook.

This book, then, offers a variety of avenues for exploring the potential of the picturebook. It is not limited to any single audience. Although many of the ideas presented will interest teachers and librarians, it is hoped that art educators and parents may find the theories and practices useful as well. The book's content should be accessible to those trained in art as well as those with very little formal training. Finally, the implications of research and the suggestions for practice that I discuss here are not limited to younger children. They are meant to embrace an audience of middle and secondary students as well as adults.

Although the format of the printed verbal text requires a linear progression from the first page to the last, as shown in the table of contents, there is a spatial quality to the book's organization that is in keeping with its subject matter. Therefore, just as the eye can enter a picture at any point, I invite my readers to choose their own point of entry into this book—to look, for example, through the pictures first or to read the practical suggestions in the last part of the book before digging into chapters on children's responses or style in picturebooks. To this end I have included a visual map of the books contents for those who are more spatially inclined.

A History of the Picturebook
The first picturebooks
A new book form
A new technology
Picturebooks for children
Advances in printing techniques
Into the 20th century

Style in Picturebooks:
A Theory of Criticism
The aesthetic nature of the picturebook
Style in art
Style in picturebooks
Evaluating picturebooks

Creating a Picturebook
The process of creation
Learning from illustrators:
Tomie dePaola, John Steptoe,
Trina Schart Hyman

The Art of the
Picturebook

Classroom Connections
Exploring the art of the picturebook
Exploring an illustrator's work
Exploring media
Book making and publishing
Folktale comparisons
Holding a mock Caldecott Award
The art of the word
Picturebooks for older students
The book arts of the Middle Ages
Beyond the classroom, into the museum

THE POTENTIAL
OF
PICTUREBOOKS

Children and
Picturebooks

Studying Children and Picturebooks
What is a picturebook?
Picturebooks as contexts for literacy learning
Picturebooks and children's preferences
Picturebooks: New directions

Children's Responses To Picturebooks
A framework for response:
How children choose picturebooks
How children look at picturebooks
How children respond to picturebooks
How children talk about picturebooks
What children see in picturebooks:
The development of aesthetic awareness

Developing a Context for
Response to Picturebooks
The role of picturebooks
The role of the teacher

ACKNOWLEDGMENTS

The picture of children, artists, and picturebooks that I present here has been a work in progress for many years. As I visited classrooms and wrote articles and chapters, my thinking about picturebooks was shaped and my perceptions deepened. Or, to use the language of the painter, an undercoat was laid, broad areas sketched out, and details colored in bit by bit. Although I am sure that my understandings about picturebooks and children's responses will continue to grow, the present volume represents an important stage of development in those understandings and would not have been possible without the help of some special people.

I must thank Charlotte Huck and Kenneth Marantz for their warm support; I don't believe that I ever would have reached this point without their unique insights about children and picturebooks. I must also thank my other important teachers, the children and adults in the classrooms I have visited over the years. Although names of children and teachers have been changed in the book, I'm particularly grateful to Marlene Harbert, Jenna Hodges, and Janine Hoke, who gave me access to their classrooms as well as insight into children's responses.

I am indebted to my friends, Dan Darigan, Susan Hepler, and Laura Smolkin for helping me make connections between picturebooks and other art forms and to Dan for creating the italic alphabet shown in Chapter 7. My appreciation is also due to Heidi Grant who gave me so much of her time, her good ideas, and her cheerful support and to the editors at Merrill/Prentice Hall, who helped me through this book with their patience, good humor, hard work, and helpful advice.

I would especially like to thank the reviewers of this text for their valuable suggestions and comments: Pose M. Lamb, Purdue University; Susan A. Burgess, Framingham State College; Patricia J. Cianciolo, Michigan State University; Judith Hillman, St. Michael's College; and Patricia P. Kelly, Virginia Tech.

Finally I want to thank my mother, Irene Shoemaker Zulandt. As a child I would take the drawings from her life drawing classes at Pratt Institute out of the closet where they were carefully stored and study them with fascination. She did not pursue a career in art as she had originally intended, but I like to think that her talents have been passed on to me in some small part, fulfilled in ways that have surprised us both but have also given us both joy and satisfaction.

AUTHOR PROFILE

Barbara Kiefer is an Associate Professor in the Department of Curriculum and Teaching at Teachers College, Columbia University where she teaches courses in Reading and Children's Literature. Originally trained in art education, she taught grades one, two, four, and five in several regions of the United States and in overseas schools. She is particularly interested in the role that picturebooks play in developing children's literacy, literary, and aesthetic understandings and has studied children's response to picturebooks extensively. She has served as chair of the Elementary Section Committee of the National Council of Teachers of English and as a member of the NCTE Executive Board, and was a member of the 1988 Caldecott Award Committee of the American Library Association. She has also chaired the Children's Book Council/International Reading Association Joint Committee which oversees the IRA Children's Choices project and the NCTE/CLA Notable Trade Books in the Language Arts Committee. She has published articles and book chapters about reading and children's literature in books and professional journals, created the cover art for *Children's Literature in the Classroom: Extending Charlotte's Web* and is co-author of the book, *An Integrated Language Perspective in the Elementary School: Theory Into Action*.

CONTENTS

I
Children and Picturebooks 1

1
Studying Children and Picturebooks 3

2
Children's Responses to Picturebooks 15

5
Creating a Picturebook   *91*

6
Style in Picturebooks: A Theory of Criticism   *115*

III
Picturebooks in the Classroom   *143*

7
Classroom Connections   *145*

APPENDIX A
Exploring the Art of the Picturebook

APPENDIX B
Exploring the Books of Tomie dePaola

APPENDIX C
Sources for Art Materials and Information

APPENDIX D
Picturebooks for Older Students

GLOSSARY

CHILDREN'S BOOK'S REFERENCES

REFERENCES

INDEX

PART

I

Children and Picturebooks

CHAPTER

1

Studying Children and Picturebooks

A mother settles herself in a rocking chair and positions a baby on her lap, nestling her in the crook of her arm. She opens the cover of Margaret Wise Brown's *Goodnight Moon* and begins to read. The child, sucking contentedly on one thumb, uses her other hand to point to the red balloon, the little mouse, and the tiny kittens pictured there as mother reads the familiar refrain. Although the child doesn't speak yet, she is participating in a communicative act, learning the forms of social interaction and seeing the symbolic representation of her world on the printed page.

A father enters the children's room of a library in the inner city followed by two preschoolers. Because they have arrived early for story hour, he picks up John Steptoe's *Stevie* from a display of books and sits down at a nearby table to read with the children. The youngest climbs on his lap, while the other sits close to his side. As he reads, their eyes are held by the vivid colors of Steptoe's illustrations. Although the children are not reading fluently yet, they are participating in a literacy event, helping to turn the pages, asking questions about the story, and sharing the enjoyment that their father has for books.

A teacher is sitting on a chair surrounded by a class of children. She takes out Maurice Sendak's *Outside Over There*. "I have a special storybook to share with you," she says. "Please come up close, very very close. It's one of *those* books." As she begins reading, some of the children do not move their eyes from the pictures for a moment. Others look first to the pictures, then back to her face in a continual, rhythmic movement. Still others, further back in the group, see the smallest detail and remember it. The teacher reads, pausing often for their comments or their silent looking.

These children are part of a community of readers. Today and in the coming days and weeks they will use language to talk and write about their reactions to the book. They will use art, drama, and other means to represent their thoughts and feelings, and over time their responses will deepen and grow. They share with the baby and the preschoolers something beyond the mere hearing of words or reading of pictures and printed text. In the event that surrounds the reading of a picturebook, each participant is called upon to engage in interchange of intellect and emotion, an experience that is at once communal and individual and that transcends time and place (Figure 1.1).

Indeed, scenes like these are timeless. We might have found a similarly rapt audience in front of the cave paintings at Lascaux, 15,000 years ago, eyes centered on the paintings of animals as a shaman narrated stories of the hunt. Or we can turn to the Warlpiri culture in the western Australian deserts today where artists create paintings on bark or in sand to reenact the "dreamings," mysteries of their culture that connect them to their ancestors and to their land.

The importance of the visual/verbal experience described is no less powerful because it is mainly experienced by children in Western culture. Suzanne Langer has argued, "Image making is the mode of our untutored thinking and stories its earliest products" (1942, p. 145). The picturebooks of today bring together image and idea in a unique and vital art form that can be explored on many levels by adults and children alike.

FIGURE 1.1
Picturebooks introduce children to literacy, literature, and art.

Source: From GOODNIGHT MOON, text by Margaret Wise Brown. Pictures copyright © 1947 by Clement Hurd. Copyright © 1975 by HarperCollins Publishers; From STEVIE, by John Steptoe. Copyright © 1969 by John L. Steptoe. Reprinted by permission of HarperCollins Publishers; From OUTSIDE OVER THERE by Maurice Sendak. Copyright © 1981 by Maurice Sendak. Reprinted by permission of HarperCollins Publishers.

WHAT IS A PICTUREBOOK?

The picturebook has taken various forms over the centuries. Today library shelves are likely to contain alphabet and counting books, "toy" books (those that can be patted, pulled, or otherwise manipulated), concept books, information books, and storybooks, all of which have pictures that play a major role. In addition, many chapter books or novels for children include illustrations. It's not surprising then that there are an abundance of definitions of the picturebook and no little confusion on the part of adults as to what constitutes a picturebook.

A question that adds to this confusion is whether picturebooks are to be considered literature (see Groff, 1974, and Landes, 1985). Certainly picturebooks are covered most often in courses in children's literature rather than in art history or modern art. Art educator Ken Marantz argues, however, that "picturebooks are not literature (i.e., word dominated things), but rather a form of visual art. . . . The picturebook must be experienced as a *visual/verbal entity* [emphasis added] if its potential values are to be realized" (1977, p. 150). Similarly, illustrator Uri Shulevitz suggests that "A true picturebook tells a story mainly or entirely with pictures. When words are used they have an auxiliary role" (1985, p. 15).

In her introduction to *American Picturebooks: From Noah's Ark to the Beast Within*, Barbara Bader explains:

> A picturebook is text, illustrations, total design; an item of manufacture and a commercial product; a social, cultural, historical document; and foremost an experience for a child. As an art form it hinges on the interdependence of pictures and words, on the simultaneous display of two facing pages, and on the drama of the turning page. (1976, p. 1)

Illustrator Barbara Cooney (1988) likened the picturebook to a string of pearls. She suggested that the pearls represent the illustrations, and the string represents the printed text. The string is not an object of beauty on its own, but the necklace cannot exist without the string. Although in picturebooks a verbal text should certainly be beautiful and bring pleasure in and of itself, Cooney's analogy supports the idea of the *interdependence* of pictures and text in the unique art object that is a picturebook.

Therefore, for purposes of discussion in this book, the umbrella term *picturebook* will include those books in which the pictures could be thought of as pearls. This term will embrace formats such as concept books or wordless picturebooks (where there is a theme or meaning that unifies the images) as well picture storybooks (in which pictures and words tell a story). Outside this umbrella lies the illustrated book, one where the occasional picture is present to add to the words but is not necessary to our understanding of the book. This is another jewel altogether.

I would argue, then, that the picturebook is a unique art object, a combination of image and idea that allows the reader to come away with more than the sum of the parts. We can no more look at a single illustration in the book or examine the words without the pictures than we can view 5 minutes of a 2-hour film or see an opera without hearing the singers' voices and say we have experienced the whole. The picturebook is unique, and our experience of it will be something magical and personal, one that will change with each reading, "each time a little different as metaphors grow richer" (Marantz, 1977, p. 151).

PICTURES AS CONTEXTS FOR LITERACY LEARNING

Having defined the picturebook as a unique form of art, we can begin to explore its potential. Indeed, as central as picturebooks are in the lives of many young children and as visually engaging as they can be for older children immersed in visual images of today's world, the opportunities for developing literacy, literary, and aesthetic understandings through picturebooks are tremendous. Too often, however, the research surrounding children and picturebooks has not recognized the full range of contributions picturebooks may bring to children's lives.

Writing and Reading

By focusing on the development of children's language, reading, and writing abilities in the context of picturebook reading, many studies of children and picturebooks have neglected what may be the book's major attribute, the visual context it provides for learning. Certainly, picturebooks have long been a staple in many homes and early childhood programs. Moreover, research shows that children who are read to in the preschool and early grades gain significantly in language and literacy development over the years (Cazden, 1966; Wells, 1986). We can assume that the type of book most often being read to preschoolers is the picturebook rather than illustrated or unillustrated chapter books or novels.

However, little is known about how the illustrations in picturebooks affect children's development in writing. Researchers have certainly shown that engagement with visual symbols is essential and integral to children's early written products. The opportunity to create art seems to offer children a context for creating both oral and written texts (Caldwell & Moore, 1991; Dyson, 1989; Graves, 1975; Hubbard, 1989). We also know that the illustrations in books can stimulate children's oral language (Gambrell & Sokolski, 1983; Manzo & Legenza, 1975). Yet few studies have looked at the contributions that the illustrations in picturebooks may make to children's knowledge of story structure, their use of vocabulary, or the inclusion of descriptive details in their writing.

The art in picturebooks is also neglected in many studies of reading. For example, studies of emergent reading often focus attention on the verbal aspect of the storybook reading sessions. In many analyses, researchers devise complex categories for discourse on the printed verbal text and limit comments about the illustrations to one or two categories (Harker, 1988; Yaden, Smolkin, & Conlon, 1989).

Even when illustrations are the focus of reading comprehension or word recognition studies, researchers often isolate words and pictures from the context of the whole book or story, destroying the aesthetic nature of the book. In one such study, Samuels presented groups of kindergartners with four words on index cards, with and without pictures. The "no picture" group gave significantly more correct responses to the printed words than did the "words and pictures" group. Samuels (1970) concluded that pictures interfered with word learning and recommended that books for beginning readers contain no illustrations.

Reading researchers of the 1960s and 1970s were so intent on helping children acquire reading *skills* at the expense of any other understanding (e.g., aesthetic) that Patrick Groff issued this scathing attack on picturebooks. "There was a time not so long ago," he lamented, "when picturebooks for preschoolers gave more space to words than to illustrations. . . . Back then the text was the important thing for the youngster who had yet to learn to read. The illustrations were used simply to clarify the text. With their bright colors they drew children to the words, the *important* [italics added] things that books are made of" (1973, p. 26). He goes on to state, "To the degree that it dilutes the opportunities for the child to respond to a word story, the modern picturebook becomes a nonliterary commodity. It can limit the child's interest in *real* [emphasis added] books and even impart a neutral or negative attitude towards words" (1973, p. 28). Although Groff argued that picturebooks were not literature, he didn't see them as an art form that could be just as important to the young child's understanding of literacy.

Fortunately, in recent years researchers have looked at reading in more holistic and natural contexts and have found evidence that illustrations in books *are* important to the reader's understanding. Schallert (1980) and Levin (1981), for example, conclude that both listening and reading comprehension were facilitated when illustrations overlapped and extended the printed words in books (a characteristic inherent in our definition of the picturebook as an aesthetic form).

Even with these understandings, however, reading researchers have not tapped the rich potential of the picture book. Instead, many studies of pictures in reading materials continue to focus on superficial analysis of the illustrations in textbook materials (Koenke, 1987; Tierny & Cunningham, 1984) rather than on understanding the possibilities that real picturebooks provide for a child's intellectual and emotional development.

Visual Literacy

Research on perception and visual literacy may be more directly related to the visual aspects of picturebooks. Fransecky and Ferguson (1973) define the visually literate person as one who is able to "discriminate and interpret the visible actions, objects and symbols, natural or man made, that he encounters in his environment" (p. 45). When responding to picturebooks, children must also discriminate and interpret what they see. This process involves their attention, their recognition, and finally their understanding.

A number of studies in perception and cognition help us to see how this process unfolds. William Miller, in a study conducted in the 1930s, concluded that young children see "relatively few of the items that make up a picture" (1936, p. 288). However, any parent or teacher who has read books like *Goodnight Moon* to children knows that even very young children pick out small details in illustrations and point them out at each reading. In describing the important role of picturebooks in the life of her multiply handicapped granddaughter, Dorothy Butler (1980) mentions Cushla's enthusiasm for finding the tiny parrot hidden in the illustrations of *But Where Is the Green Parrot?* by Thomas and Wanda Zacharias (Figure 1.2). When the book was first introduced to Cushla at about 18 months of age, she had to have help locating the bird. However, "thereafter she scanned each picture carefully, finding the parrot with great satisfaction" (p. 37).

Indeed, research has since shown that children *do* see small details. In fact, they seem to scan pictures differently than do adults. Coles, Sigman, and Chessel (1977) investigated the eye movements of preschool children (ages 3½ to 6½) and adults in an attempt to describe scanning strategies for geometric patterns. They found that

FIGURE 1.2
Children love finding the small details in books like *But Where Is the Green Parrot?*

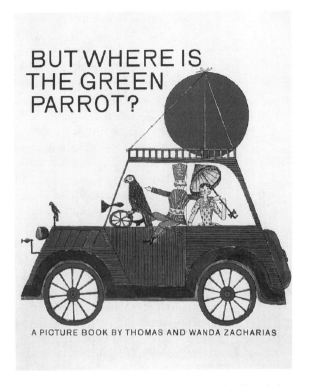

Source: From BUT WHERE IS THE GREEN PARROT? by Thomas and Wanda Zacharias. Translation copyright © 1968 by Sigbert Mohn Verlag in Gutersloh. Used by permission of Bantam Doubleday Dell Books for Young Readers.

adult scanning was more systematic and organized and that the youngest children were the least systematic and had longer eye fixations. They suggest, however, that this lack of systematicity "could be simply that the child is answering a different question to that understood by the adult; or it could be that he is deprived of two important aids—an adult tutor and his finger!" (pp. 126–127). Their findings may help explain why children ask for repeated readings of favorite storybooks. Their careful scanning of each page may represent a learning technique rather than a lack of maturity.

Another factor in becoming visually literate is the ability to recognize representations in a picture. There has been some argument about whether this ability is innate or learned. Hochberg and Brooks (1962) declared that by age 2 children can recognize representations in pictures when they have little or no prior experience with pictorial materials. In other contexts and cultures, however, this is not always the case. Sigel (1978) concluded that picture recognition was a cultural convention, although it was easily learned.

The seeds of this learning may lie in the cultural rituals like the nightly picturebook reading event. For example, Ninio and Bruner (1978) point to mother-and-child interactions during picturebook reading as a stepping stone to understanding representation, not only in pictures but in language as well. This early experience with pictures in the meaningful and supportive context of picturebook reading may be necessary to lay the foundation for visual literacy as well as literary and aesthetic understanding.

Such understandings may not be as easily acquired as perceiving and recognizing pictures. Jahoda, Deregowski, Ampene, and Williams (1977) suggested that difficulties in *comprehending* pictures are encountered when children must interpret relationships and activities depicted in pictures. Sigel (1978) cited a number of studies in which children had difficulty classifying and categorizing pictures. It seems unlikely, however, that directly teaching such skills would improve picture comprehension (Cocking & Sigel, 1979). If, as Mandler and Robinson (1978) suggest, the schemata for comprehension are formed during real life experiences with stories, then the deepest understanding of pictures would come through real life experience with picturebooks.

Unfortunately, experts in the field of visual literacy have often neglected the potential of picturebooks to develop visual literacy, just as reading and writing researchers have overlooked the opportunities for language and literacy learning provided by picturebooks. Children live in a highly complex visual world and are bombarded with visual stimuli more intensely than most preceding generations. Yet few teachers spend time helping children sort out, recognize, and understand the many forms of visual information they encounter, certainly not in the same way teachers deal with print literacy (Considine, 1987).

Developments in teaching visual literacy, however, have often paralleled the skills-based approach found among reading specialists. In the mid-1960s, for example, Debes proposed a hierarchy of 35 visual competencies. They ranged from the ability to distinguish light from dark to the ability to read emotions in body language in pictures (Debes, 1970).

More recently, researchers have recognized the potential for the picturebook in developing visual learning strategies, yet visual literacy curricula often resembles the more traditional skills-based hierarchies. These hierarchies include such categories as the ability to observe details; the ability to infer and perceive; the ability to identify symbols, shapes, and colors; and the ability to generalize information. All these skills bring to mind the scope and sequence of skills found in reading textbooks (Murphy, 1992).

Some researchers suggest that visual literacy skills are meant to apply to the "reading" of all visual media, which would include road signs, advertisements, film, and video, as well as picturebooks (Considine, 1987). Even those who recognize that the picturebook can provide children with the basis for developing visual literacy suggest that "visual interpretations begin with the literal, the concrete, and then move to more abstract concepts" (Goldstone, 1989, p. 595).

Although well meaning, such approaches may underestimate the power of the picturebook to give rise to a variety of intellectual and emotional responses. These flow naturally from each child without regard to skill levels. Indeed, aesthetic understanding—the ability to ask "What is art?" and "What is my response to it?" (Brandt, 1989)—does not lend itself to skill levels. It evolves out of extended and personal experiences of and with art.

PICTUREBOOKS AND CHILDREN'S PREFERENCES

Over the years, then, the full potential of the picturebook has been neglected by literacy researchers. Yet, those who have purported to be interested in the art of the picturebook have also misunderstood both the picturebook's uniqueness as an art object and the child's ability as a meaning maker. We can begin to see this in the argument over the picturebook as literature or art. Too often it is reviewed as literature by those who know very little about art (Marantz, 1977). Reviews of picture books, for example, often give short shrift to the illustrations, mentioning them in a phrase or sentence and rarely taking into account their ability to convey meaning.

Moreover, for the better part of this century researchers studying children's reactions to the artistic qualities of the picturebook were simply asking what children liked. They most often tried to determine children's preferences in style, media, or content of illustrations for book publishers and purchasers. They used their findings to recommend that publishers produce books that met children's desires. But to determine whether, for example, children liked color or black and white pictures, researchers reduced their testing instruments to single pictures or slides. These controlled for the variables being studied and asked children to choose the picture that they liked best (Martin, 1931; Rudisill, 1952; Smerdon, 1976). Such studies found that children preferred color over black and white, realism over abstraction, and, in content, humorous rather than serious and familiar over fantastic or unfamiliar subject matter.

These studies, however, often lack an understanding of the integrated nature of picture and text that lies at the heart of our definition of the picturebook. Moreover, in many of these studies, children's reactions were observed only momentarily and not in the natural context that surrounds most book-reading events.

For example, Gerald Smerdon (1976) set out to investigate children's preferences for realism and abstraction. For his parameters, he used the representational illustrations in Ladybird Books (the closest U.S. equivalent are the illustrations in the Basal reading series of the 1950s) and the more abstract work of British illustrator Charles Keeping. Smerdon asked an illustrator to prepare 12 black and white drawings of a castle on a continuum from realistic to abstract. He then had a panel of adults rank these, and he identified the six pictures most often chosen to represent this continuum. Smerdon then flashed these pictures on a screen in pairs for 5 seconds (Figure 1.3). The 381 children from ages 6 to 15 were then asked to mark their

FIGURE 1.3
Smerdon's study used drawings from (a) realistic to (b) abstract to represent styles of illustration.

Source: From G. Smerdon (1976), "Children's preferences in illustration," in *Children's Literature in Education*, *20*, pp. 17-31. Reprint by permission of Insight Books, an imprint of Plenum Publishing Corp.

preferred picture in a response booklet. In this fashion, the artistic object and the picture-viewing event were simplified.

From this, Smerdon concluded that children preferred what the artist and most adults called "realistic" art, although younger children and some adolescents seemed to prefer less realistic forms. In defending his reasons for eliminating color as a variable, Smerdon stated that he hoped to reduce the emotional elements in their choices. Such meddling with artistic products, however, only removes the object of study further from its original form. Here, the investigator not only violated the artistic integrity of the picturebook, but he failed to consider that emotional response may be part of the child's interaction with the book, and, indeed, that reaction may need longer than 5 seconds to develop and deepen.

A problem with preference studies is that researchers do not take into account the complex nature of aesthetic response. It involves affective as well as cognitive understandings, and it may change over time (Beach, 1993; Purves & Beach, 1972; Rosenblatt, 1976). Nor do they consider the social and cultural nature of the picturebook reading, which is part of children's experience with picturebooks (Heath, 1983; Hickman, 1981).

Finally, many researchers may have neglected the power of the picturebooks to evoke emotional response. For example, some researchers work to understand how meaning is constructed linguistically in the context of picturebook reading (Sulzby, 1985; Teale, 1984; Wells, 1986). They certainly have contributed to our understanding of how pictures support or extend the meaning of the verbal text, but less about how books capture children's hearts as well as their minds. Yet the power of art to evoke emotions may be the picturebook's most significant contribution to children's cognitive and aesthetic understanding. Langer (1953) argued that artwork is an expression of the artist's idea.

> . . . something that takes shape as he articulates an envisagement of realities which discursive language cannot properly express. What he makes is primarily a symbol to capture and hold his own imagination of organized feeling, the rhythms of life, the forms of emotion. (p. 392)

This powerful quality of the visual art of the picturebook may be its greatest potential. We must consider this aspect of the picturebook as well as its power to instruct or inform, so that the question to ask ourselves is not, "How do picturebooks help children learn to read?" or "What kind of pictures do children like?" but "To what kind of picturebooks do they respond most deeply?" For it is this deeply felt response that may lead to children who develop a lifelong interest in books and a lifetime appreciation of art.

PICTUREBOOKS: NEW DIRECTIONS

Thus far we have looked at studies that have, for the most part, neglected to consider the potential of the illustrations in picturebooks and in many cases even failed to consider the very essence of the picturebook as an art object. Yet researchers in reading cognition and literature have contributed important understandings that may be applied to the study of picturebooks and may illuminate some of the approaches we might take to sharing picturebooks with children.

Educators realize that children are meaning makers, learning in active engagement with their surroundings (Halliday, 1975; Wells, 1986). These beliefs, founded on the work of John Dewey, Jean Piaget, and Lev Vygotsky, have been reaffirmed and supported by reading researchers who have shown that getting meaning from print involves an orchestration of strategies. The reader then becomes a co-constructor of meaning with the author, using knowledge of language systems (phonological, syntactic, and semantic), stories and other texts, and the world in general to understand the words on the printed page (Anderson, Reynolds, Schallert, & Goetz, 1977).

Even before the work of psycholinguists and sociolinguists led to the interest in "whole language," Louise Rosenblatt set the stage for parallel understandings in the field of literary response. As Rosenblatt argued in *Literature as Exploration*,

> The literary work exists in a live circuit set up between reader and text; the reader infuses intellectual and emotional meanings into the pattern of verbal symbols and those symbols channel his thoughts and feelings. Out of this process emerges a more or less organized imaginative experience. (1976, p. 25)

Rosenblatt's work has helped us to ask what children bring to the aesthetic experience and what their responses might tell us about the aesthetic process. In recent years, research in literary response has certainly revealed what a complex process this may be. Purves and Beach (1972), for example, suggest

> Response consists of cognition, perception, and some emotional or attitudinal reaction; it involves predispositions; it changes during the course of reading; it persists and is modified after the work has been read; it may result in modification of concepts, attitudes or feelings. (p. 178)

Presently these assumptions lie at the heart of many theories of response to literature and have important implications for any form of artistic response. Indeed, theory and research in the field of aesthetic response supports the complexity of the process, its basis in individual experience, and its roots in emotional as well as cognitive understanding.

CONCLUSION

This chapter has defined the picturebook and reviewed research relating to children and picturebooks. This research, with theories of literary and aesthetic response, sets the stage for looking at children, artists, and picturebooks from a new direction, one that values the child as a meaning maker and the picturebook as a rich source of intellectual and emotional meaning. In subsequent chapters we will see that the picturebook does indeed have great potential for engendering such meaning. We'll examine children's response to picturebooks in natural settings and explore the qualities of the picturebook that may lead children beyond visual literacy to the deepest aesthetic understandings.

CHAPTER

2

*Children's Responses
to Picturebooks*

When I turned to the picturebook as topic for research, the first question I asked was, "What kind of pictures do children like?" I soon discovered that many researchers before me had asked this question. However, as I read their research I found that this was a superficial question. Just as a nutritionist would be more interested in the dietary value of food than in what food children like, an educator is primarily concerned with the literary and artistic responses of children as part of a very complex process. Children might be lured to a table of books with the things they "like," but they would not make a very substantial meal with only The Berenstain Bears series (Berenstain) or *The Babysitter's Club* (Martin) night after night. Nor is it likely that such preferred fare would provide the essential ingredients for becoming lifelong, discerning readers.

It soon became clear that the questions I needed to ask were much more complex. Many studies did not see the picturebook as an art object in which images and text work together to create a product that is more than the sum of its parts. Researchers controlled for variables like color or content or realism and tested children with single pictures apart from the context of the whole book. Weiss, 1982, for example, presented words in meaningless strings, controlled for typeface and size, and manipulated picture placement by using blue rectangles to represent the illustrations. The study found that boys preferred the illustrations on the top of the page, and girls preferred the pictures on the bottom. Although it seems that only a Freudian psychoanalyst might be interested in such findings, Weiss suggested that teachers and librarians should be aware of such preferences and that book designers "should place illustrations either at the top or bottom of the page" (p. 405).

As the result of such studies, I decided that questions about children and picturebooks needed to take a new direction. I was fortunate to begin my studies when language and literacy researchers were starting to question traditional studies that sought to control complex variables, to provide "treatments," and to establish norms rather than uncover uniqueness.

Thanks to the work of psycholinguists and sociolinguists such as Ken and Yetta Goodman, Frank Smith, Courtney Cazden, and Del Hymes, literacy educators in the 1970s began to call for research in natural classroom settings, research that valued the complexity of linguistic processes and described those processes rather than pinpointed cause and effect. At the same time, Howard Gardner was developing his theory of multiple intelligences with colleagues at Harvard's Project Zero and researching the arts as ways of knowing (Gardner, 1982, 1988). The work of Louise Rosenblatt (1976, 1978) was receiving renewed attention, and Arthur Applebee (1978) was examining children's sense of story, relating their developing understanding of literature to Piagetian and Vygotskian notions of cognitive development.

In this climate, Janet Hickman (1979, 1981) conducted one of the first naturalistic studies of response to literature in an elementary school setting. She studied children in grades K through 5 in a school that used children's literature as the core of the curriculum. Hickman's work has served as a model for much of the literary response research conducted since then and has helped to frame my own thinking about studying children's response to picturebooks.

As a result of this research, I realized that instead of asking what children's probable preferences for styles of art, media, or pictorial content were, we needed to understand what was *possible* as they interacted with picturebooks. Such questions could only be answered by observing children in real classrooms, interacting with a variety of picturebooks, in contexts that would allow for full interchange among children, peers, and teachers over time.

To begin such a study I chose two first/second grade classrooms in alternative public schools in a suburb of Columbus, Ohio. The classrooms were modeled on the British informal system and might now be described as "whole language." Children's literature formed the core of the curriculum, with learning activities organized around themes. The use of reading, language arts, or other textbooks was not required, but there were between 300 and 500 picturebooks in the classroom libraries, supplemented by school library books when necessary.

The classroom day was organized around class meetings and integrated work times with time outs for "specials" such as art, music, and physical education. Several times a day the teachers read aloud to children and took time to discuss books with them. In addition, children had opportunities to read alone and with other children and to talk about books with each other throughout the day. They were also expected and encouraged to respond to books through art, writing, drama, and many other avenues and to share these book responses with each other and with the entire school. Classroom and hallway space was regularly filled with the colorful results of the children's responses to books and provided a lively display of their learning.

I entered these classrooms as an observer, for 10 weeks the first year and for 12 weeks the following year. At first, to let the children get used to me and to help me to understand what I was looking at and looking for, I stayed in the background. I noted behaviors and comments during read-aloud sessions and during individual and group work times in my field notebook. Transcriptions of taped class read-aloud sessions and discussions also became part of the data that I examined day after day.

After I had begun to identify several themes or domains of response, I also conducted and taped interviews with children. In one set of interviews, for example, I used two picturebooks that differed in style and content: Lloyd Bloom's black and white paintings for Chaffin's *We Be Warm Till Springtime Comes* and Janina Domanska's colorful abstracts for the predictable and poetic *What Do You See?* As I met with individual children, I asked them to show me how they liked to look at a new picturebook and to talk about each book as they looked through it.

I later read the class a Grimm's fairy tale without showing them the pictures and asked them to try to imagine pictures in their heads as I read aloud. Later I showed pairs of children three versions of the tale illustrated in different styles and media and asked them to talk through the books, asking questions like, "What are you thinking about as you look at these pictures?" (Figure 2.1).

As I reviewed field notes and transcripts of discussions and interviews, I first identified several general themes that I used to describe children's responses to picturebooks. Initially these themes or domains centered on the variations rather than similarities in children's responses, the changes in responses that I observed over time, and the stylistic and content differences among the picturebooks that were the focus of their studies and their responses. Later, as I conducted further observations and interviews, these initial categories were further refined, and I developed a descriptive framework for children's responses to picturebooks that I continue to find useful today (Figure 2.2).

Although I never attempted to quantify children's responses within this framework, it shaped my observations in other settings and with other populations. These

FIGURE 2.1
What Do You See? and *We Be Warm Till Springtime Comes* represent different styles and content.

Source: Reprinted with the permission of Macmillan Publishing from WHAT DO YOU SEE? by Janina Domanska. Copyright © 1974 Janina Domanska. Reprinted with the permission of
Macmillan Publishing from WE BE WARM TILL SPRINGTIME COMES by Lillie D. Chaffin,
illustrated by Lloyd Bloom. Illustrations copyright © 1980 by Lloyd Bloom.

further observations were conducted in a third/fourth grade combination classroom
in the same school I had initially visited in suburban Columbus; in a University
preschool in Houston, Texas; in a second grade class in an urban Houston school
with a multicultural population; and in a below-grade-level multi-cultural fifth grade
classroom in a suburban Houston school.

These observations and interviews suggest that picturebooks can be rich
sources for learning and response in all classrooms. The responses of children at various ages highlight developmental differences in their awareness of stylistic factors in
picturebooks. These differences can help teachers to develop children's critical aesthetic awareness and to deepen individual responses to picturebooks (Kiefer 1982,
1988).

The remainder of this chapter will detail the dimensions of children's responses
to picturebooks and the developmental factors relating to the art of the picturebook.

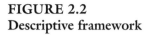

FIGURE 2.2
Descriptive framework

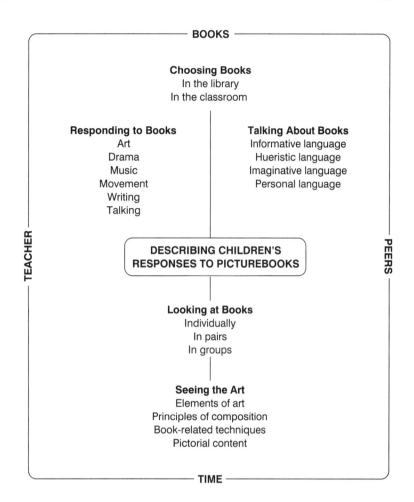

THE FRAMEWORK FOR RESPONSE: HOW CHILDREN CHOOSE PICTUREBOOKS

In most of the classrooms where I conducted observations, the children had many opportunities to choose and to read books. When, however, basal readers were the focus of lessons and there were few picturebooks in the classroom, I was able to collect only a limited amount of spontaneous data regarding children's responses to picturebooks. It seemed that the more picturebooks present and available to children, the greater the variety of responses.

This was true even among fifth graders, who might have been expected to consider picturebooks as books "for babies." The classroom was filled with picturebooks as part of a study arranged by their regular teacher and art teacher. The students chose picturebooks regularly and enthusiastically, talking about the books, writing about them in their journals, visualizing their responses, and conducting illustrator studies, all tied to that year's announcement of the Caldecott Award for distinguished illustration.

Even in classrooms and schools with extensive libraries, children often chose books that the teacher or librarian recommended or read to them. Many teachers created special displays to highlight books or offered books to children after they had been read aloud. One teacher would often close the read-aloud session by holding the book up and saying, "Who wants this book?" Invariably four or five hands would shoot up. If the teacher didn't volunteer the book, someone was sure to ask, "May I have that book?"

At other times children chose books because they were deeply interested in the topic, such as horses. They also gravitated to books that were displayed attractively, cover facing forward. In fact, the book shelves where they could see only the spines of books tended to be the last place the younger children would go to choose a book. On one occasion I watched several first and second graders head to the "S" books after the librarian had highlighted a book by Peter Spier. They were not looking for other books by Spier; they simply seemed to need some subtle adult guidance in choosing their books.

Children often used peer recommendations or relationships in choosing books to read. One first grade boy, getting ready to check out his library book, explained that he selected it simply because it was on the same shelf as the one his friend had picked. Indeed, Hepler and Hickman (1982) have emphasized the importance of creating a community of readers where peers opinions are valued and supported.

In many classrooms, books often get passed from child to child in a type of underground network that operates pretty much apart from the teacher. I found such a case with Hill's *Ms. Glee Was Waiting*, a book about a girl who seems to be making every attempt to get to her piano lesson at Ms. Glee's, but one disaster after another keeps her from arriving. The book, whose pictures contradict the events described by the printed text, did not make much of an impression the first time that it was read to first and second graders. However, when the teacher returned to it as part of a unit on time, one child noticed the changes on the clock from picture to picture. Several children found other "clues" in the pictures, and soon the book was being passed from child to child so that everyone could find the "secrets" in the pictures. Soon a group of children asked to create a mural of the book, and several children swore they had passed Ms. Glee's house on a field trip. The teacher played a subtle role in extending responses to the book, but the enthusiasm was certainly fired by the community of children who chose to pass this book around among themselves (Figure 2.3).

HOW CHILDREN LOOK AT PICTUREBOOKS

Observing children during read-aloud sessions and during individual or buddy reading provided information about the many ways that children used their eyes to look at books.

During read-aloud sessions with younger children, teachers usually sat on a chair in an open space in the room, gathering the children together at their feet. Teachers held the book at their shoulders with the pages facing outward, only occasionally placing the book in their laps where the children couldn't see the pictures as the words were read. During these sessions most teachers encouraged children to talk by asking questions or inviting questions and comments. The teachers did not

FIGURE 2.3
Children noticed the small clock and other details in
Ms. Glee Was Waiting.

Laura was late and Ms Glee was waiting,

Source: From MS. GLEE WAS WAITING by Donna Hill. Illustrations by Diane Dawson. Copyright ©
1978 by Donna Hill and Diane Dawson. Reprinted by permission of Atheneum Press.

seem to worry that children might "lose" the whole of the story. They often read the book again, or they summarized at the end of the reading.

During these sessions some children sat close to the teacher, their eyes intent on the pages or moving back and forth between the teacher's face and the book. Other children sat further away and appeared to give less attention to the book. Even these children, however, seemed to note small details in the illustrations despite their distance from the book, and they often called these details to the attention of their classmates. A second grade boy who had been sitting about 12 feet away from the teacher and who only seemed to be paying sporadic attention to Eric Carle's illustrations for Norma Green's *The Hole in the Dyke* nevertheless noticed that the small figure in the picture was wearing wooden shoes, a detail that most adults might have trouble seeing from that distance.

Children looking at books on their own also had idiosyncratic approaches. Some children looked through the entire book from front to back; others preferred starting at the back. Among first and second grade students, many of the "emergent" readers tended to preview the illustrations in the entire book before they read. Then, as they turned to each new page, they would also look at the picture before reading the printed text. When they came to a word or phrase they didn't know, they would often glance at the illustrations for help.

More fluent readers, on the other hand, seemed to proceed directly to the printed text on opening a book and gave less attention to the pictures. I observed two second grade boys reading Van Allsburg's *Jumanji* during their "buddy" reading time (a regular alternative to Sustained Silent Reading, where children read with a friend). When they first began reading the book, one of them covered most of the pictures with his elbow and the two would glance quickly at the illustration as they turned the page. Only as the story neared its climax did they turn to the illustrations and give them more attention.

HOW CHILDREN RESPOND TO PICTUREBOOKS

In many of the classrooms I visited, children were invited to respond to books in a variety of ways. These responses often took the form of class discussion or informal conversations. In addition, younger children often responded with physical movements or sound effects. For example, as a primary teacher read the words, "she charmed them with a captivating tune," from *Outside Over There* (Sendak), two boys chimed in with a rhythmic "duh, duh, duh." Later as the class discussed Sendak's rendering of a dog, a boy responded with a cheerful "Arf, Arf."

More elaborate responses to picturebooks often involved writing, art work, displays, puppetry, and dramatic presentations. Sometimes the format of the illustrations inspired the form of the response. For example, after several first graders had read Tomie dePaola's *The Comic Adventures of Old Mother Hubbard,* whose scenes are set behind a proscenium arch, the children decided to put on a puppet show of the story.

At times, teachers guided children toward a project. A fifth grade teacher, for example, asked children to use a comparison chart or a Venn diagram to evaluate the books they were judging as part of a mock Caldecott Committee. Just as often, however, children would suggest their own choices.

When the children chose to create art in response to a book, the choices included paintings, collages, murals, bas relief sculptures, soft sculptures, stitchery, and dioramas. Younger children seemed to use the illustrations in the book as a springboard for inspiration, although their finished products did not always resemble the original book. For example, children who created a mural from Pat Hutchins' *Clocks and More Clocks* included some of the details from the original story. However, their clock was filled with curlicues, and Hutchins' clock is angular and straight. Yet, they seemed to want to have the book close by as they worked; at one point the project came to a halt because *Clocks and More Clocks* was lost.

Older children, however, seemed to be more interested in studying the techniques of the artist. Third, fourth, and fifth graders often chose a medium that resembled the artist's original medium (e.g., chalk, collage, pastel, watercolor) and their responses often bore a striking resemblance to the original book. This may have been a learning technique. Certainly many artists have learned their craft by copying techniques of the old masters. This sort of response to a picturebook may help sharpen their technical understanding of art media at a time when they might otherwise become discouraged that their lack of technique interferes with their inner vision (Gardner, 1982) (Figures 2.4 and 2.5).

FIGURE 2.4
A first grader's response to
A Story, A Story by Gail
Haley

FIGURE 2.5
A fourth grader's response
to *The Crane Wife* by
Sumiko Yagawa

HOW CHILDREN TALK ABOUT PICTUREBOOKS

Children in all settings displayed an enthusiastic willingness to immerse themselves in the contents of their picturebooks, and verbal language seemed to give them the tools to understand these complex art objects. Thus, their verbal responses to picturebooks accounted for the greatest amount of data, which helped me understand the dimensions of response.

My field notes and transcripts of read-aloud sessions and interviews show that children used language for many different purposes as they talked about books within the larger social context of their classroom. These children were indeed "meaning makers" when it came to understanding the art of the picturebook. This realization recalled M. A. K. Halliday's work on language development, *Learning How to Mean* (1975). Several of his functions of language described the kinds of verbal responses that I was seeing in children.

Eventually I adapted four of Halliday's functions of language—the informative, heuristic, imaginative, and personal ones—to describe children's verbal responses to picturebooks. Using Halliday's general descriptions of each function, I developed a taxonomy that was refined as I reviewed data from subsequent studies. This is not a hierarchy, but a way of systematically describing the richness of the verbal data I examined (Table 2.1).

Informative Language

The first category, informative language, often served a telling function for children, with many of them literally pointing to the pictures as they spoke. A first grader looking at Ilse Plume's version of *The Bremen Town Musicians* (Grimm Bros.) pointed to the picture and stated, "Here's the dog and here's the cat and here's the donkey." Looking at Donna Diamond's illustrations for the same story, another first grader pointed to what was included in the pictures—"Here's the hen on the roof"—and what wasn't included—"This has no stars."

Other children used the pictures to retell or reconstruct events in the story. A first grader explained that in Domanska's *What Do You See?* "The water's sorta dark and the background is sorta dark and they have him diving in and then they're on the boat." Looking at Paul Galdone's version of *Hansel and Gretel*, a fifth grader explained "Here you see the witch looking right through the curtain. You don't even see the witch talking to them. You just see them sleeping there and the witch leaving and then you see her trying to get her [Gretel] to go in."

Informative language also encouraged children to compare the illustrations to other books or to the real world. Some wanted to point to what was on the page and then touch something similar in the world around them. A second grade child noticed the small game box under the tree on the title page of Van Allsburg's *Jumanji*. "That's like his other book," she told me, and indeed the box, an inch across, did seem to have the topiary figures that decorated the cover of Van Allsburg's first book, *The Garden of Abdul Gasazi*.

Comments such as "This looks like wood" or "This reminds me of that other book" were found at all age levels. Children often seemed to use these comparisons as a reality check. First and second graders, for example, looked at Domanska's expressionistic animals in *The Bremen Town Musicians* (Grimm Bros.) and stated, "Cats aren't usually pink and orange" or "I never seen a purple donkey" (Figure 2.6).

TABLE 2.1
Verbal responses to picturebooks

Primary Function	Subcategories	Examples
1. *Informative:* Provides information, a pointing or telling function.	1.1. Reports the contents of the illustration. 1.2. Provides information about art styles or techniques. 1.3. Describes or narrates pictured events. 1.4. Compares contents of the illustrations to something in the real world. 1.5. Compares one book to another.	"There's the witch." "He used brown." "You just see them sleeping there and the witch leaving and then you see her talking to them." "This looks like wood." "This looks like *Jumanji*."
2. *Heuristic:* Problem-solving function, includes wondering about as well as offering solutions.	2.1. Wonders about the events or contents of the illustrations. 2.2. Makes inferences about events, the setting, or a character's personality, motives, or actions. 2.3. Makes inferences about cause and effect or possible outcomes. 2.4. Makes inferences about the preparation of the illustrations—what the artist did. 2.5. Makes inferences about the illustrator's intentions.	"Couldn't they just sell the bed and buy food?" "This looks deep." "She looks mean." "If they stepped on a twig they would of got real hurt." "It looks like he used a little pencil line to just do little sketches for it." "He liked to use darker colors."
3. *Imaginative:* Recalling, creating, or participating in an imaginary world.	3.1. Enters into the world of the book as a character or onlooker. 3.2. Creates figurative language. 3.3. Describes mental images.	"The father looks like he's saying, 'Why do we have to leave them?' and she's going, 'Hah hah.'" "These [leaves] look like tropical birds." "This doesn't look the same as I thought."
4. *Personal:* Connecting to individual experience, reporting emotions, stating opinions.	4.1. Relates personally to events, setting, or characters. 4.2. Expresses feelings or describes personal effects of art elements. 4.3. Expresses opinions or evaluates the illustrations.	"I wouldn't of went up there with a snake up there." "Here she's yelling. My mom does that." "That makes me sad." "Darker colors give you a feeling of being scared." "He shoulda put a wart on her nose." "The pictures don't look so good here—it looks like he repeated. He just used orange and a grey."

Source: Reprinted by permission of Barbara Kiefer. In *Journeying: Children Responding to Literature*, edited by Kathleen Holland, Rachel A. Hungerford, and Shirley B. Ernst (Heinemann, a division of Reed Elsevier Inc., Portsmouth NH, 1993).

FIGURE 2.6
Children compared illustra-tions in *The Bremen Town Musicians* to their knowl-edge of the real world.

Source: Illustration from THE BREMEN TOWN MUSICIANS by the Brothers Grimm, translated by
Elizabeth Shub. Illustrations by Janina Domanska. Illustrations copyright © 1980 by Janina
Domanska. Reprinted by permission of Greenwillow Books, a division of William Morrow &
Co., Inc.

Many children were interested in the illustrator's techniques, and some used informative language to talk about the process of picture making as well as the content of the pictures. Not only did they talk about the elements of art ("He used brown"), but they remarked on also the particulars of picture layout and composition. For example, a first grader mentioned that Donna Diamond "gave a border to the picture" in *The Bremen Town Musicians*, and two fifth graders discussed eye movement in Lisbeth Zwerger's illustrations of *Hansel and Gretel* (Grimm Bros.) (Figure 2.7).

Kristen:	Here it looks sort of like a hill—how they've brought the color up.
Mark:	Maybe to shift your eyes.
Interviewer:	Do they kind of do that for you? Shift your eyes?
Kristin:	It depends on where the main part of the picture is . . .
Mark:	You see this [a tree] and then you follow there [to the right] and then you see the girl and then you're crazy to turn the page.

Heuristic Language

To reassure those who establish visual literacy checklists for higher level skills, we would only need to look at the many forms of the second function, heuristic language, generated by children in response to picturebooks.

FIGURE 2.7
Children talked about eye movements in Zwerger's illustrations for *Hansel and Gretel*.

Source: From HANSEL AND GRETEL illustrated by Lisbeth Zwerger. Illustrations copyright © 1979
by Lisbeth Zwerger. Reprinted by permission of William Morrow and Company.

Halliday (1975) referred to heuristic language as "the 'tell me why' function" (p. 20). For example, the second grader who asked "How could she fly?" about Maurice Sendak's heroine in *Outside Over There* received a quick reply from a classmate: "Because it's a magic cloak." A fifth grader questioned a discrepancy between the parents' poverty mentioned in the text of *Hansel and Gretel* and the rather cheerful setting pictured in an illustrated version. "I don't see why they don't have enough food. It looks like expensive beds. Couldn't they just sell the beds and buy seeds and plant food?" These remarks are typical of children who use the heuristic or problem-solving function to ask questions about illustrations or to make inferences or predictions about the events in a story or a character's motives.

Two fourth graders suggested that the storm at sea pictured in Sendak's *Outside Over There* represents the inner emotions of the heroine. "She has to take care of the baby and that's her responsibility and she feels bad and that's why the storm is there," they argued.

Two fifth grade boys discussed the children's lack of shoes in Galdone's version of Hansel and Gretel.

Colby:	I think they would have some kind of shoes for them because if they stepped on a twig they would have got real hurt.
Jay:	Well they were poor so they may not have been able to afford them.

Colby: See, they would have stepped on those pebbles and they'd be
                                 going down the path in real pain with those pebbles.

Anthony Browne's modern-day illustrations of *Hansel and Gretel* (Grimm
Bros.) evoked much speculation on the part of the fifth graders who examined the
book (Figure 2.8) Looking at the bedroom scene featured early in the book, one
child inferred, "It looks like the mom isn't really responsible because she throws her
clothes around." Another fifth grader suggested why the stepmother may want to
get rid of the children:

> In this story, she's the one getting all the attention and the money spent on her. See the
> makeup on her face? See how she's dressed and she has makeup and her hair is done? Is
> that a cigarette? And she's wearing high heels out in the forest and the leopard coat.
> They [the family] may be running out of money because all the money they spent on
> her.

In addition to using it to understand a story's elements, children used heuristic
language to make inferences about art techniques or the illustrator's intentions.
Looking at Zwerger's *Hansel and Gretel* (Grimm Bros.), a fifth grader explained,
"This looks like water color because how the bottom's real dark and it's, like, wet." A
fifth grader interpreted Paul Galdone's pictures for *Hansel and Gretel*.

FIGURE 2.8
Illustrations helped children
make inferences about the
stepmother in Anthony
Browne's version of the
Grimm's *Hansel and Gretel*.

Source: From HANSEL AND GRETEL by Anthony Browne. Copyright © 1981 by Anthony Browne.
         Reprinted by permission of Alfred A. Knopf, Inc.

FIGURE 2.9
A first grader guessed that
Lloyd Bloom had used paint
to do the illustrations as she
looked at this page from
Chaffin's *We Be Warm Till*
Springtime Comes.

For Jackie, Nikki and Christa Chaffin—
may they always have springtime
—L.D.C.
For Cyndy, my wife
—L.B.

Source: Reprinted with the permission of Macmillan Publishing from WE BE WARM TILL SPRING-
TIME COMES by Lillie D. Chaffin, illustrated by Lloyd Bloom. Illustrations copyright © 1980
by Lloyd Bloom.

It looks like he used a lot of line . . . like he used a pencil line to just do little sketches
and then he put a little color in because he thought everything would be white at first
and he just took a pencil line and sketched it in.

A first grader speculated that Lloyd Bloom had used paint in *We Be Warm Till*
Springtime Comes (Chaffin) because she could "see the brush strokes coming down."
Indeed, the thick impasto paint of the original art reproduces well in the book's final
printed form. Her inference is probably correct (Figure 2.9).

Imaginative Language

Imaginative language, the third category, allows children to enter the world of the
book or to transform the illustrations in imaginative ways. Although some experts
argue that the illustrations in books interfere with children's ability to use their imagination, I found that picturebooks inspired imaginative experiences for children.
Their language in response to picturebooks allowed them to participate in the imaginary world created by the author and artist or to create their own mental images.

Younger children often "chose" a character that they wanted to be as they read or looked through a book.

Nina: Look at this dog—it's like a different dog.
Amanda: Yeah—I think I wanna be the cat now. What do you want to be?
Nina: I wanna be the dog.

Some children assumed the roles of characters and created dialogue as they viewed the illustrations. A third grader lowered her voice and said gruffly, "So here you are you old sinner. I've been looking for you all this time and this is where I find you," as she looked at the woodsman confronting the wolf in Trina Schart Hyman's version of *Little Red Riding Hood* (Figure 2.10).

Two fifth graders improvised the following exchange as they looked at Hansel and Gretel walking behind their parents in Paul Zelinsky's version of the Grimm Brothers story.

Kristen: Right here the expression on his face he says like, "I know, I'll pick up these rocks and we'll find our way back."
Mark: Yeah like, "Heh heh, look what I'm gonna do now. They won't lose us."

At times, children described how their mental images differed from the illustrator's version. A fifth grader made the following comments upon looking at

FIGURE 2.10
Hyman's woodcutter in *Little Red Riding Hood* inspired a third grader to improvise dialogue.

Source: From *Little Red Riding Hood*, retold and illustrated by Trina Schart Hyman. A Holiday House Book. Copyright © 1983 by Trina Schart Hyman.

Zwerger's *Hansel and Gretel*: "I thought the witch's house would be in a clearing and all you'd see was gingerbread and candy."

On several occasions children described mental images evoked by the pictures. A first grader, looking at Donna Diamond's black and white illustrations for *The Bremen Town Musicians* (Grimm Bros.), noted that when he had first listened to the story he had pictured it like Diamond's pictures. "When I first heard the story," he reported, "I thought of something like a real story of real animals and that was the story [pointing to Diamond's book]. But then I asked my mind to change it into color."

Two first graders were also looking at Diamond's book when one said that it reminded her of Chris Van Allsburg's *Jumanji*, another book done in black and white (Figure 2.1). One of the girls went to get the Van Allsburg book, and as they looked at the two books side by side they stated:

Nina:	They look pretty different.
Interviewer:	They do, don't they. How they are different?
Nina:	Because this [*Jumanji*] has a little bit more colors in it—like . . .
Interviewer:	Colors?
Nina:	See—the game board . . .
Amanda:	It looks like different colors doesn't it.
Interviewer:	Uh huh.

FIGURE 2.11
Children talked about seeing colors on this black-and-white page in Van Allsburg's *Jumanji*.

Nina: And like when you just turn it and you can see white—and
                                 you can see a little bit red.

The interesting aspect of this exchange is that the illustrations discussed were only black and white. Thus these statements clearly describe mental images rather than what the children saw on the page. Other teachers have told me that when *Jumanji* was out of sight, their students also argued that Van Allsburg's pictures were in color.

The imaginative function seemed to encourage children, particularly younger children, to use verbal imagery in formulating unusual comparisons, and I noted many instances of metaphorical use of language. A first grader, for example, looked at ripples behind a boat in Uri Shulevitz's *Dawn*. "That's like whipped cream that men put on to shave," he explained. On other occasions first and second graders described Tomie dePaola's distinctive clouds as "pumpy" or "like mashed potatoes."

Personal Language

The fourth category of verbal responses relates to language resulting from connections to children's personal lives, their feelings, or their opinions about picturebooks.

On many occasions books reminded children of part of their unique personal experience. A story event or illustration often triggered a personal connection that might seem to have little relation to the book itself. For example, looking at Domanska's pictures in *What Do You See?* a first grader declared, "We got bathroom wallpaper colored like that." Zwerger's hazy watercolors in *Hansel and Gretel* reminded a fourth grader of her T.V. "It's broken and when you turn the contrast it gets all fuzzy." A fifth grader pointed out the witch's red eyes in Zelinsky's *Hansel and Gretel* (Grimm Bros.). "She can't see that good cause her eyes are real red. You can't see that good cause after you get out of the swimming pool—you can't see that good and your eyes are still red." A first grader looking at Bloom's illustrations for *We Be Warm Till Springtime Comes* (Chaffin) was reminded of her own desire for spring to come.

> Cause you know, they were wishing spring would come, but it was winter. Just like I'm hoping spring will come—that's when my communion is and that's when my birthday is. . . . It's going to be a communion and so on because I'm inviting lots of people and I hope it will be good weather cause we're probably going to go to Da Vinci's [a restaurant] and it's probably gonna be very expensive.

Picturebooks also engendered connections to people in children's personal lives. Plume's dog character in *The Bremen Town Musicians* (Grimm Bros.) reminded another first grader, "I love dogs. They're so cute. We were going to get one but my grandma had to come [live with us] because she kept messing up the [her] house." A fifth grader pointed to Browne's picture of the stepmother in *Hansel and Gretel* (Grimm Bros.). "Here she's yelling. My mom does that."

The pictures also evoked expressions of emotion. As they looked at a close-up of a dog's face filled with porcupine quills in Carrick's *Ben and the Porcupine*, first and second graders exclaimed, "Don't show that picture. It makes me so sad" (Figure 2.12).

FIGURE 2.12
A close-up in Carrick's *Ben and the Porcupine* evoked strong feelings from children.

Source: From BEN AND THE PORCUPINE by Carol Carrick. Illustrations copyright © 1981 by Donald Carrick. Reprinted by permission of Clarion Books/Houghton Mifflin Co. All rights reserved.

Third, fourth, and fifth graders spoke about the effects that the color in pictures had on their emotions, reporting that bright green made them feel happy or that browns and grays made them feel sad or scared.

At all grade levels, children were willing to express opinions about books and to think about them critically. The younger children often evaluated books using their own subjective criteria rather than relying on some objective quality in the book itself. When asked to explain why she had stated that Domanska's *What Do You See?* was a good book, for example, a first grader replied, "Because I liked it."

Third through fifth graders were more apt to back up their subjective reactions to a book with objective criteria. Looking at one of the versions of *Hansel and Gretel* (Grimm Bros.), a fifth grader, for example, complained that Galdone "didn't take her [*sic*] time with this book. She used too much of this brownish stuff and it doesn't look good." Later he came back to the book and said, "I didn't like that one. It didn't look good. The pictures, she coulda took her time with it."

In comparing *The Wave* by Margaret Hodges with illustrations by Blair Lent and *The Burning Rice Fields* by Sarah Bryant with illustrations by M. Funai, two illustrated versions of a Japanese folktale, a fourth grader wrote:

I really notice the difference in the language and the illustrations of the two books. In *The Wave* the language is [*sic*] very exquisite and very delicate—the words carefully picked one by one and in *The Burning Rice Fields* the words are slopped on the page. The illustrations in *The Wave* is cardboard cuts carefully cutted [*sic*] to resemble objects in the story and in *The Burning Rice Fields* the pictures are done in a child's version of crayon drawings. Unfortunately I like *The Burning Rice Fields* better because its [*sic*] in more detail.

In fact, detail was often used to judge a book's quality. When her teacher asked her to guess who had done the illustrations for Krasilovsky's *The Cow Who Fell in the Canal*, a second grader wrote

I chose Peter Spier because of the small pictures and the details in them. He had details in the grass and the leaves on the trees. He would try to draw every single little leaf. I saw that on his fences he drew the line of the wood that made it look real. The waves look very pretty.

Two fifth graders looking at Paul Zelinsky illustrations in *Hansel and Gretel* (Grimm Bros.) had this discussion:

Patrick:	I like the end pages in this one. I think from the end pages that I'm going like it better than the two I've read so far.
Interviewer:	What makes you feel that way?
Rhonda:	Clouds
Patrick:	Yeah, it looks bright . . . and it's got some dark but not as dark as that whole thing [Anthony Brown's version] and I like books where they're like happy.
Rhonda:	And this looks like you're really standing outside and seeing birds and clouds.
Patrick:	I think the illustrator did a good job because I like realistic illustrations.
Interviewer:	And you don't think the others were realistic huh?
Rhonda:	Not that much.
Interviewer:	What is the difference?
Rhonda:	The details and the colors.
Patrick:	And they look really poor because look at his pants. They're all torn. . . . He used a lot of detail because the walls are cracked.
Rhonda:	And look at their faces (Figure 2.13).

Their discussion demonstrates the fluid and dynamic ways in which children use language; one function quickly gives rise to another as one child supports or extends the understanding of another. What is important here is not that we can delineate and identify specific functional categories, but that the awareness is heightened. By inviting children to make meaning through picturebooks, we can provide important contexts for language and thinking. In addition, we open up artistic and aesthetic ways of knowing as well.

FIGURE 2.13
Children appreciated details in Zelinsky's illustrations for the Grimm's *Hansel and Gretel*.

Source: Illustration by Paul O. Zelinsky. Reprinted by permission of G. P. Putnam's Sons from HANSEL AND GRETEL retold by Rika Lesser, illustrations copyright © 1985 by Paul O. Zelinsky.

WHAT CHILDREN SEE IN PICTUREBOOKS: THE DEVELOPMENT OF AESTHETIC AWARENESS

Children's responses to picturebooks show they are eager to talk about their responses to the books that they are reading, and they are also aware of the visual elements of these books. Indeed, as children at different grade levels responded to picturebooks in different ways, I found that they developed more critical thinking about cognitive and aesthetic factors. This awareness was different depending on the age of the child.

Perhaps this critical awareness grew out of the way children looked at the illustrations. If children and adults scan visual material differently, then the children's interest in the artist's use of detail may arise from the way their eyes scan the illustrations. Whether this way of scanning is, indeed, a learning technique, these children taught me how to look at picturebooks.

One of the first things I noted was that children picked up the smallest details that many illustrators include in their pictures and that we adults often overlook. A second grader compared the inch-wide box on the title page of Van Allsburg's *Jumanji* to the topiary figures from *The Garden of Abdul Gasazi* (Van Allsburg). Other children noticed that the toy dog in *Jumanji* also appeared in the shadows in Van Allsburg's *The Wreck of the Zephyr*. On another occasion, a first grade boy noticed that the tiny book on a hassock in the crowded room in Shulevitz's *Oh What A Noise* had the book's title printed on its spine. Other children found mushrooms growing under the Strawberry Snatcher's feet in Molly Bang's *The Grey Lady and the Strawberry Snatcher* or the tiny mouse in Peter Spier's *Gobble Growl Grunt*.

The rewards of looking carefully at illustrations to find what one teacher called "secrets" may in turn help children become more sensitive to the artistic qualities in picturebooks. For example, older children were more aware of the real "live" artist behind the book than were the younger children. Although even kindergarteners and first graders talked about illustrators by name, I found that some of them were confused about who actually created the pictures. Some thought that machines made the pictures rather than an artist who created an original work that was then photographed and printed by machines.

Other young children were unsure about variations in individual styles or the stylistic choices made by artists in the process of illustration. When asked if the three different versions of *The Bremen Town Musicians* were by different artists, one first grader assured me that they were and pointed to their names on the cover. Another first grader, however, explained that he knew they were by different artists by looking at the copyright pages. "This is from New York, and this one in the United States of America, and this one is made in New York, New York," he assured me.

Often, a child's attention to the artist's style was idiosyncratic. One first grader argued that *Mother, Mother, I Want Another* by Maria Polushkin was illustrated by the same artist who did *I Saw a Ship a-Sailing* (Domanska). I was puzzled by his conviction because the two books differed greatly in artistic style. Perhaps the fact that there was a mouse on each book helped make the connection? "No" he explained, "The words." I still did not understand because the words in the titles were different. As I looked more closely, however, I discovered that both books had been set in Abbott Old Style, a rather distinctive typeface. The student had, in fact, over-generalized the style of the printed letters to the entire art work (Figure 2.14).

FIGURE 2.14
A first grader thought *Mother, Mother, I Want Another* and *I Saw a Ship A-Sailing* were illustrated by the same artist.

Source: From MOTHER, MOTHER, I WANT ANOTHER by Maria Polushkin Robbins, illustrated by Diane Dawson. Text copyright © 1987 by Maria Polushkin. Illustrations copyright © 1978 by Diane Dawson. Reprinted by permission of Crown Publishers, Inc. From I SAW A SHIP A-SAILING by Janina Domanska. Copyright © 1972 by Janina Domanska. Reprinted with the permission of Macmillan Publishing Company.

Older children, however, seemed to know that a real person lay behind the creation of the pictures. Many older children were aware that the artist existed in the real world and could be the subject of dialogue or study. Looking at Chris Van Allsburg's *The Wreck of the Zephyr*, a third grader suggested, "Those are nice pictures. We ought to write to Van Allsburg." A fifth grader remarked that he had decided to do a study of Van Allsburg "because he does black and white in some of his books and I like the way he puts his details in with black and white, like making it light or dark."

At all ages, many of these children used an expert lexicon; that is, they used artistic and technical language relating to book production. For example, even first and second graders used terms like *technique, media, watercolor, India ink*, and *endpapers* as they talked about picturebooks. When they lacked the correct term, however, they readily improvised. A first grader looking at woodblock prints told me that the artist had used "color concussion." He knew that, he assured me, because he had "looked carefully at the pictures with a magnifying glass." A third grader referred to Ann Jonas' black and white pictures in *Round Trip* as "obstacle" illusions. And although all children had trouble with abstract terms like *Impressionism* or *Expressionism*, they often created appropriate descriptors like *sprite* (for Hyman's *Little Red Riding Hood*) or *lushy* (for Sendak's *Outside Over There*).

Children's talk about illustrations also revealed differences in the way they understood the elements of art, which are the artist's means of expression (see Chapter 6). All children seemed to be familiar with elements like lines, shapes, and colors, although they didn't always have the correct nomenclature. Kindergartners, first, and second graders talked about "squiggly" lines, "twisty" lines, or "construction paper" shapes (referring to shapes with sharp edges). Many of these youngsters confused colors that were bright in intensity with those that were light in value and used the term *light* to indicate brightness. Although they didn't often use the word *texture*, children of all ages referred to qualities of texture by using terms like *rough* or *smooth*. And, although even the older children rarely used the term *value*, they seemed aware of this element by discussing "dark pictures" or an artist's use of "sunlight."

Unlike the younger children, children in grades three and above seemed to be aware not only of the elements of art but also that the artist chose these elements to convey meaning to the viewer. These children talked about an artist's role in evoking emotional responses through the elements of art, and they commented on artists' technical choices. Looking at Paul Galdone's *Hansel and Gretel*, a fourth grader stated, "The lines sorta make it look detailed and the detail makes it look scary." The element of shape in Toshi Maruki's *Hiroshima No Pika* caused a third grader to remark, "The pictures look sad. They don't have a certain shape to them" (Figure 2.15).

Further proof that children recognize the emotive power of the elements of art was evident in this fourth grader's comments. As she compared illustrations in Yagawa's *The Crane Wife* to those in another version of the folktale, Matsutani's *The Crane Maiden* (Figure 2.16), Heather wrote:

> In *The Crane Wife* the paper used is rice paper and the painting is done by taking soft light shades of watered ink and brushing it on with light strokes. In *The Crane Maiden* the artist chose simple shapes with watercolor and the color sort of blue.

When I asked her which one she liked better, she replied,

FIGURE 2.15
A third grader understood that the artist's use of shape in *Hiroshima No Pika* affected her feelings.

Source: Cover illustration from HIROSHIMA NO PIKA by Toshi Maruki. Copyright © 1980 by Toshi Maruki. Reprinted by permission of Lothrop, Lee and Shepard Books, a division of William Morrow & Co., Inc..

FIGURE 2.16
A fourth grader responded to the artists' different use of shape in *The Crane Maiden* and *The Crane Wife*.

Source: Illustration from THE CRANE WIFE retold by Sumiko Yagawa, translated from the Japanese by Katherine Paterson, illustrated by Suekichi Akaba. Illustrations copyright © 1979 by Suekichi Akaba. Reprinted by permission of Morrow Junior Books, a division of William Morrow and Company.

The Crane Maiden is too block like, like it's all straight, made up of squares. *The Crane Wife* is made up of circles. It fits the story better because it's a smooth story and a ball rolls and a square won't.

In addition to recognizing that an artist could use elements of art to convey meaning, older children also seemed aware of the meaning-making potential of the artist's technical choices, such as endpapers, page layout, and choice of original media. For example, as he opened Zwerger's version of *Hansel and Gretel* (Grimm Bros.), a fourth grader looked at the rust-colored endpapers and commented, "They look reddish brown like somebody's put something there and just forgot about it and never got it up again. They put it in the forest and left it there forever." For him, the endpapers evoked a feeling and set the mood for retelling this old tale.

Several of the third, fourth, and fifth graders who looked at the layout of Zwerger's illustrations noticed the abrupt cut-off of several of the illustrations, leaving large areas of white at the edge of the page. This interferes with the swirling fluidity of the watercolors used in the original art and breaks the somber mood created by the colors' dark values (Figure 2.17). Two fourth grade boys speculated about the artist's reasons.

Matt: Maybe he did this while he was on a trip or something. He saw those people that looked like his characters and he had a special size of paper and he couldn't blow it up.

Jason: They shoulda put something there [in the margin], a bird or something.

On another occasion, two fifth graders had a different answer:

Mark: This page has white over there and these pages he just paints right to the end. I doubt it's blanked out or anything.

Kristin: He probably did it on purpose.

Interviewer: Why?

Kristin: Well he might have said in the end of the thing you know when they copy the pages . . .

Mark: And he might have wanted you to see them [the characters] instead of . . .

Interviewer: So he was kind of spotlighting the people?

Mark: Like there was nothing else out there.

A third grader's remarks about the illustrations and page layout in *Hiroshima No Pika* is indicative of how children's understanding of the meaning-making power of visual art grows. Maggie had been looking at the small vignettes and single page illustrations in the first part of the book and remarking on the rather cheerful colors. Then she turned to the point in the story where the atomic bomb is dropped, a double page spread with no printed text, done in tones of red, rust, and black. "It gives me the impression that the illustrator's just seen the bomb happen and she just choked and doesn't want to talk about it and she'll show you a picture of what happened," she stated. She understood that art has a unique ability, not only to convey ideas but to reach the heart.

Their experiences with picturebooks helped children like Maggie understand the aesthetic nature of the picturebook in ways that transcended any adult attempts

FIGURE 2.17
Several children questioned the layout of Zwerger's illustrations for the Grimms' *Hansel and Gretel*.

Source: From HANSEL AND GRETEL illustrated by Lisbeth Zwerger. Copyright © 1979 by Lisbeth Zwerger. Reprinted by permission of William Morrow and Company.

to have them classify books according to "schools" of art. Indeed, many children were unsure of how terms like *Expressionism* or *Realism* should be applied to picturebooks. A first grade boy insisted, for example, that the flattened stylistic paintings in Aardema's *Bringing the Rain to Kapiti Plain* were "real" because "in real life giraffes have big spots." He said that Domanska's decorative grey bird in *What Do You See?* looked real because "it's got normal colors that a bird has" (Figure 2.18).

When allowed to formulate their own meanings regarding picturebooks, children's comments were uncannily intuitive about elements of artistic style. For example, in *Outside Over There*, with its wide vistas and dramatic figures, Sendak pays homage to German Romantics of the early 1800s, such as Philipp Otto Runge, as well as to Renaissance artists like Pieter Bruegel. Seeing the book for the first time, a first grader asked, "Is that from the Bible?" Other primary children called the pictures "lushy" and referred to goblin babies as "Jesus babies" (the child explained that they were like the paintings his art teacher had shown him at Christmas time). Illustrator Chris Van Allsburg began his artistic career as a sculptor. Although they did not know this, the children looking at *Jumanji* or *The Wreck of the Zephyr* made comments like "it looks like clay" or "the wave looks like it's a stone wall."

Such insights suggest that trying to make children label books according to abstract terms from the field of art history is neither necessary nor useful. Indeed, the child who insisted that the pictures in *Bringing the Rain to Kapiti Plain* were "real" may have been referring not so much to style of art but to his experience with the book.

FIGURE 2.18
A first grader argued that the bird in Domanska's *What Do You See?* **looked real.**

Source: Reprinted with the permission of Macmillan Publishing from WHAT DO YOU SEE? by Janina Domanska. Copyright © 1974 Janina Domanska.

CONCLUSION

Studying children's responses to picturebooks in these classroom settings has convinced me that picturebooks can and do provide children with purposeful talk, increase their literacy, deepen their response to books, and open up their awareness of art and aesthetics. Indeed, the ways in which these children came to make meaning is a profound reflection of the theory of aesthetics so beautifully articulated by Suzanne Langer (1953), who argued:

> The exhilaration of a direct aesthetic experience indicates the depth of human mentality to which that experience goes. What it [the work of art] does to us is to formulate our conceptions of feeling and our conceptions of visual, factual, and audible reality together. It gives us *forms of imagination* and *forms of feeling* [emphasis added] inseparably; that is to say it clarifies and organizes intuition itself. That is why it has the force of a revelation, and inspires a feeling of deep intellectual satisfaction. (p. 397)

In the following chapters we will explore the ways in which the full potential of picturebooks can be realized to achieve such satisfactions.

CHAPTER

3

Developing a Context for Response to Picturebooks

The rich tapestry of children's responses to picturebooks described in Chapter 2 was woven from a number of threads. Although these factors were never quantified, I believe that by describing practices that seem to give rise to children's literacy, literary, and aesthetic understandings through picturebooks we can engender equally complex responses in other settings.

In my studies, the individual children, their age (and perhaps their gender), and their peers' reactions all probably played a role in the talk, writing, art, and other responses to picturebooks. Perhaps the most important element in the context for response were the picturebooks that they looked at and thought about and the teachers who directed their eyes and ideas.

THE ROLE OF PICTUREBOOKS

It may be unnecessary to point out that the presence of picturebooks was crucial to the wide variety of responses that I found among children. But some picturebooks in particular seemed to evoke the deepest responses in children, responses that changed and grew over time.

Certainly, teachers tried to accumulate extensive classroom libraries, and in some cases they had 200 to 300 books. In primary classrooms, this collection consisted almost entirely of picturebooks and included a variety of topics and genres—wordless picturebooks, picture storybooks, poetry, information books, alphabet books, and counting books. Even in upper grade classrooms teachers included a broad range of picturebooks for children to choose from, particularly picture storybooks, folktales, poetry, and information books.

Several books seemed to rise to the surface of these extensive libraries and catch the children's imaginations in ways that I found both unexpected and deeply satisfying. In all cases, these were books that I considered exceptional art forms—that is, in all of them, pictures and text (or images and idea) worked together to provide unique aesthetic experiences. Yet many adult critics suggested they were not books for children at all. Kimmel (1982), for example, argues that books such as Molly Bang's *The Grey Lady and the Strawberry Snatcher*, Chris Van Allsburg's *The Garden of Abdul Gasazi* and *Jumanji*, and Maurice Sendak's *Outside Over There* are "far too unusual or sophisticated to attract many children" (p. 37), while Hankla (1982) calls *Outside Over There* "paranoid" and a "shallow icy surrogate for a literature which will benefit humanity" (p. 347).

In addition, books such as these were *not* those that children ought to like, according to preference studies (Martin, 1931; Rudisill, 1952; Smerdon, 1976). Based on the study results, we could predict that children would not like *The Grey Lady and the Strawberry Snatcher* because the pictures are surreal rather than realistic. They would not like *The Garden of Abdul Gasazi* and *Jumanji* because the illustrations are in black and white rather than full color. They would not like *Outside Over There* because the content is fantastic rather than familiar.

Yet these books, as well as Richard Kennedy's *Song of the Horse* and Donna Hill's *Ms. Glee Was Waiting*, inspired a wealth of responses in the children I observed. If these books did not please children, they certainly puzzled them, piqued their curiosity, and began a chain of events that led to the depth of thinking and feeling that can constitute the most profound aesthetic experience.

Ms. Glee Was Waiting

As mentioned in Chapter 2, first and second graders did not seem to care for Diane Dawson's book, *Ms. Glee Was Waiting*. The book was not done in full color. The illustrations, which contradicted the meaning of the verbal text, showed the main character, Laura, moving in a setting that grew more and more bizarre.

After the children's lukewarm reaction, however, the teacher returned to the book when the children were studying time. The theme may have alerted one of the children to the clock pictured on the cover and on many subsequent pages. Once one youngster noticed this small detail, others began to look more carefully at the pictures. One discovered that on the title page illustrator Donna Hill shows us a picture of Ms. Glee's white house, and on the dedication page a map shows that Ms. Glee's house is only across the bridge (Figure 3.1).

These clues give away the secret that Laura is doing everything she can to avoid going to her piano lesson, and indeed this secret became the class mystery. Their teacher used the mystery to invite children to try to find out what was hidden in the pictures. In the days following that read-aloud session she'd ask, "Has everyone found the secrets in *Ms. Glee*? If you haven't, you're really missing a treat." Of course, no one could resist that kind of invitation, and I'd often find several new children pouring over the book. The book became so popular that it often was miss-

FIGURE 3.1
A map gives away the secret in *Ms. Glee Was Waiting*.

ing, and everyone would stop what they were doing until it had been located. As a result of this experience, several children did a mural of scenes from the book. Ms. Glee, her house, and the clues to her mystery went on to become part of classroom lore.

The Grey Lady and the Strawberry Snatcher

The experience with *Ms. Glee* was likely part of the cause of the response that Amy, a second grader in the same class, had to Molly Bang's *The Grey Lady and the Strawberry Snatcher*. This wordless picturebook begins quite innocently with a highly representational depiction of a basket of strawberries sitting among other fruit on a farmer's market table.

This everyday image soon gives way to surrealistic ones. The Grey Lady, who is clothed in the grey of the negative background space, purchases the strawberries only to be stalked by a strange-looking fellow with a purple hat, bright blue skin, and mushrooms growing under his feet. He chases her across town and into a jungle. He finally is diverted by a raspberry patch so that the Strawberry Lady can get safely home. Bang violates visual expectations throughout the book with the surrealistic images, the juxtaposition of background and foreground space, and even the violation of traditional picturebook paging (Figures 3.2 and 3.3).

Amy's initial reaction to the book was not particularly enthusiastic. Her teacher had placed the book on a table next to a basket of real strawberries and a sign that read, "The Grey Lady Loves Strawberries. Do You?" I had positioned myself close by, eager to see if anyone would take the bait, so I was there to watch Amy's reaction. She picked up the book and leafed through it from back to front.

Interviewer:	What did you think?
Amy:	Strange pictures—people [pause] like vanishing. You can only see their ears. [pause] That must be the Strawberry Snatcher. [pointing and leafing through it again] Yeah, that must be the Strawberry Snatcher.

FIGURE 3.2
Strange images abound in
The Grey Lady and the Straw-
berry Snatcher.

Source: Reprinted with the permission of Four Winds Press, an imprint of Macmillan Publishing from THE GREY LADY AND THE STRAWBERRY SNATCHER by Molly Bang. Copyright © 1980 by Molly Bang.

FIGURE 3.3
Molly Bang violates expectations of space and layout in *The Grey Lady and the Strawberry Snatcher*.

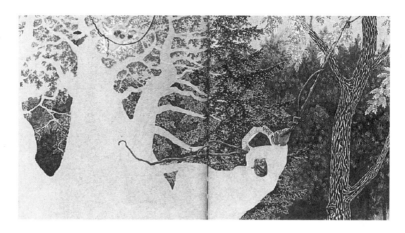

Source: Reprinted with the permission of Four Winds Press, an imprint of Macmillan Publishing from THE GREY LADY AND THE STRAWBERRY SNATCHER by Molly Bang. Copyright © 1980 by Molly Bang.

At this point she put the book down and walked away. Her teacher had also been keeping her eye on the book, however, and asked Amy what she was thinking. Amy went back to the book and picked it up again.

Amy:	They're strange looking characters. You can tell this guy's the Strawberry Snatcher.
Mrs. Hall:	You know what this reminds me of? When you finished *Ms. Glee* you asked me to find more books like that.
Amy:	You can find clues?
Mrs. Hall:	Have you found clues?

Mrs. Hall's question became an invitation to take another, more careful look at the book. Amy returned that morning to talk through it with me, verbalizing her predictions and inferences ("I betcha he lives in the forest, see that's how he gets mushrooms coming out of his feet") and personalizing the events to her own experience. ("Hey Mrs. Hall, he fell in the lake and got all smeary. . . . That's what happens to me. I get red all over my fingers at my Grandma's cabin.")

On subsequent days the teacher's subtle question led Amy to share the book with other classmates, to go to the library to find other books by Molly Bang, and to find other "secret" connections among those books. Eventually she prepared a display of Bang's books for the rest of the class and created a play of *The Grey Lady and the Strawberry Snatcher*. For this child, an initial rejection of a "strange book" turned into a long-term appreciation with the help of her sensitive teacher.

Song of the Horse

Another book that provoked intense reactions among third and fourth graders was *Song of the Horse* by Richard Kennedy. The book is a stream-of-consciousness account of a child's horseback ride. The narrative is full of contrast, moving back and forth between the fenced-in barn and the freedom of the open countryside, the outward calm of the rider and her or his inner passions.

Marcia Sewall's illustrations support the poetic text perfectly. The black and white drawings reinforce the contrast, and the rough scratchboard textures set against smooth white paper echo the inner and outer emotions of the rider. The forms of horse and rider are solid, yet not overly representational; they do not interfere with the lyrical mood set by the words by being too detailed. In fact, this lack of detail may be why girls assumed that the main character was female and boys saw a male.

Even the pictorial layout reinforces the themes and rhythms of the text. The first pictures are placed on the right side of the double page spread, but once horse and rider leave the fenced-in yard, the illustrations burst across the page with multiple images of horse and rider visually recreating the horse's galloping strides (Figures 3.4 and 3.5).

Almost from the first page, the book inspired debate among the children as the teacher read it aloud. Describing the horse, the narrator says, "He is always waiting for me, standing still and thinking about me. Standing upright in his sleep he dreams about me and he never dreams of anything else" (p. 4). One of the boys asked, "How does he know that that horse knows all that?" Patrick, the realist in the group, declared, "He's crazy. He's reading other people's—animal's thoughts and he doesn't even know what they are. He's dreaming." Tricia replied, "She's not dreaming. A lot of times when you look at a dog or something and his eyes are bright but you can tell he's happy."

FIGURE 3.4
Song of the Horse begins with tranquil images.

Source: From SONG OF THE HORSE by Richard Kennedy, illustrations by Marcia Sewall. Copyright
© by Marcia Sewall, illustrations. Used by permission of Dutton Children's Books, a division
of Penguin Books USA Inc.

FIGURE 3.5
Horse and rider move swift-ly across the page in *Song of the Horse*.

Source: From SONG OF THE HORSE by Richard Kennedy, illustrations by Marcia Sewall. Copyright
© by Marcia Sewall, illustrations. Used by permission of Dutton Children's Books, a division
of Penguin Books USA Inc.

As the horse and rider become lost in the excitement of their ride, the narrator
states,

> We run into a place where all is perfectly still, and there is no difference in anything and
> no sameness in anything, and in this great empty moment, a song is singing. The song
> has words that are ancient and strange, and music like newborn water, tumbling all
> together, but I can't remember any of it. (pp. 24–25)

Patrick insisted, "Oh he's telling his dream because he says I can't remember it or
something." Tricia replied, "No it's not like that when you go to some place and
you're all by yourself and it's a special place and you're like totally leaving the other
world." Patrick argued, "Like in his head he's dreaming and when the feelings you
have inside you is the inside world and the outside world is the place where things
really happen." Tricia replied, "Okay, I think that when she was running with the
horse that she had a special feeling 'cause sometimes you get it when you're around
nature." Heather added, "I always get that feeling when I'm playing the piano or
singing a real sad song."

At this first reading, other children mentioned the author's use of metaphors
and compared it to the books that they had been reading. Some were illustrated in
black and white, others were about horses, and still others were about dreams. Several children had been doing sketches and writing in their journals while the teacher
was reading, and one girl shared the poem and drawing she had done.

When the discussion had finished, the book was quickly put into the hands of
one of the children who'd asked for it, and in the next few days, like *Ms. Glee Was
Waiting*, it became one of those "missing books." Their teacher explained "I loved
that—we couldn't find it. It was hiding in someone's box and it was passed around."
Heather explained the reason for this. "The illustrations catch your eye, and then
you don't want to let it go. You just want to get a hold of that book and keep it until
you've done all the illustrations."

As the children began to display the writing and art that they were doing in
response to the book, it became clear that they were most often writing poetry. The
teacher had not suggested this style; the book just naturally invited poetry. Two boys
wrote the following poems (Figure 3.6):

Gone with the Wind

A Horse and his boy
go so fast
the wind is a whipping
breeze close behind them.
The horse's mane
is wild while
he is galloping.
The boy's mother
calls but he
does not hear
because he is
gone
gone with the wind.

A Boy and His Horse

The boy hops
on the
great stallion standing
restlessly in his
stall and they start off
the horse and the boy
know they are a
blaze to everyone
leaving a black
stroke in the air like
a paint brush

FIGURE 3.6
A child's response to *Song of*
the Horse

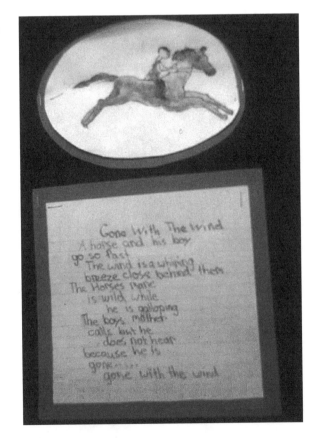

FIGURE 3.7
Song of the Horse inspired
third and fourth graders to
create poetry and art.

To add to these first efforts, the teacher brought in other picturebooks about horses, an information book by McClintock called *Horses As I See Them*, Lee Bennett Hopkins' collection of poetry, *My Mane Catches the Wind*, and Paul Goble's Native American folktale, *The Girl Who Loved Wild Horses*. Other children found novels about horses in the library, and more and more art and poems about horses appeared until a display of all their responses was arranged. Tricia's watercolor painting of two horses, one black and one white, and her poem show the cumulative result of all the discussion, reading, and creating that began with this one book (Figure 3.7).

> *The sun is setting*
> *it was time*
> *The sound of hoof beats*
> *disturbed the silence of the night*
> *the wild horses filled the*
> *canyon. Prancing and calling, the*
> *horses raced. . . . it is their*
> *time now, and no one could*
> *take that time.*
> *They ran in their own*
> *world the wind whistling*
> *behind them*
> *forever*
> *and*
> *ever*

Outside Over There

I had another opportunity to observe initial reactions to a "strange" book deepen and grow when Maurice Sendak's *Outside Over There* was read to first and second graders. These were the same children who had been studying the theme of time, and they were intrigued by this book from the outset. This may have been due to Mrs. Hall's enticing summons, "I have a special new storybook to share with you. Please come up close. . . . It's one of *those* books." If she'd hoped to invite them to look closely and think deeply about the book, she certainly succeeded. Indeed, the book is both visually and verbally compelling, and, in spite of the fairly brief printed text, the children spent 45 minutes talking through the book. They ended then only because the lunch bell rang.

As Mrs. Hall read, they predicted, wondered, inferred, and made connections as Sendak's unique vision opened up their own imaginations. They were fascinated by the visual subplots that Sendak included, particularly with a ship that appears outside the window. It is shown first caught in a storm, then sinking, and then reappearing with the goblins who have stolen Ida's sister. As Ida sets off to rescue the baby, the children wondered about her magic "raincoat" and speculated where her absent sea captain father and her mother might be.

When the story was finished, Mrs. Hall drew their attention back to the total book, asking, "What does this book make you think about?" She listened to their responses, drawing out their initial ideas with further questions. Thus this extraordinary teacher initiated an exploration of Sendak's book that would take some of these children into deeper understandings of the art of the picturebook, as well as of themselves.

In the next days and weeks, she brought in more books by Sendak and invited children to talk and compare. She also read the book again several times. Some of the children suggested that time was of great importance in the book because they had noted movement through day and night and also of the positions of the moon (a recurring symbol in Sendak's books). Children who noticed five tiny butterflies on the pages after Ida rescues her sister assured me that the five goblins had turned into the butterflies. Two second grade boys who had poured over the pictures decided at this juncture that Ida's experience was really a dream. They knew this, they told me, because they had seen the shepherd asleep on one of the double-page spreads. It was a dream because you "count sheep when you dream" (Figure 3.8).

When I returned to Mrs. Hall's room a year and a half after completing my first visit, she had just read *Outside Over There* for the fifth time following an illustra-

FIGURE 3.8
Second graders speculated about the shepherd pictured in *Outside Over There*.

"If Ida backwards in the rain would only turn around again and catch those goblins with a tune she'd spoil their kidnap honeymoon!"

Source: From OUTSIDE OVER THERE by Maurice Sendak. Copyright © 1981 by Maurice Sendak. Reprinted by permission of Harper & Row.

tor study of Sendak. At this time she was teaching a combination third/fourth grade, and many of the children whom I'd observed in her first/second grade class were now in this older group. She told me that in studying the book this time, "more feelings came into play, the feelings of the child, and they really noticed the parents and the father. They were caught up in it, so it took a long time to reach that. There again it's that group of different people, sharing these ideas."

Two of this group, eight- and nine-year-old girls, sat down with me and the book, eager to tell me what they thought it was really about (Figure 3.9).

Terri:	She's [Ida's] so happy, and then she notices the baby's gone— then she gets kinda mad.
Tina:	There's the father's ship.
Interviewer:	How can you tell?
Terri:	We can't, but that's what we're thinking.
Tina:	She's getting mad, and the flowers keep growing, and then there's the shipwreck out there.
Terri:	It's kinda like if she's mad, outside here it's mad.
Tina:	She has to take care of the baby, and that's her responsibility.
Terri:	She feels bad, and she's all mad and that's why the storm is there.

FIGURE 3.9
Two girls used the illustrations to understand the heroine's feelings in *Outside Over There*.

The ice thing only dripped and stared,
and Ida mad knew goblins had been there.

FIGURE 3.10
Children enjoyed spending time looking at *Jumanji*.

The girls' personal recognition of the possibilities of meaning in this book are every bit as profound as any of the adult critiques that I have read. I would guess that Sendak would be satisfied with their explanation, whether or not it matches his own.

Indeed, I found that books that engendered such deep understandings were not necessarily the books executed in a manner that the children "liked." When pressed, most children admitted that they preferred books in color. But when I asked first and second graders whether it was okay to do illustrations in black and white, one replied, "Pictures don't have to be in color. . . . It's harder when it's in black and white. It takes more time and you don't just whip through the book." He pointed to the cover of Van Allsburg's *Jumanji* and explained that the monkeys hiding in the closet would have been easy to see if the book had been in color. But, he explained, "You like to take time." Older children also agreed that an important criteria for a picturebook was not one that was "easy for you to find things" but one that "makes us think more" (Figure 3.10).

Taking time with a book and thinking more about books are certainly worthy goals for any reading program or for any educational program, for that matter. Maxine Greene (1978) has referred to this type of deep reflection as "wide awakeness." Aesthetic experiences such as these help provide children with what Greene calls "a ground for the questioning that launches sense-making and the understanding of what it means to exist in a world" (1978, p. 166).

Yet, the books that make students think more are not always the books that children will discover on their own. The important lesson to be learned from the experiences discussed here is that with many books, children need a teacher (or a librarian or parent) who will open up the possibilities hidden there, and who will allow time for those deep understandings to rise to the surface of their consciousness. Thus, the remainder of this chapter is devoted to the teacher's important role in engendering responses to picturebooks.

THE ROLE OF THE TEACHER

The fact that teachers in these classrooms were able to inspire the kinds of long-lasting responses to picturebooks that we have seen is not due to any special artistic training. They were not art experts, but they *were* enthusiastic about picturebooks and interested in learning from children as well as teaching them. In addition, they shared other characteristics that helped set the stage for the breadth and depth of children's literacy, literary, and aesthetic understandings.

Inviting Children to Picturebooks

Teachers seemed to feel that it was important for children to have access to a variety of books in their classrooms. In fact, to provide children with many books, teachers often spent their own money.

One teacher reported that she stretched her dollar by looking for books to add to favorite themes or to special collections such as folklore or poetry. Another teacher volunteered to collect and process all the book club money if she could have the bonus books in return. Teachers also frequented garage sales and second-hand book stores. The teaching staff in the alternative school finally convinced their school board to give them the money normally spent on textbooks to buy trade books for their school and classroom libraries. Others successfully persuaded their principals to let them buy real books rather than workbooks or ditto masters even when the district refused to give up the basal readers.

Successful teachers of picturebooks also had supportive school librarians who were enthusiastic sources for books and who were willing to help with book selection and give book talks to children. When librarians had helped plan a unit or knew of a teacher's special interest in picturebooks, they would set aside special books that the teacher might like to see. In many places, municipal libraries have special teacher loans, allowing teachers to take out up to 50 books at a time, for example, and to keep them longer than normal.

Once these teachers collected books for their classroom libraries, they actively promoted books and helped individual children select books. They arranged special spaces for books so that children had a comfortable library corner in which they could look at, choose, and sit down to read their books. Teachers tried to place books with the cover facing outward, on special book racks or simply anywhere a book would fit. They did brief book talks to promote books or offered books to children following a read-aloud. They also encouraged other children to talk informally about the books they were reading and to pass favorites on to a friend. They created special displays for special books. As Mrs. Hall explained, "I think some books in particular just sit there, and sometimes I think children need some help to look at them in a different way and to really appreciate them."

Taking Time to Talk About Picturebooks

Reading aloud every day, several times a day, was a common practice among teachers, who took this time to talk with children about books and to listen to their comments. These discussions were, I believe, when personal reactions were extended and deepened. Teachers knew, for example, that this was a time when important connections could be made for children. Mrs. Hall suggested that giving children time was essential for their development as readers.

> Little by little, [I'm] feeding the fire, so to speak, and continuing an interest. Then one sparks another one to do something else and the networking—the connection, that's what I think the totality of it is. It's not stark or sterile. They're so broadened by it, and it just becomes automatic. You know immediately they think of other books or they think of other illustrators or their own experiences.

Teachers also helped me to see that listening to children was an important part of talking with them. Just as it was not necessary to have formal art training to talk about picturebooks, it was not necessary to have a detailed lesson plan before you read and discuss a picturebook with children. I really came to understand this as I looked over transcripts of two different first/second grade teachers reading *Outside Over There* aloud.

I considered both of these teachers master teachers. Their rooms were filled with books, and children chose from many authentic experiences to explore themes and ideas in these classrooms. However, I found instructive two very different approaches to reading this particular book, which resulted in very different outcomes.

Mrs. Jay was looking at *Outside Over There* as part of a mock Caldecott Award committee she had set up for this and seven other picturebooks (an activity that provided me with a wealth of data for my study). Among the books the children were looking at were several illustrated in black and white, an alphabet book, a book of poetry, and folktales and fantasies. Just as the Caldecott Committee of the American Library Association chooses the most distinguished work of illustration in a given year, the children were told, "What I want you to do . . . is look at the books, don't just pick it up and look through it fast. If you were on the Caldecott Committee and it was your job to select the best picturebook, what would you be looking for?"

To help the students think about their choices, she had created a large comparison chart with categories such as "Use of Color," "Media," "Shape or Size (Placement of Words)," and "Type of Illustration." Each day after she read one of the books, she and the children would talk about the illustrations and fill in the chart. Thus when she introduced *Outside Over There*, she simply told the children it was another of the books that they were going to consider for the Caldecott Award. Excerpts from the transcription of their read-aloud session, however, show that Mrs. Jay's agenda didn't always match what the children were trying to talk about.

Mrs. Jay: [Reading the opening lines that tell Papa is away at sea and Mama is sitting in an arbor.] See what—Where is Mama sitting? Does anyone know what kind of plant that is?

[Comments from many children.]

Mrs. Jay:	Grapevine arbor. How does it start to grow? [pause]
[More comments]	
Mrs. Jay:	Then it just grows up the side like.
Adam:	Yeah we have some of that in our yard.

[Mrs. Jay reads the pages where Ida is not watching her sister and the goblins climb in the window.]

Children:	[Comments] Ooooo . . .
Sara:	I know what happens.
Mrs. Jay:	Look at the baby's face. Is she enjoying the music do you suppose?
Children:	Yeah. Yeah.

[Mrs. Jay reads further. The goblins snatch the baby and leave an ice baby behind.]

Stella:	The eyes are gross.
Sara:	I know what's going to happen to that baby.
Mrs. Jay:	Big eyes—kinda bulgy.

[More ahhs and oooohs from the children.]

Mrs. Jay:	[Reads on.] The pictures show Ida hugging the ice baby and then realizing that her sister is gone. To her right is a large window and we see a ship and then a storm. It appears that the ship has sunk.
Kate:	What is that?
Adam:	The ship.
Mrs. Jay:	Look at Ida. How is she feeling?
Children:	*Mad*.
Mrs. Jay:	How is the sea feeling?
Children:	Angry.
Mrs. Jay:	How do you know the sea is feeling angry? Adam?
Adam:	Because the waves are starting to close in on the ship, starting to get rough on the sea.
Mrs. Jay:	Right. What kind of weather do we have?
Children:	Storm.
Adam:	A big storm.
Josh:	Bad weather.
Kelly:	A windstorm.

The children continued to express an interest in the ship, which appears on subsequent pages. Mrs. Jay directed their attention to other aspects of the illustrations.

Mrs. Jay:	Look at the flowers. They even look like they're going [to climb] in the window. [She reads the page where Ida puts on her mother's rain cloak and makes a "serious mistake."]
Tommy:	What was the mistake?
Kate:	Oh! It's gone [referring to the ship].
Adam:	It sunk.
Jason:	It either sunk or it was burnt.

| *Amanda:* | How did she make it sink? |
| *Mrs. Jay:* | Oh I don't think Ida made it sink, do you? |

The children continued to argue about the boat, but Mrs. Jay resumed reading. Toward the end of the book, Mrs. Jay read the page where Ida plays her horn and the goblins dance into a frenzy. The sea is visible once more, the moon is reflected in the water but the ship is still missing.

Adam:	And the ship's gone.
Nina:	It docked. It got—
Mrs. Jay:	See the reflection on the water?

Looking through these comments, we can see two different conversational topics struggling to emerge. (In fact, this dialogue represents a common classroom discourse pattern called IRE. The teacher **I**nitiates, children **R**espond and the teacher **E**valuates.) But in trying to direct the children's attention in this case, the teacher lost it. With it she lost the kind of predicting, questioning, and inferencing we value in children. Instead, she was left with fairly literal, one-word answers to her questions.

Among the second group of children, whose responses to the book were detailed earlier in this chapter, a different pattern of talk emerged. Mrs. Hall's introduction to *Outside Over There*, for example, recreates the intimacy of a parent-child read-aloud, and she makes sure to draw the children's careful attention to the book with her opening comments and questions. Her introduction invited children to look carefully at all parts of the book, to make connections, and to make predictions about what they might find between the covers.

Mrs. Hall:	I have a special new storybook to share with you. Please come up close, very, very close. It's one of *those* books. What did you say about this book, Hildy?
Hildy:	Is that from the Bible?
Mrs. Hall:	[pauses] The author—
Child 1:	Maurice Sendak.
Child 2:	I know! Ohh she also wrote *Where the Wild Things Are*.
Mrs. Hall:	Maurice Sendak. Look what I just did. I flipped to the back pages. Why?
Child 3:	They tell something.
Mrs. Hall:	I thought there might be a picture of Maurice Sendak and wanted to see. [The end flap was blank.] Maurice Sendak is a man, and I thought we might have some information on the back pages.

After the children made further comments about the book, Mrs. Hall leafed through the title and dedication pages and asked, "What would you expect to find in this story just from looking?" They had many predictions: "flowers," "little people," "boats," "a whole bunch of babies." As she began to read, the children continued to comment, and her own comments dropped out almost entirely. She also welcomed the children's silence; sometimes she let as much as a minute go by until someone spoke. Children continued to build meaning as they talked through the rest of the book. Like other first and second graders, they were fascinated by the richness of visual detail, and they speculated about the storm, the sunflowers, and the hidden caves and paths (Table 3.1).

On completing the last page Mrs. Hall closed the book and asked the children to reflect on their experience.

Mrs. Hall:	What does this book make you think about? What does this book make you think about, Missy?
Missy:	Well the water, 'cause there was a whole bunch of water.
Mrs. Hall:	Anything else? What does it make you think about? Jenny?
Jenny:	It made me feel sad.
Mrs. Hall:	Why would you say that?
Jenny:	Because they took the baby away. They did a couple things that were sad but the ending made me feel better.
Mrs. Hall:	Hildy?
Hildy:	Well, it's sort of like in the old times because of the pictures and stuff.
Mrs. Hall:	What did the pictures make you think about?
Hildy:	Well, they're sort of lushy and stuff.
Mrs. Hall:	Lushy, Hmmm. That's lovely. Laura, what did this book make you think about?
Laura:	It made me feel happy.
Mrs. Hall:	Mmm? Which part made you feel happy?
Laura:	When that little girl . . .
Child 1:	Ida.
Laura:	. . . Ida got the creatures turned into water.
Mrs. Hall:	When they turned into what? [The text reads "when they quick churned into a dancing stream."]
Laura:	Like—um—like—um . . .
Mrs. Hall:	Think about it. It will probably come. Tommy?
Tommy:	Okay, ummm—it . . . There's time in it because it starts from the day—it goes all through night and back to day again.
Child 2:	And the moon—it changes.
Mrs. Hall:	The moon does. [Pause]. Does the moon really change?
Tommy:	No, it was just in different positions.
Child 2:	All it ever did was change.
Child 3:	The moon never changes.
[Lunch bell rings]	
Mrs. Hall:	Who wants this book?

This picturebook reading experience encourages collaboration rather than competition among these participants in classroom discourse, and the children's talk sets the stage for further understandings to develop and grow. Instead of a list of questions meant to satisfy some scope and sequence of comprehension skills that are found in reading textbooks or in many literature "response guides," the teacher's questions were simple ones. Yet questions like, "What does this book make you think about?" or "How does this book make you feel?" and a willingness to listen were crucial to the deep understandings and important responses that followed.

TABLE 3-1
Partial transcript of reading aloud *Outside Over There*

The Book	Teacher	Children
pp. 8–9 Mama and the children are sitting in the arbor.	[Reads the text.]	**Child 1:** Look there's those people [the goblins]. **Child 2:** They're taking stuff from her. **Child 3:** They're on every page and there's a boat in the water. **Child 2:** And they're taking stuff. **Child 4:** And there's a dog and children.
pp. 10–11 The goblins are climbing in the window. Ida looks the other way.	[Reads the text twice.]	**Child 1:** I think they're trying to scare her because they got up on the ladder—the ladder to move something—they can go around and get up to take the ladder. **Child 2:** And they're trying to scare her.
pp. 12–13 The goblins take the real baby and leave one made of ice.	[Reads the text.] Look at the eyes. Tommy?	**Child 1:** I was going to say that because they took her and then I was going to say it was a doll cause like they wanted to do something with her. **Child 2:** Goblins. **Child 3:** It's like that one story Mrs. Hall told—they took him away and were gonna do something to her and then bring 'em back cause [unintelligible] . . . **Child 4:** Oh I know [whispers]. **Child 5:** Look at the baby's eyes—they look [unintelligible] . . . **Tommy:** Um—they're getting more flowers like in the picture see there and there [turns the page] more flowers are coming.
p. 14 Ida hugs the ice baby. A ship is seen through the window.	[Reads the text.]	**Child 1:** Ohh. **Child 2:** There's still more flowers see there's [excited] . . . **Child 3:** There's the sea and there's the boat and it's wrecked. **Child 4:** Yeah. **Child 5:** It could have been his Papa's. **Child 6:** And right there—There's lightning in there.
p. 15 Ida realizes her sister is gone. A storm has sunk the ship.	[Reads the text.]	**Child 1:** Ooooh—See—and there's that boat. **Child 2:** We just said that. **Child 1:** It's like that goblin poem. **Child 3:** "The goblins'll get you if you don't watch out." [More comments.]

The Book	Teacher	Children
pp. 16–17 Ida vows to rescue her sister. She grabs her mother's yellow cloak and "made a serious mistake."	[Reads the text.] What do you think the mistake might be?	[A gasp and muffled comments.]
pp. 18–19 Ida climbs out the window backwards "into outside over there." The double-page spread shows Ida falling out her window. To the left, a ship is sitting near a bridge, and stairs lead to a stormy sky with the moon peaking through. The goblins are crossing the bridge carrying the baby.	[Reads the text.] A path to where? I like that, don't you?	**Child 1:** Look at that shadow. **Child 2:** Like they're going to *take her*. **Child 3:** Ummm—Is that a crack there? Is that a crack? **Child 4:** It looks like there's a special light there and it's there—maybe that down there it gets to the ship, the light in the picture. **Child 5:** And it has a moon coming up and everything. **Child 6:** It could be a path. **Several children:** Yeah. **Child 6:** I don't know—goblin kingdom. **Child 7:** It—oh . . . **Child 8:** Outside over there. **Child 7:** Yeah—into outside over there. **Child 9**: I was gonna say that.

Providing Time to Respond to Picturebooks

In addition to providing children with a variety of picturebooks and giving them time to read picturebooks and talk about them, most teachers also provided time for written, artistic, dramatic, and musical responses to books. They seemed to intuitively recognize that in addition to talking about a book children needed to know their books in other ways.

Thus teachers gave children a place to write, a box of props for creative dramatics, simple musical instruments, and an art corner with art supplies. In addition to crayons, these supplies included inexpensive watercolor sets and tempera paints, charcoal, pastel chalk, oil pastels, and "found" materials and paper for collages. These materials were similar to those illustrators used in their original art, and children were free to experiment and learn about these media in their own work.

Sometimes teachers helped children undertake studies more directly related to the picturebook art. Several teachers asked children to make their own Caldecott Award selections, and fifth graders wrote to that year's committee with their recommendations. Illustrator studies were common. A first second/grade class did a study of Peter Spier books, and third and fourth graders explored the books of William Steig. Fifth graders conducted their own research studies, each choosing an illustrator they wanted to learn more about. The classroom teacher often collaborated with the art teacher on projects or themes. The fifth grade teacher helped children study Japanese folktales and poetry to coordinate with the art specialist's unit on Japanese art. The art teacher helped children develop a set of criteria for judging the Caldecott books in their classroom study.

At other times teachers suggested more specific ways to explore picturebooks. Comparison charts were a common way to help children compare and contrast the books they were reading. Teachers' guidance included suggesting categories the children might consider. A kindergarten teacher, for example, asked two boys to compare Galdone's *The Three Bears* with Brinton Turkle's wordless version, *Deep in the Forest*, in which a little bear breaks into Goldilocks' house. The teacher asked the boys to fill in the following categories: "List the characters in the story," "What are the colors in the illustrations?" "Who lives in the house?" and "Who breaks into the house?"

The fifth grade teacher talked about the art elements that the children might look for in their picturebook. When they had determined a list as a group, she asked each child to compare several Caldecott books using those categories or to develop a Venn diagram that looked at differences and similarities. Just as often, however, categories emerged as children talked about their books together. Along with elements of the story, they elected to compare elements of the illustrations.

In most cases, however, responses grew out of each child's personal choice. The teacher might simply suggest that each child could choose a book and a way to respond to it as part of a study or unit. The children were not expected to do a project for every book they read, nor were they told how to respond. That is, the whole class was not assigned to create dioramas, but children were free to *choose* that form of response.

When they chose to respond with art projects, the final products might incorporate a few details from the picturebook or it might pay close homage to an illustrator's style and medium. In addition, the elements of art often showed up in their writing. During a study of Japan, George, a fourth grader, created a collage in response to Gerald McDermott's folktale, *The Stonecutter: A Japanese Folktale* (Figure 3.11). To accompany his art, he wrote:

> I did a collage from *The Stonecutter* by Gerald McDermott. First I started out with blue green and blue purple chalk. Then I used green shiny fancy paper for the mountain. The spirit of the mountain is done in waxy green paper. Next I made the stonecutter's hut out of felt-like royal blue paper. Also I cut a crescent shaped moon from waxy light blue paper. Last I finished off with the stone cutter. He is made of shiny aqua turquoise paper.

George had not copied the medium of the original book but was inspired by the art to create something uniquely his own. His work shows how the art of a picturebook and the chance to respond to it through art can influence children's writing.

Moreover, despite the fact that experts such as Bruno Bettleheim (1975) argued that illustrations interfered with children's ability to form their own visual images, the writing and artwork that resulted from their experiences with picturebooks may have enhanced children's abilities to create mental images. Even when older children read unillustrated prose and poetry they chose to interpret their responses through art. Mrs. Hall reported that when she began Jill Paton Walsh's science fiction novel, *The Green Book*, children didn't want to see the few black and white illustrations by Lloyd Bloom. Instead, she recalled:

FIGURE 3.11
A fourth grader's response to McDermott's
The Stonecutter

One person said, "Can I get my journal?" and I said, "Certainly you can get your journal." And then someone else said, "Can I get mine?" So it started. Every day there would be an increasing number who chose to get their journals.

Many of the children chose to draw in their journals while she read, and this was the first time she remembered this happening. Toward the end of the book, some of the children decided that they did want to see Bloom's pictures, but "very few chose to do so," Mrs. Hall recounted. But from that time on, many of the children chose to sketch as they listened to her read.

At times, the experience *surrounding* the book and not specifically a single book provided the impetus for art and writing. As part of a class unit on Japan, third and fourth graders had been studying World War II and the bombing of Hiroshima. Their teacher read Eleanor Coerr's *Sadako and the Thousand Paper Cranes* aloud, and the children collected other books and materials about the war.

These experiences were an important introduction to Toshi Maruki's *Hiroshima No Pika*, a moving account of the bombing as told by a survivor. Tina, a fourth grader, created a picture of the atomic dome in Hiroshima and wrote:

FIGURE 3.12
Maruki's *Hiroshima No Pika* inspired a
fourth grader's art and writing.

As the evening sky turns to the dark night sky we light paper lanterns and let them float freely on the open pond with the spirits of our ancestors. The purples, pinks, and blues of the sky reflect onto the atomic dome which in 1945 August, the atom bomb blew up on top of. Today is August 6 1982 and we are celebrating peace day. I wrote on the lanterns the name of a dear friend and relative that died of the atom bomb.

Her art and her writing reflect the very personal way in which she has responded to reading. It also exemplifies how an aesthetic experience can inform a child's feelings and ideas (Figure 3.12).

I believe that the chance to respond to books in different ways is important to deepening children's responses to books. Although some would argue that responses other than discussion are not authentic and have no place in child-centered class-rooms, I have found that it is natural for both children and adults to choose *many* diverse ways to return to a book to know it more deeply. The important thing is to recognize the teacher's important role in helping children make the choices that will deepen response.

CONCLUSION

Maurice Sendak (1993) tells of receiving a 14-page letter from a 12-year-old girl telling him how much she hated *Outside Over There*. As he read through her letter, in which she detailed her dislike page by page, it became clear to him that by the end of her letter she clearly understood the meaning he had been trying to convey through the art and words. Although she disliked the book, the important thing for him was that she had considered it so carefully and felt so deeply about it.

Maxine Greene has argued that "art education, like aesthetic education, can create domains where there are new possibilities of vision and awareness. Art educators can help awareness feed into an expanding life of meaning, can make increasingly available moments of clarity, moments of joy" (1978, p. 196). Certainly the classrooms described in this book provide a model for the domains Greene envisions, and the teachers we have seen understood how to create these possibilities for their students.

Louise Rosenblatt (1978) has suggested that aesthetic response consists of multiple strands that need to be allowed for and developed in readers. In one strand, the reader "responds to cues, adopts a stance, develops anticipatory frameworks, senses, synthesizes, and reorganizes." In a second strand, the reader reacts to the work, registering "approval, disapproval, pleasure, shock, acceptance/rejection." In the third strand, the reader recognizes "technical traits of the text, of the author's [illustrator's] role" (p. 69).

If we are to allow all these strands to develop in response to picturebooks, we need to lead children back into the books to deepen and extend initial reactions. Teachers who understand the complexity of this process will provide children with good picturebooks, give them time to read, take time to talk with them about the books, and provide them with a variety of ways to respond to picturebooks in collaborative classroom communities.

PART

II

The Art of the Picturebook

CHAPTER

4

*A History of the
Picturebook*

*A*young child clutches a favorite picturebook to her chest like a well-loved doll. A group of youngsters sits rapt before a picturebook. It often seems as if this art object works a magic spell upon children. Perhaps *magic* is the best word to describe the bright connection between audience and art, but it is not only with children and not only in this century that such magic has been worked.

Part I of this book was based on observations of children's day-to-day interactions with picturebooks that took place in some special classrooms. The children and adults in these contexts were my teachers, and their responses to picturebooks were described to suggest possibilities for classroom practice in other settings. In Part II, I hope to add to these possibilities by exploring the potential of the picturebook as an art object, detailing its history, proposing a theory of criticism based on its uniqueness, and describing the approaches of contemporary illustrators to its production.

In this century the picturebook has been the province of young children. Aside from the publication of small-press, limited-edition art books meant for an adult audience, the production of picturebooks has been aimed at preschool and primary grade children, and the marketing of picturebooks has been directed toward parents, librarians, and teachers who purchase books for these children. Even today, adults tend to place picturebooks on library shelves labeled "easy reading," and older children may refer to them as "baby books." Yet many modern picturebooks are intellectually and visually sophisticated and may demand a range of experience and developmental understandings that are beyond many young children.

Many teachers are recognizing this, and picturebooks are showing up not only in the upper elementary school grades but also in middle school and high school classrooms. In addition, adults seem to be discovering picturebooks; several of those published for the children's market have reached the adult best-seller list of *The New York Times*. It is my guess that these adults aren't buying them for children but that they, too, find picturebooks a satisfying and perhaps enriching aesthetic experience.

This should not really be surprising, for throughout its long and varied history, the picturebook has had a broad audience and a wide appreciation as an art object in its own right. That aesthetic experience arises from images and ideas combined in some complete form that is remade as an audience brings to it their own personal intellectual and emotional understandings. Sometimes such experiences occur alone, but often the company of others provides opportunities to know the picturebook even more deeply.

The picturebook itself, then, may have changed over time due to social, cultural, and technological factors, but the *experience* of it seems remarkably unchanged. We can compare children's responses and our own to traditions that date back thousands of years. We can also appreciate that although the picturebook has remained a vital art object because the form has evolved over the centuries, it still remains a work of art that speaks to our imagination. We respond to it with the deepest reaches of our emotions as well as our intellect.

THE FIRST PICTUREBOOKS

If we understand the picturebook experience as one in which participants engage both intellectual and emotional resources with a visual/verbal art form, we can trace the first picturebooks back perhaps as far as 40,000 years. Evidence suggests that the Australian aborigines have practiced "dreamings" for at least that long (Crumlin &

Knight, 1991; Hughes, 1988). Today these dreamings take the form of sculptures and rock, sand, or bark paintings. Rock engravings that date back to 30,000 B.C. suggest that this is the oldest continual art form in existence. These dreamings intermingle myth with the attempt to give visual form to that myth. Robert Hughes (1988) explains that dreamings are for the aborigine the world's spirit ancestors, and the deeds of these ancestors form a huge narrative or artifact of the intellect. The paintings and sculptures that result are an individual artist's attempt to capture the "maps of landscape and the ancestors it contains" (p. 80).

Certainly this intermingling of picture and myth, narrative and image must have been present in the caves of Lascaux in France or Altamira, Spain, 15,000 years ago. Joseph Campbell (1986) argues, "Just as every shrine and ceremony in the ancient world, . . . had its origin in legend so must these sanctuaries of the old stone age have had theirs" (p. 311). The paintings of bison, horses, and deer on the cave walls were probably the focus of magical hunting and puberty rites in which legends and words hinged upon the pictured forms. Campbell speculates that the power of these ceremonies must have been immense. He imagines the long descent into the inner chambers of the cave, leaving the bright world behind.

> A terrific sense of claustrophobia and simultaneously of release from every context of the world above, assails the mind . . . where darkness no longer is an absence of light but an experienced force. And when a light is flashed to reveal the beautifully painted bulls and mammoths, flocks of reindeer, trotting ponies, wooly rhinos, and dancing shaman of those caves the images smite the mind as indelible imprints. (1986, p. 66.)

Thus those ancient participants might have begun their involvement in a deeply powerful human experience. Although the artistic product does not resemble today's picturebook, it may represent a similar aesthetic process.

Using the products of technology available (there was of course no paper, no written alphabet, no printing presses or book binderies), the artists created products similar to the picturebooks of today.

The paintings were likely a result of a cultural need—the need to represent through image and myth the basic aspects of survival of the individual and the race. The rituals surrounding the cave paintings were probably social. The paintings were not experienced in solitude but as part of a group ceremony and interaction. Individual response, however, must have been present in this group setting and was likely to change and deepen as participants returned to the scene on some systematic basis. There is reason to believe that these "stories" were retold again and again, for the images are painted on top of earlier images, indicating a repeated "reading" or re-experiencing of the art form (Campbell, 1986). Thus these technological, cultural, and social underpinnings provide the basis throughout history for the individual's response to image and idea now found in the picturebook.

In intervening centuries, visual art on walls, canvas, or other decorated objects continued to combine with story or idea to play a profound role in human culture and society. Even after the advent of writing and books, frescoes, paintings, reliefs, and many other art forms retained a strong storytelling propensity.

The first objects, however, that had the attributes associated with a modern picturebook emerged in several locations around 2700 B.C. At this time, people of the Mesopotamian region were using marks pressed into wet clay, and the Chinese were writing on long strips of bamboo or wood. In Egypt, papyrus, made from the stems of the papyrus plant that grew along the Nile River, provided a technological advance. By placing strips of the papyrus stem in layers and putting them under pressure, the crushed strips were matted into porous, loosely textured material. This gave the Egyptians an advantage over other Middle and Far Eastern societies because the papyrus scrolls were much more easily transported and stored than the unwieldy wood or clay tablets, and in the dry desert climate the scrolls were nonperishable.

In the Egyptian papyrus, the descendant of the cave paintings and the ancestor of the modern picturebook may be found. These papyri, especially those referred to as the *Book of the Dead*, combined pictorial image and verbal story. This portable and permanent object was accessible to those who knew the writing system, but it was also revered by those who didn't (Figure 4.1). The placement of pictures and words is remarkably similar to what we see in today's picturebooks. The pictorial images are predominant, while the words are part of the overall composition and are pleasingly balanced and integrated with the images. Often what appears to be a decorative border accompanies the central scene, anticipating the beautifully designed borders of the illuminated books of the Middle Ages or the modern-day picturebooks of artists like Jan Brett or Trina Schart Hyman.

The purpose of these books may be very similar to that of the cave paintings, however, because the *Book of the Dead* was a personal guide prepared for and interred with important personages. The book consisted of "a collection of spells, incantations and rituals which eased the soul's passage through the nether world" (Harthan, 1981, p. 12). The book's audience probably remained a wide one, for even those who were not literate may have had access to the books in communal celebrations. Individual and social response thus may have continued to be part of the aesthetic experience that centered on this picturebook.

While the *Book of the Dead* continued the ritualistic tradition of the cave paintings, a more secular type of picturebook emerged as early as the 12th century B.C. Among these were animal fables, books of astronomy and magic, and satire and erotica. Around 500 B.C. the Greeks and then the Romans adapted the scroll books of the

FIGURE 4.1
Funerary papyrus *(Book of the Dead)* **of Hunefer, circa 1310 B.C.**

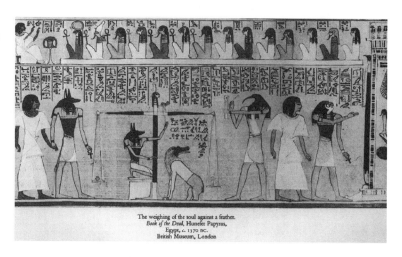

The weighing of the soul against a feather.
Book of the Dead, Hunefer Papyrus,
Egypt, c. 1370 BC.
British Museum, London

Egyptians. Although few of these survive, Weitzman (1947) proposes that the Homeric poems and dramas were illustrated with as many as 700 illustrations. Bland (1958) suggests that literary illustrations probably followed scientific and portrait illustration, surfacing for the first time about the fourth century A.D. We cannot be sure because the great fires in the library at Alexandria destroyed any hard evidence of these forms.

The layout or composition of the visual image with printed text was an important factor in these early books. According to Bland (1958), composition took three forms in the earliest Egyptian books: the frieze picture, in which smaller illustrations ran along the top or bottom of the scroll; the column picture, in which the picture is placed within a column of writing and is usually the same width as the text; and the full-size picture, also referred to as the miniature. These various types of layouts are familiar from today's picturebooks and are logical within the restraints of the technicalities of printing. However, there were no such restraints on these early book designers. Because the books were done by hand, the layout could have taken any direction. Bland suggests that the introduction of such features "must have been one of the great decisions in the history of the book" (p. 25).

A NEW BOOK FORM

A second major advance in picturebooks came in the fourth century A.D. when the Romans invented the codex. Based on the multi-leaved clay tablets used in Greece and Rome at the time, this technique allowed bookmakers to cut pieces of papyrus or parchment into sheets, which were folded and sewn together in the fold, then bound with thin pieces of wood covered with leather. The codex was much easier to use than scrolls and allowed both sides of the page to be used. Harthan (1981) points out that the complete text of Virgil's *Aeneid* would have required 12 papyrus rolls of 30 to 35 feet each but could have been written on a single codex. Moreover, the codex encouraged a more disciplined sense of layout and design in picturebooks. The full-page, framed illustrations—sometimes alone, sometimes facing a page of printed text—was the result of this form. The invention of the codex, according to Harthan, "affected book production as profoundly and permanently as did the invention of printing in the mid-fifteenth century" (p. 12).

The codex also allowed a wider rage of style and media to be used in the illustrations. Rolled scrolls required mostly line drawing since layers of paint would crack when rolled and unrolled. In addition, parchment or vellum, made of animal skins, gradually replaced papyrus, which rapidly disintegrated in the Mediterranean climate. The change in these forms and materials allowed the use of rich colors, including gold (Janson, 1991). The style of illustration was influenced by the style of painting used at the time, yet these pictures seem remarkable forerunners of the illuminations of the Middle Ages and of many of the picturebooks of today. Janson (1991) describes the Virgil manuscript:

> . . . the picture, separated from the rest of the page by a heavy frame, has the effect of a window and in the landscape we find remnants of deep space, perspective and the play of light and shade. (p. 262)

Harthan (1981) also remarked on the surprising modernity of these early Roman picturebooks and stated, "The theory that the ancestry of the picturebook is to be sought not only in Egyptian papyri but also in narrative cycles found in wall frescoes, vase paintings, sarcophagi, and metalwork seems here to find confirmation" (p. 140). The combination of image and story found on the cave walls at Lascaux was very different in form from the codexes of the fifth century, yet the emotional and intellectual experience surrounding each remained remarkably similar. Although they are now less the object of a communally shared event, picturebooks are still likely to evoke highly personal aesthetic responses in readers. "The magical properties of books," Olmert argues, "is universal" (1992 p. 23).

As the Roman empire drew to a close, the picturebook was evolving in many areas of the world. In China the invention of paper and printing happened independent of Western events. *The Diamond Sutra*, the oldest printed picturebook, printed from woodblocks on a scroll, was written about 868 A.D. At about this same time, the book became central to Islam and contributed in two important ways to Western art and book traditions. First, the art of calligraphy was central to Islamic art, admired above all the other arts, according to Avrin (1991). Olmert (1992) suggests that Christian monks producing manuscripts in the West must have been acquainted with some of these beautiful scripts. Second, because the Koran could not depict human and animal figures, geometric and plant forms were used to decorate the book's pages. This contributed to what Olmert suggests is "one of Islam's gifts: abstraction" (p. 53) and perhaps to the highly decorative botanical borders that would emerge in Western manuscripts later in the Middle Ages.

Between 300 B.C. and 1500 A.D., the Maya created codices that consisted of bark, pounded and covered with a thin layer of lime plaster. These sheets formed long screen-folded manuscripts that were visually similar to Egyptian scrolls (Figure 4.2). Olmert (1992) declares, "The most remarkable part about these codices is their design, the way the scribe controls space" (p. 35). He also suggests that the reading of the books may have been part of a royal ceremony. He imagines them being read "on court occasions by scribes or priests wielding decorative pointers, the texts themselves little more than elegant aide-memoirs to long tales cunningly embroidered on

FIGURE 4.2
Mayan Codex Madrid, circa 1250–1450 A.D.

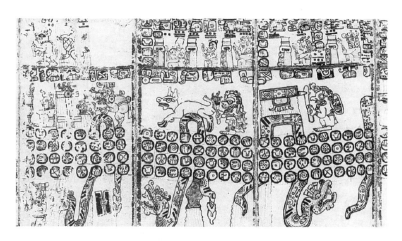

Source: From Akademische Druck-u. Verlagsanstalt Grasz-Austria. Reprinted from *The Smithsonian Book of Books*, copyright © 1992.

a tropical night" (Olmert, 1992, p. 35). In addition, although we have no artifacts that date back that far, native tribes in North America may have developed picturebooks of their own, similar perhaps to the buffalo hide paintings common to Plains tribes of the 19th century.

In Europe, the picturebook survived and flourished in two major European centers. In Byzantium, the Emperor Constantine commissioned scriptures written and illustrated on parchment codices. The books that grew out of this Eastern European tradition relied on Greco-Roman style, which gradually merged the motifs that came to be associated with the stylistic, uniform pictorial symbols of early Christian art. These included the elongated, angular figures and stiff poses seen in Byzantine frescoes, stained glass windows, and paintings.

During this same time, book illustration in Western Europe, particularly in England and Ireland, evolved in an independent school, reflecting styles and motifs of "barbaric" invaders such as the Celts. These were predominately ornamental and included interlacing, beast ribbon designs, and spiral patterns such as those found in the *Book of Kells* (800 A.D.) or the *Lindisfarne Gospels* (690 A.D.). In these books, a visual story was sublimated to visual decoration; very few portraits or landscapes appear aside from stylized portraits of saints (Figure 4.3).

Although the term illuminated is applied to any decorated manuscript beginning with Egytian papyri, the manuscripts of the Middle Ages are best known as

FIGURE 4.3
Initial page of the Gospel of St. Matthew, Lindisfarne manuscript

Source: From *The Lindisfarne Gospels* by Janet Backhouse. Copyright © 1981 by Phaidon Press Limited. Reprinted by permission.

"illuminated" because of the gold that was often used in their execution. Bland (1958) argues that during these years illustrations that sought to clarify were replaced with illuminations that sought to beautify. That is, the original purpose of the uniform stylized picture of early Christian art may have been to present recognizable pictures that would spread the Gospels to an illiterate and linguistically diverse audience. These later forms show a move toward art for art's sake and also a move toward the expression of more individualistic painting styles.

In A.D. 800, Charlemagne invited the monk Alcuin to journey to Europe from York in Northern England to help unify his empire. As a result, the artistic traditions in the Irish and English manuscripts began to merge with classical forms from the East. In addition, Alcuin helped devise the Carolingian alphabet, which was "used in some of the most beautiful and legible texts ever written," according to Olmert (1992, p. 74). It also was a great improvement over the less legible Gothic lettering widely used (Figure 4.4).

Western illustration thus became more individualized and dynamic, beginning, perhaps, with the *Utrecht Psalter* in the early ninth century. Bland (1958) suggests that "with its unadorned impressionistic line, its fluttering draperies, and its figures

FIGURE 4.4
Page from the Grandval Bible, circa 840 A.D.

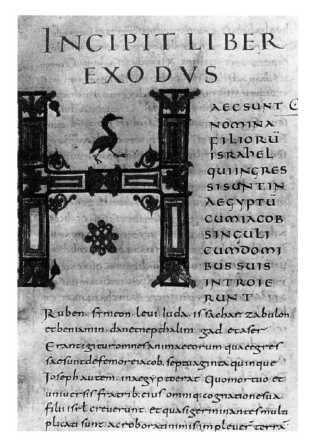

all in violent motion it must have produced on the contemporary eye an overpowering contrast to the static, highly-coloured illumination of the time, the more so as it was applied to the same traditional subject matter" (p. 44). This book may have been one of the first in which the illustrator took on more than the role of craftsman to become a creator in the true artistic sense (Figure 4.5). Certainly its influence on Romanesque and Gothic styles was profound, as was the influence of the picturebook on other art forms during the period.

Whatever the styles of these books, the Church became responsible for the continuation of the picturebook, not only to present and glorify the message of the church but also as a center for the craft of bookmaking. In addition, church scribes continued to preserve and illustrate secular works, although religious texts primarily were judged worthy of illumination. During this period, the picturebook regained some of the mystical qualities of its earliest ancestors. Among a largely illiterate population, the illustrations retained their power to effect a profound religious experience as the individual participated in the rituals surrounding stories of the old and new testaments.

In the 13th century, however, the picturebook began to move into the province of the secular world. Universities and a more widely literate populace increased the demand for books. This trend led to the illustration of many more secular texts: histories, epic poems, and romances. The Irish *Tain*, a Celtic epic that introduced the hero Cuchulain, was written by an Irish scribe in 1106. It was part of a manuscript called *The Book of the Dun Cow* because of its dark cowhide binding (Olmert, 1992).

The 14th century saw the appearance of four poems by the Gawain poet, among them *Sir Gawain and the Green Knight*. In 1410 *The Canterbury Tales* were illustrated in the Ellesmere manuscript with Geoffrey Chaucer appearing in its pages riding his horse, perhaps to Canterbury (Figure 4.6). Readers of children's literature will recognize that all these works have their modern-day counterparts in books like Tomie dePaola's *Fin M'Coul: The Giant of Knockmany Hill* (Cuchulain is the villain);

FIGURE 4.5
Utrecht Psalter, ninth century

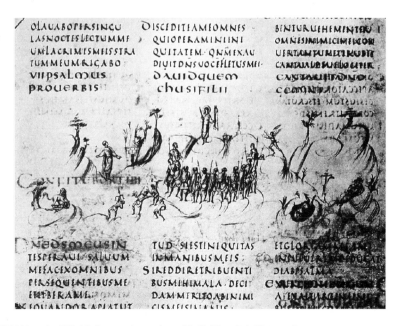

Source: From UNIVERSITY LIBRARY, Utrecht, MS 32, f. 4r, as reproduced in D. Bland, *A History of Book Illustration: The Illuminated Manuscript and the Printed Book*, 1958, World Publishing.

FIGURE 4.6
The Ellesmere manuscript of *The Canterbury*
***Tales* featured a drawing of Geoffrey**
Chaucer.

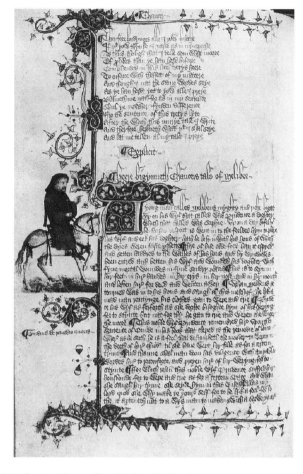

Source: This item is reproduced by permission of The Huntington Library, San Marino, California.

Walter Wangerin's *The Book of the Dun Cow*; Selina Hasting's *Sir Gawain and the Green Knight*, illustrated by Juan Wijngaard; and Barbara Cohen's adaptation of Chaucer's *The Canterbury Tales*, illustrated by Trina Schart Hyman.

Harthan argues that "after the long near monopoly of religious subjects, illustration was at last becoming popular, instructional, and recreational in a manner we can recognize as anticipating modern attitudes" (1981, p. 48). With this shift of focus, the illustrations began to reflect the real world of the time, adapting forms from contemporary architecture, sculpture, and painted windows in more realistic portrayals. Some illustrations included the interiors of contemporary homes; others used the device of the window to look out on contemporary landscapes. In an illumination from the 15th century manuscript, *The Hours of Mary of Burgundy*, for example, a woman dressed in the costume of the time is sitting in front of a window in the lower left foreground reading a book, with a small dog resting on her lap. On the windowsill are accouterments of her home, a necklace, several loose carnations, and a vase of irises. Through the window we see an interior of a church where the Madonna and Child are paid homage (Figure 4.7). This scene, too, has its connec-

FIGURE 4.7
The Hours of Mary of Burgundy, 15th century

Source: By permission of Österreichische Nationalbibliothek, Austria as reproduced in M. Olmert
(1992) *The Smithsonian Book of Books*.

tion to modern-day picturebooks set in Medieval time and is recalled in unique ways by Nancy Burkert and Trina Schart Hyman in their illustrations of The Grimm Brothers' *Snow White and the Seven Dwarfs* (Figure 4.8).

Although ornament remained an important component of the illustrations until the end of the Middle Ages, it evolved into different forms. For example, Flemish artists in the 14th and 15th centuries began to treat the decorated border like a frame, with the picture set in the middle. Often this device brought the text forward and set the picture in the background. The exceptionally detailed flowers and borders in these manuscripts, as well as the inclusion of real landscapes in the increasingly popular books of hours, are thought to have influenced Dutch still-life and landscape painting in the late 16th century. They have certainly spoken to modern illustrators like Juan Wijngaard, who has used such motifs in his illustrations for Selena Hastings' *Sir Gawain and the Loathly Lady* (Figure 4.9).

During this period in Europe there was little difference between the products of illustrators and painters besides the size of the artwork and the fact that strict guild laws forbid the two from trespassing on each other's territory. The "miniatures," as the paintings in books were called, were still done by hand (not printed) just as paintings, altar pieces, and frescoes were. The status of the two artists was equal, and the book arts had important influences on the art of painting. According to Olmert (1992):

FIGURE 4.8
Opening pages from two illustrators' versions of the Grimm Brothers' *Snow White*: (a) Hyman and (b) Burkert

Source: Figure a from SNOW WHITE by Paul Heins. Text copyright © 1974 by Paul Heins; illustra-
          tions copyright © 1974 by Trina Schart Hyman. By permission of Little, Brown and Com-
          pany. Figure b reprinted by permission of Farrar, Straus & Giroux, Inc: Illustration by Nancy
          Ekholm Burkert from SNOW-WHITE AND THE SEVEN DWARFS by the Brothers Grimm,
          translated by Randall Jarrell. Illustrations copyright © 1972 by Nancy Ekholm Burkert.

As the demand for illustrated books increased, it caused seismic changes in the way books were produced. The distinction between scribes and craftsmen who decorated books was increasing, and over time the latter were to become more important. Modern art, it could be said, began in the scriptorium in the work of rubricators, who added fancy initial letters, usually in red ink, to the text; of illuminators, who applied goldleaf, silver, or colored paint to the page; and of miniaturists who peppered each page with flowers and grotesques and painted historiated initials—big letters containing portraits and landscapes. (p. 84)

During this time books also came to be valued, not for their magical or religious qualities, but as objects of art in themselves. By the 15th century books of hours, collections of hymns, prayers, and psalms meant to be read at eight hourly devotions, were among the most profitable in the book trade. Harthan reports that wealthy burghers and even some students could now afford to buy books. "Book

FIGURE 4.9
Comparison of (a) *Sir Gawain and the Loathly Lady* and (b) *The Boucicaut Hairs*

Shuddering with horror he slowly turned his head. Standing before him was the most beautiful woman he had ever seen. She had long golden hair hanging to her waist, her figure was slender as a fairy's, her pale skin as perfect as a piece of polished ivory.

collecting and with it an aesthetic appreciation of books in their own right had arrived" (1981, p. 42).

Two major technological advances took place during the early Middle Ages that affected book availability and production. The first was the development of paper, which may have spread to Europe from China through Islamic countries. This material, made by hand from rag pulp, was not as strong as parchment, but it was much cheaper, and this may have further widened the audience for the picturebook while it reduced the quality of the original artwork. At about the same time inks the proper consistency for woodblock printing were developed. This method of printing, in which letters and pictures were cut into a single block, appeared in Europe in the early 15th century and was the precursor of movable type.

A NEW TECHNOLOGY

The great revolution in book printing came with the invention of the printing press during the 1450s. This invention signaled the end of the hand-illuminated book and the beginning of picturebook-making as a commercial rather than a purely aesthetic process. In fact, the early printers were probably not as much concerned with the beauty of the finished product as they were with making a profit.

But the advent of a method by which books could be mass produced quickly on fairly inexpensive paper for a wider, less privileged audience further supports the argument that the nature and audience of the picturebook changes as a result of social, cultural, and technological changes. This period in history, which saw the rise of the middle class as well as a more even distribution of wealth and power, was reflected in the picturebooks of the time. As may be expected, the themes of the picturebooks appealed to popular as well as religious tastes. Among the titles of these first mass-produced books are Boccaccio's *Decameron* and Aesop's fables.

The illuminated book did not, of course, disappear overnight; it coexisted for many years with typeset forms. Initially, too, the mass-produced picturebook searched for an identity of its own and perhaps for an audience. The plates printed on the presses were often cast to resemble handwritten books. Other mechanically printed books were illustrated by hand even though the woodblock was widely known and ideally suited to the typeset text. At other times, the wood block was used for illustrations, but only to produce the simplest of outlines, which were then colored in by hand.

Eventually, however, the Gothic lettering style developed for the handwritten manuscripts of the early Middle Ages was replaced by the Roman alphabet. This style, along with Italian sensitivity for the layout of pictures and text, spread to the rest of Europe. Bland (1958) also suggests that a more subdued sense of book decoration may have given rise to the value which Renaissance scholars began to place on the literary qualities of the book at the expense of the pictorial qualities valued in earlier periods. Perhaps this was also due in part to a phenomenon that gave rise to a new audience for the picturebook: the recognition of childhood as a separate culture.

PICTUREBOOKS FOR CHILDREN

Prior to the 16th or 17th century, picturebooks were created for an adult audience. Children were not considered a group apart, separate from adults in entertainments or other artifacts of culture. Early paintings of the nativity, for example, show the infant Jesus as a miniature adult; babies' different physical proportions were not recognized. Aries (1962), for example, explains that the artists of "the tenth and eleventh centuries did not dwell on the image of childhood, and that that image had neither interest nor even reality to them" (p. 34). Other paintings show that children dressed in the same clothes as adults, and adults played the same games that we now associate with childhood. Aries speculates that this may have been due to the terrible toll taken by disease in these dark ages. Parents emotionally could not afford to pay much attention to children if their chances of survival was small.

Although Avrin (1991) mentions that alphabet books created to teach children Hebrew had been found in Egypt at a much earlier time, the first children's book is generally accepted to be the *Orbis Pictus*, an alphabet book intended to "entice witty children." Published in 1658 by John Amos Comenius as *Orbis sensualium pictus (The Visible World in Pictures)*, it might more accurately be called the first basal reader because Comenius' aim was to teach, not to entertain (Figure 4.10). Furthermore,

FIGURE 4.10
A page from the *Orbis Pictus*

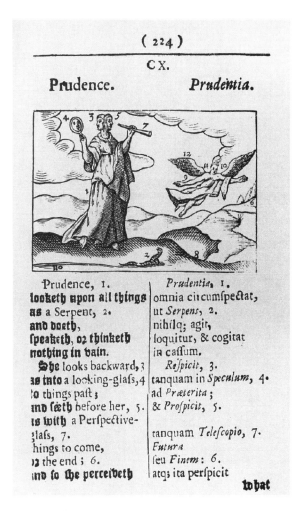

Source: From the Folger Shakespeare Library. Reprinted from *The Smithsonian Book of Books* by Michael Olmert.

although picturebooks continued to be published for the edification and entertainment of adults, for many more years children's picturebooks retained an educational purpose. Aside from little chapbooks (inexpensive, condensed versions of old tales crudely printed and bound and sold by peddlers), most children's picturebooks of the 17th and 18th centuries were meant to instruct them in moral behavior and Christian duty. For example, the first children's book published in America, in 1656, was titled *Spiritual Milk for Boston Babies in Either England Drawn From the Breast of Both Testaments for Their Soul's Nourishment* (Norton, 1991).

By the 1700s however, the popularity of collections of fairy tales and fables and the continuing success of chapbooks convinced British publisher John Newbery to consider publishing books for children solely for their amusement. Influenced by John Locke, Newbery was an "advocate of a milder way of educating children" (Norton, 1991, p. 51). He published *A Little Pretty Pocket Book* in 1744, the first of many books for children.

ADVANCES IN PRINTING TECHNIQUES

Newbery's success with this and other books propelled the field of publishing for children forward. However, advancements in printing technology as much as cultural mores or societal practices were responsible for the breakthrough in publishing high quality picturebooks for children in the late 1800s.

Following the invention of the printing press and movable type, illustrations in books were produced by one of several printing methods. Wood block printing or engravings were among the earliest forms. English printer William Caxton, for example, used this method to print the first book in English around 1480. These illustrations were at their most beautiful in the works of masters like Albrecht Dürer in the early 1500s (Figure 4.11).

Wood cuts and wood engravings are both relief techniques, meaning the design stands out from the background. As the background is cut away, the design remains raised above the surface to receive the ink, which is then printed on the paper. In another relief technique, *intaglio*, the design is incised into and below the surface of metal. Etching, developed in Europe in the 1500s, was a variation of metal engraving. The metal plate was covered with wax, and tools drew the design into the wax. When the plate was dipped in acid, the metal where the wax had been removed was eaten away (Harthan, 1981).

Variations on these printing techniques were used well into the 1800s until lithography was invented by Aloys Senefelder in 1798. In this process, a design is drawn or painted onto a smooth stone with a waxy substance, much like drawing on paper with a crayon. After the design is covered with a fixative (a mixture of gum arabic and acid), the stone is wet with water and then inked. The ink adheres only to the wax and can then be printed onto paper when pressure is applied. Lithography made possible the printing of a much more painterly style of illustration. It also allowed for the reproduction of musical tomes and math and chemistry volumes, which required the use of special symbols (Olmert, 1992).

Reproducing many prints was difficult, so printers kept searching for effective and inexpensive color reproduction techniques. Aside from studio experiments like the colored etchings of William Blake, color had to be added to prints by hand, using brush or stencil. Scarfe (1975) suggests that the need for color was particularly felt in picturebooks published for children. He argues:

> The story of children's books is intimately bound up with the search for methods of colour printing, and in this the very necessity for colour spurred artists and printers to solve the problems. It is thus that children's books have had an important role in graphic art as a field for experimentation. (p. 9)

FIGURE 4.11
"Visitation," from *The Life of the Virgin* **woodcut by Albrecht Dürer**

Source: From Oeffentliche Kunstsammlung, Kupferstichkabinett Basel. Reprinted from *The History of the Illustrated Book* by John Harthan, copyright © 1981, Thames and Hudson, Ltd.

INTO THE 20TH CENTURY

The credit for achieving mass-market color reproduction and thus for ushering in a golden age of children's picturebooks must go to publishers like Edmund Evans. By the 1860s, when color printing techniques had begun to stabilize, Edmunds, an artist himself, made a real effort to refine the process. Alderson (1986) suggests:

> There is no gainsaying the care which Edmund Evans gave to the early print-runs of his picturebooks, if not always the later ones. The "clever artist" in him recognized the need for printing techniques to match the illustrator's work as closely as possible and he was one of the pioneers in applying photographic processes to the preparation of woodblocks. He was also sensitive to colour-values and how they could be mingled through the overprinting of tints, and he exercised great care in his choice of pigments for his inks. (p. 75)

With this attention to detail, Evans convinced artists like Walter Crane, Kate Greenaway, and Randolph Caldecott to create works especially for children. Caldecott's first book, *The Diverting History of John Gilpin*, was published in 1878. He is called the father of the modern picturebook because his drawings reflected the exuberant liveliness that characterized children's responses (Figure 4.12). Moreover, as Moebius (1986) suggests, it was due to Evans' sense of design that the picturebook would become the unity of pictures and text that it is today. In England, the field of illustration for children would go on to attract now-legendary figures like Beatrix Potter, Arthur Rackham, Leslie Brooke, and Ernest Shepard, while America would give us Howard Pyle, N. C. Wyeth, and Jessie Wilcox Smith. Their work is still held up as an example for illustrators who followed and for illustrators to follow.

In 1926, *Clever Bill*, considered the first children's picture story book, was written in England by William Nicholson (Figure 4.13). Wanda Gag's *Millions of Cats* followed in the United States in 1928. These stories were told with very little text and relied heavily on the illustrations to convey meaning. This format predominates in children's picturebooks today.

FIGURE 4.12
Caldecott's lively style is evident in *The Diverting History of John Gilpin*.

Source: From THE DIVERTING HISTORY OF JOHN GILPIN by William Cowper, illustrated by R. Caldecott. Copyright © 1977 by Frederick Warne Ltd.

FIGURE 4.13
In William Nicholson's
Clever Bill, the pictures tell
the story with a little support from text.

Source: Although every effort was made, we were unable to trace all copyright holders for this figure.

For the greater part of the 20th century, the character of picturebooks was
shaped both by the emerging audience of young children and the technology available for reproducing these highly visual books. By the early 1900s, techniques such
as offset printing, in which an image was transferred to the printing plate by photo-
graphic negative, had replaced hand-colored engravings as the method for translating
original art to the printed page. According to Ward (1978), these methods allowed
more faithful reproduction of the original artwork than did letterpress printing. In
addition, the paper used in offset printing more closely resembled the paper used for
the original artwork.

For a full-color book, even the streamlined processes of offset printing often
required many tedious hours of color preseparation on the part of the artist, and full
color was still expensive to reproduce. For this reason, many books were done in
black and white or in only two or three colors well into mid-century. Even so, illustrators like Virginia Lee Burton, Wanda Gag, Clement Hurd, Robert McCloskey,
Esphyr Slobodkina, Lyn Ward, and Leonard Weisgard produced works of art that
reached out to touch, entertain, and enthrall their audiences (Figure 4.14). Many of
their books are still in print today, and they serve as examples of their creators' innov-
ative techniques and vibrant imaginations.

Since the early to mid-20th century, picturebooks have continued to prosper
and to change. At the end of this century, new techniques in laser printing have
streamlined the process of book production and allowed the picturebook to continue
to develop as an art form. Today's picturebooks attract an audience of readers of all
ages and intrigue artists who have discovered the picturebook as a challenging
medium for their talents. Moreover, the picturebook has never been the product of
only one culture; it seemed to develop independently from culture to culture around

FIGURE 4.14
The Little Fireman by Esphyr
Slobodkina represents an
artful blending of pictures
and text.

Source: From THE LITTLE FIREMAN by Esphyr Slobodkina. Copyright © 1938/1993 by Esphyr Slobodkina. By permission of HarperCollins Publishers.

the world. Now, however, the rise in multicultural picturebooks in the United States and the burgeoning international interest in picturebooks has allowed illustrators from many cultures to represent their unique experiences in images for all to see.

CONCLUSION

Through the centuries, the artist's role has been to understand the needs of society and, using the technology at hand, to convey some meaning through the pages of a picturebook. Although culture, society, and the character of the book may have changed, I'd like to think that these artists have remained remarkably alike. Throughout the years they have been people who had some inner need to tell about their world through pictures. They may have shared the longing of Cormac, a young peasant living in the ninth century in Mary Stolz' *Pangur Ban* who wants to draw in the dirt with sticks instead of dig in the fields for food. His desire to draw, expressed by a modern day writer for readers of today, is not very far removed from the artists and audiences of the past. Stolz based her character on a real person, a nameless artist living in ninth century Ireland who paused in his labors over the Gospels to include a poem to his cat within the beautiful borders he had drawn (Olmert, 1992).

Stories of such playfulness are found throughout the history of book illustration. Printer William Caxton included an engraved frontispiece in his first printed book, picturing himself presenting the book to his patroness Margaret, Duchess of Burgundy. He is on his knees, holding the book up to Margaret, and in between the two is Margaret's pet monkey, facing Caxton in exactly the same pose. In an engraving titled "Visitation" from *The Life of the Virgin*, Albrecht Dürer included a small dog sniffing the dirt in the foreground, his nose not far from a hornbook, one of the first book forms for children. On the hornbook are Dürer's initials. Perhaps this, too, was one of those books with secrets (see Figure 4.11).

In the collection of illuminated manuscripts in the Morgan Library is a book of hours done by Don Guilio Clorio in 1546. One of the scenes shows a gathering of the nobility, and off to the left is a dwarf in painter's clothes, the artist's pun on the

FIGURE 4.15
The dwarf in Hyman's illustrations for *Saint George and the Dragon* makes eye contact with the audience.

Source: From SAINT GEORGE AND THE DRAGON by Margaret Hodges. Text copyright © 1984 by Margaret Hodges; illustrations copyright © 1984 by Trina Schart Hyman. By permission of Little, Brown and Company.

term *miniature* that was applied to all book art. Four hundred and forty years later, Trina Schart Hyman would win the Caldecott Medal for distinguished illustration for Hodges' retelling of *St. George and the Dragon*, a story from that time period. Her illustrations echo the jewel-like colors and vibrant compositions of those earlier illuminations, and on the last double-page spread, among the nobility gathered for the celebrations, a dwarf at left looks out at the audience as if to share a secret smile at this bit of magic (Figure 4.15).

Indeed, perhaps it is the magic of picturebooks that conjoins the audience, the object, and the artist over the years. As Olmert so eloquently states, "The arc that connects medieval Canterbury and modern New York is clear. . . . The illustrator's enthusiastic response to the story is what lifts a tale—and us the reader—off the page. And that is any illustrator's goal" (1992, p. 252).

CHAPTER

5

Creating a
Picturebook

*I*f over the centuries it has been the illustrator's goal to lift the tale and the reader off the page, it is just as surely the illustrator's *inner* need that begins this process. Langer (1953) has proposed that the making of a work of art is the creative process that engages an artist's "utmost technical skill in the service of his [her] utmost conceptual power, imagination" (p. 40). This shared process—the exhilaration of creation and the acceptance of failure that goes with it—is an emotional experience as much as an intellectual one, and it is the emotions that infuse good art and our response to it.

This chapter, then, looks at the process of picturebook creation and at several illustrators who are representative of the larger field in their approach to their work, in their connections to the history of art and the art of the picturebook, in their appeal to children, and in their connections to classroom practice. In doing so, I hope to provide a deeper understanding of the aesthetic potential of the picturebook and how it is realized through the artist's imagination.

THE PROCESS OF CREATION

Although each illustrator brings something unique and personal to the picturebook, illustrators share certain requirements of the art form and certain steps in the procedure of creation. First, in most cases, comes a story or concept; it is rare for the pictures to be created first and then have a written text added. At the very least the artist has to start with some concept or mental construct. Chris Van Allsburg reports, for example, that his writing impulse grows out of a vague feeling about time and place, one that seems to combine a visual premise with a psychological one (Kiefer, 1987).

In many cases, of course, the illustrator is not the writer. He or she is presented with an author's finished manuscript, which is sent by an editor who thinks the two would be a good match. The illustrator takes over the job of giving visual life to the author's words. In many cases authors have no say in who will illustrate the manuscript, nor do they have any contact with the artist while the illustrations are in progress. This can result in real agony or great delight when the writer sees the final work. Well-established writers may be more involved in choosing their illustrators, but they do not always work together during the process. Exceptions exist in the collaboration of writers and illustrators like Richard Egielski and Arthur Yorinks or Don and Audrey Wood, who have collaborated successfully on a number of books.

Whether they are illustrating their own stories or concepts or someone else's, illustrators often start the process with meticulous research. Many illustrators conduct extensive library research, combing archives for sources like old photographs, maps, or prints for details to bring authenticity and deeper meaning to their picturebooks. Compare, for example, photographs of immigrants in the late 1800s, as seen in Russell Freedman's *Immigrant Kids*, to Diane Goode's illustrations for Levinson's *Watch the Stars Come Out*, set in turn-of-the-century New York City. You can see how an illustrator's research can lend authenticity to her unique artistic interpretation.

Even for artists who are not working with historical or cultural settings, however, research is an important part of the creation process. Lois Ehlert, whose bold, bright graphic designs are highly up-to-date, reports that for *Planting a Rainbow* "I visited flower gardens and parks. I spend a long time checking my facts before I begin to paint" (Cummings, 1992, p. 40).

Once they are through the pre-illustration stage, most illustrators begin their artwork with a storyboard, which gives an overview of the entire book on one flat surface. (The glossary at the end of this book includes printing and art terms.) Most picturebooks are 32 pages, two "signatures," or groups, of 16 pages each. For a 32-page picturebook, the artist would sketch out 17 rectangles: one each for the opening and closing single pages that face each end page and 15 double-page spreads (Figure 5.1). On the storyboard, the artist sketches in the major shapes, or forms, and the areas of dark, and light. Here the artist can look at the layout of each page and see how it flows into the next, and so on. This is the best stage to consider the overall design of the book and how it will hang together visually.

To see how the book will look when it is printed, the artist also makes a dummy—a mock-up of the finished book. This can be in very rough form, perhaps just a few inches in width with pictures roughly sketched in. At other times the dummy may be the actual size of the finished book with either rough sketches or fairly finished artwork. When Uri Shulevitz first began illustrating, he created a finished dummy to make up for his lack of experience. Other artists feel that this takes energy away from the final artwork (Shulevitz, 1985).

FIGURE 5.1
A sample storyboard for a picturebook

The dummy also allows the artist to decide how the verbal text will be segmented and paced through the book and to make sure that space is used satisfactorily throughout the pages. If a single picture covers two pages in a double-page spread, the artist has to be aware of the gutter, where the facing pages meet in the binding. When the final book is bound, details placed too close to the gutter or lines or images running across both pages can be lost, misaligned, or distorted.

The dummy also is a good place to consider how the endpapers will be executed and what will appear on the full title page and dedication pages. Depending on how many pages are needed to execute the story itself, the book may also have a half-title page, where only the title appears with no author or publisher information. Sometimes copyright and other information appears on the back pages rather than at the front of the book as a result of this process.

Once major decisions have been worked out in the dummy, the final artwork is executed. For some illustrators, changes may still be made during this stage of the work. Others find that once the work engages them they have to keep moving through the entire work and can't stop to make changes. Maurice Sendak reports that his earlier picturebooks like *Where the Wild Things Are* entailed conscious intellectual engagement throughout. However, once he began the artwork for his more recent endeavor, *We Are All in the Dumps with Jack and Guy: Two Nursery Rhymes with Pictures*, "this book just exploded" (Sendak, personal communication, 1993).

The media that the illustrator chooses for the original artwork can include any medium available to any artist, including sculpture. Modern-day printing techniques make it possible and relatively inexpensive to reproduce such three-dimensional originals as Molly Bang's cut-paper sculptures for *The Paper Crane*, Barbara Reid's modeling clay art for *Two by Two* (Figure 5.2), or Jennie Baker's collage constructions in *Where the Forest Meets the Sea*. Other artists use mixed media: Paul Morin mixed cloth, natural objects, sand, and oil paint in *The Dragon's Pearl* by Julie Lawson.

FIGURE 5.2
Original art such as Barbara Reid's plasticine reliefs in *Two by Two* can be reproduced using modern-day printing technology.

Source: From TWO BY TWO, 1977, author/illustrator Barbara Reid. Reprinted by permission of Scholastic, Inc.

Although today's illustrators also work in a variety of more traditional media—like cut-paper collage, charcoal, pastel, watercolor, acrylic, oil paints, and print techniques like wood block, linoleum prints, and etching—some artists have developed these in uniquely personal ways. For example, Brian Pinkney begins his illustrations with scratchboard drawings. These are created by painting black ink on a smooth white surface that takes ink easily. When the ink is dry, the drawing is scratched into it. Pinkney then uses oil pastels, a drawing medium that combines the vibrancy of crayon with the blending characteristic of pastel chalk. He rubs these into the scratched areas and then rubs some of the color back off with a medium called Liquin. In books like Robert Sans Souci's *Sukey and the Mermaid*, his approach lends a subtlety of hues and a rich sense of texture to his books' pages and also sets up a lively contrast between the scratched textures of the forms and the smooth whiteness of the rest of the page (see color insert).

Floyd Cooper brings a luminous glow to his character's faces by layering washes of oil paint on canvas board. He then works back into the paint with a kneaded rubber eraser, a soft malleable eraser often used with charcoal or pastels. As he lays on subsequent washes and then works back into them, he builds up a subtle tonal variation that is particularly suited to moving human dramas in books like Eloise Greenfield's *Grandpa's Face* (Figure 5.3).

Artist choose from a variety of media, depending on the needs of a story. Leo and Diane Dillon have used pastel, oil, watercolor, and acrylic as well as wood, air-

FIGURE 5.3
Floyd Cooper's illustrations for *Grandpa's Face* glow with color.

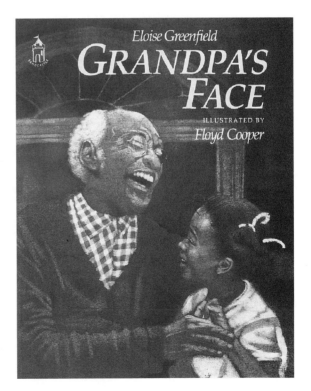

Source: Illustration by Floyd Cooper, reprinted by permission of Philomel Books from GRANDPA'S FACE by Eloise Greenfield, illustrations copyright © 1988 by Floyd Cooper.

brush, embroidery, and stained glass at one time or another (Cummings, 1992). Chris Van Allsburg excels in his use of drawing media like pen and ink, charcoal, pastel chalk, oil pastel, and conte crayon, choosing the media based on the demands of the ideas he wishes to execute.

While the artwork is in progress and after it is delivered to the publisher, there are many decisions to be made about technical matters like typeface, cover, dust jacket, and end pages (Figure 5.4). These matters are often decided by the artist and the book designer or art director, a crucial behind-the-scenes figure who oversees the final printing and who often makes important suggestions about the overall book design.

Although illustrators may share in the procedures of bookmaking, the process of creating a picturebook is, of course, also a very personal experience, sometimes taking decades to reach fruition. Such is the story of Maurice Sendak's *We Are All in the Dumps with Jack and Guy: Two Nursery Rhymes with Pictures*. The book is Sendak's visual realization of two old nursery rhymes from the Opie collection (Opie & Opie, 1951). The author calls it "a story about children surviving and how difficult it is to get on with life" (Sendak, personal communication, 1993). Although he had first tried to illustrate the rhymes back in the 1960s when being "down in the dumps" meant being depressed, he was dissatisfied with the result and put the work aside. His interest in the rhymes was renewed after he collaborated with Iona Opie on *I Saw Esau* and read a newspaper story about children abandoned in the dumps in Rio de Janeiro. Later, when he came across an image of naked feet hanging out of a cardboard box, he had the beginnings of the new book (see color insert).

We Are All in the Dumps with Jack and Guy was a tremendous challenge for Sendak because the two rhymes are unrelated. He admits, "I loved the two because they're incoherent." His task was to visualize specific phrases like "We are all in the dumps, for diamonds are trumps" and also to provide a unity to words through the images. The baby pictured throughout the pages represents that challenge, "the state of helplessness that is not incongruous with the beginning of a work of art," reports Sendak.

He managed to attain that unity through a number of elements—color, composition, and, among other details, the recurring, changing image of the moon. The book is also filled with images of hungry, homeless, mistreated children, with the crematorium at Auschwitz, with dark overtones and strange images, and with references to Renaissance art, particularly that of Andre Mantegna. It is his own "songs of experience, he has no innocence any more." He feels "the world is on the edge" and "homelessness is a metaphor of the danger" he sees in the world. At the same time, Sendak explains, "Taking care of kids means telling them the truth," and in the end the book provides a sense of hope, an understanding that children can feel safe if they have some sense of community. "Family," says Sendak, "is someone taking care of someone else" (Sendak, personal communication, 1993).

We Are All in the Dumps with Jack and Guy is "one of those books," one that will intrigue, puzzle, and ultimately reach children and adults with important truths. Sendak (1993, personal communication) wants his audience to go through this book "and feel excited and wonder what's going to happen, to absorb the root of the book and its nonverbal" meaning. This is accomplished not just in the totality of images and words but also in the entire book design. Working with his art director, Sendak arranged to have the book printed on recycled paper. The book is bound with a

Basically the life history of a book runs like this:

1. The text is accepted and the author is contracted.

2. Decisions are made in-house about the best type of format, extent, and illustrations—a request for costings (including as much information as possible) is sent to the production department. Unit cost is crucial in the future planning and production of the book. Artists are considered and samples are looked at.

3. The costings are received. The book is edited and designed (if the artist is to be provided with galleys to work from).

4. The artist is commissioned and contracted. (If the book is a picture book the artist may well discuss layout and illustrations with the author, editor—and art director at this stage, and may work from the manuscript, deciding on typographic as well as illustration style.) The artist gets a full brief and all support material.

5. The artist submits roughs, which are discussed and approved with or without further additions and alterations. Text galleys are corrected and film, or paper repro, is ordered.

6. The artist delivers the finished artwork, occasionally in full camera-ready copy (CRC) form—but usually as finished illustrations with a rough layout.

7. The designer prepares a full CRC dummy or make-up dummy to show position of all text and illustrations. The text will appear as film or repro. All instructions for the printer are included on the dummy.

8. Color proofs—in imposed pages or as scatter proofs—arrive from printer to be checked against originals by artist and art director or editor. All positions of illustrations and text are checked on imposed proofs. Color proofs are returned.

9. Revised color proofs are ordered, if needed. Final film is sent from the repro house to the printer, then "blue" ozalid proofs are checked for order placement. The book is passed for press.

10. The books are printed. Running sheets are sent for final color check.

11. The books are bound.

12. The books leave the factory on their way to the publisher's warehouse.

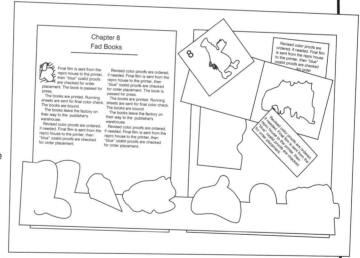

A make-up dummy spread to show position of text illustrations.

FIGURE 5.4
Life history of a book

Source: From HOW TO WRITE AND ILLUSTRATE CHILDREN'S BOOKS AND GET THEM PUB-LISHED by T.P. Bicknell & F. Trotman, copyright © 1988 Quarto Publishing, PLC. Published in the USA by North Light Books, an imprint of F & W Publications. Used with their permission.

heavy, "boxy" cover, with wrapping paper end pages to evoke the cardboard boxes of the homeless. It is a unique work of art from one of the masters of the art of the picturebook.

LEARNING FROM ILLUSTRATORS

By studying picturebooks like *We Are All in the Dumps with Jack and Guy* and by listening to artists talk about their work in books like Pat Cummings' *Talking with Artists*, we can increase our understanding of this special art form and of our own creative processes as well. This book cannot do justice to the many illustrators who have contributed to the art of the picturebook. That is the purpose of other books. But classroom studies of an illustrator's work may reveal the delightful details of an artist's unique personality while it helps children understand that any creative process entails hard work, a willingness to make changes, and a discovery of inner strengths.

The following books about illustrators and picturebooks are good resources for such a study. A section in Chapter 7, Exploring an Illustrator's Work, provides additional ideas for classroom studies of illustrators. The profiles of artists provided in the remainder of Chapter 5 are meant to highlight the ideas, methods, and personal approaches to picturebooks of three very different but highly talented illustrators.

BOOKS ABOUT ILLUSTRATORS OF PICTUREBOOKS: A SELECTED LIST

Bader, Barbara. *American Picturebooks: From Noah's Ark to the Beast Within*. New York: Macmillan, 1976.

Blegvad, Eric. *Self Portrait, Eric Blegvad*. Reading, MA: Addison-Wesley, 1979.

Brown, Marcia. *Lotus Seeds*. New York: Charles Scribner's Sons, 1986.

Cummings, Pat. *Talking with Artists*. New York: Bradbury, 1992.

Cummins, Julie. *Children's Book Illustration and Design*. New York: PBC International, 1993.

Hyman, Trina Schart. *Self Portrait, Trina Schart Hyman*. Reading, MA: Addison-Wesley, 1981.

Kingman, Lee; Hogart, Grace Allen; & Lontoft, Ruth Giles. (Eds.). *Illustrators of Children's Books 1967–1976* (fourth volume in a series). Boston: The Horn Book, 1978.

Lanes, Selma G. *The Art of Maurice Sendak*. New York: Harry Abrams, 1980.

Marantz, Kenneth, & Marantz, Sylvia. *Artists of the Page: Interviews with Children's Book Illustrators*. New York: Garland, 1988.

Marantz, Sylvia. *Picture Books for Looking and Learning: Awakening Visual Perceptions Through the Art of Children's Books*. Phoenix, AZ: Oryx Press, 1992.

Martin, Donald. *The Telling Line: Essays on Fifteen Contemporary Book Illustrators*. New York: Delacorte, 1989.

Meigs, Cornelia. *A Critical History of Children's Literature*. New York: Macmillan, 1987.

Meyer, Susan E. *A Treasury of Great Children's Book Illustrators*. New York: Harry Abrams, 1983.

Miller, Bertha Mahoney; Latimer, Louise Payson; & Formsbee, Beulah. (Eds.). *Illustrators of Children's Books 1744–1945* (first volume in a series). Boston: The Horn Book, 1947.

Schwarcz, Joseph H. *Ways of the Illustrator*. Chicago: American Library Association, 1982.

Sendak, Maurice. *Caldecott and Company*. New York: Farrar, Straus & Giroux, 1988.

Williams, Helen E. *Books by African American Authors and Illustrators for Children*. Chicago: American Library Association, 1991.

Zemach, Margot. *Self Portrait, Margot Zemach*. Reading, MA: Addison-Wesley, 1978.

Tomie dePaola

In studying the work of Tomie dePaola, children find an artist whose roots lie across a broad span of art history. He acknowledges the importance of 20th-century masters like Georges Rouault and Ben Shahn and their concern with design, and their manipulation of color planes and lines can be seen in dePaola's compositions. He also has been influenced by the art of the Italian Gothic period and artists like Giotto and Fra Angelico. Certainly the frescoes on the walls of the churches of this medieval period are echoed in dePaola's subdued colors and beautifully posed figures in books with a religious theme, like *The Clown of God* (Figure 5.5). DePaola acknowledges his debt to these early artists, saying that what he takes from them is their absolute simplicity.

> And I really care about two dimensional design. I do what the Sienese painters did but not in the same way. I almost reduce figures to a symbol. And yet I think of my own faces as good and warm. I try to show expression in the very few lines. If you look at Fra Angelico and Giotto, they're able to do that with a very stylized (I don't want to say formulaic) convention. I really like design, simplicity, and tranquility of their character. And of course they all use line very simply. (Hepler, 1979, p. 298)

DePaola's unique style also may have grown out of his Italian/Irish heritage or the time he spent in a Benedictine monastery. He draws on childhood memories for his books, specifically using autobiographical material in books like *Nana Upstairs, Nana Downstairs; Now One Foot, Now the Other*; and *The Art Lesson*.

At this point in his career he seems to be so comfortable with his work that he "stands in front of a blank canvas, puts paint on it and sees what happens" (dePaola, personal communication, 1993). In truth, more planning is involved, and he relies on his art director, Nanette Stevens, for advice throughout the process. But he seems to be happy and willing to take risks, not an easy thing with the medium of transparent watercolor, which doesn't easily forgive mistakes.

Once his verbal text is finished, he is ready to begin the artwork. Using a handmade 140-pound watercolor paper, he measures out the sheets he will need, usually cutting at least 25 sheets rather than only 17. He puts the typed text down with masking tape and then sketches in the illustration with pencil. Then, using a brown ink that he mixes himself, he paints in the lines, finishing the sheet with washes of watercolor and ink and sometimes tempera paint.

Some of dePaola's first visual storytelling was painted on the walls of churches in New England rather than within the covers of a book, but he brings the same sense of dignity and respect to childhood that he must have given to those churches. DePaola has translated his unique background and training into his own style and mastered many picturebook forms with equal success. He has created wordless books, contemporary fiction, folktales and legends, and information books. His

FIGURE 5.5
Tomie dePaola's (a) *The Clown of God* recalls scenes from Giotto's frescoes in the Arena Chapel in Padua, (b) "The Marriage of the Virgin."

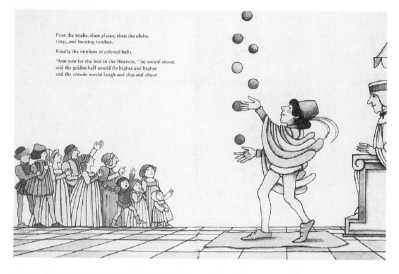

First the sticks, then plates, then the clubs, rings, and burning torches.

Finally the rainbow of colored balls.

"And now for the Sun in the Heavens," he would shout, and the golden ball would fly higher and higher and the crowds would laugh and clap and cheer.

Source: Excerpt and illustration (a) from THE CLOWN OF GOD, copyright © 1978 by Tomie dePaola, reproduced by permission of Harcourt, Brace & Company. Reproduction (b) from Scala/Art Resource, NY.

style, while recognizable, is not static, and he is able to alter his use of line, color, pattern, and other elements to fit the needs of each particular book.

DePaola is adept at creating memorable characters through words and pictures that bring readers back to his books again and again. Indeed, favorites such as Strega Nona and Big Anthony have appeared in several volumes including *Strega Nona*

Meets Her Match (see color insert). The adventures of these two are always engaging, yet it is their expressions and their poses, executed with such simplicity, that evoke our greatest pleasure.

Throughout his work dePaola maintains a warmth and sense of joy that had appealed to people of many ages for so many years. This is true in all his books but particularly in those with contemporary settings such as *Tom*, a recollection of his childhood relationship with his maternal grandfather (Figure 5.6).

In all dePaola's books, his economic use of line, his arrangement of pictorial space, and his masterful handling of pure rich colors work together to create images and feelings that last after the pages of the book are closed. This perhaps is what accounts for his success with children and adults.

In addition, dePaola's appeal comes from his strong connections to the child in himself and his continuing involvement with children through projects like the Center for Holistic Studies. He believes that pictures are stimulating rather than stifling to a child's imagination. "In pictures there are all kinds of elements which can send the child into a further embroidering of ideas. I think the artist makes the invisible visible, the image has great power" (Hepler, 1979, p. 297).

DePaola fears that children are becoming automatons, sitting in front of the television and video games, and that the schools are doing little to develop children's natural art abilities. He tells of an incident when, in one kindergarten class, he asked which children could draw, and *everyone* raised their hand. Yet, when he asked the same question of fourth graders, only five children put their hands up. He argues that "we don't have to teach first graders how to read pictures; they already know

FIGURE 5.6
DePaola pictures warm relationships in books like *Tom*.

Source: Illustration by Tomie dePaola reprinted by permission of G. P. Putnam's Sons from TOM, copyright © 1993 by Tomie de Paola.

how. What we need to do in schools is help teachers learn more from children so that it's not a matter of teaching visual literacy but of maintaining it" (dePaola, personal communication, 1993).

John Steptoe

An artist who will undoubtedly help children deepen their visual understanding is John Steptoe. Bradley (1991) argued that Steptoe "functions as a significant change agent—an archetype for pushing and redefining cultural ethnic and artistic boundaries" (p. 12). Tragically, he died in 1989 at the age of 39. He left behind 16 books, unforgettable images of African Americans and Africans, and most important a legacy as a risk taker, an artist who was always struggling to understand what it meant to create art.

Steptoe was born in Brooklyn in 1950 and grew up in the Bedford-Stuyvesant area of that borough. He attended the High School of Art and Design but dropped out after his junior year. He quickly broke into the children's book field, however, publishing his first book, *Stevie*, in 1969 at the age of 19. Like dePaola, he wrote many of his own texts and also illustrated the stories of others.

His stories and images are firmly rooted in his culture. In his early career, he was influenced by the Black Action movement, and his work during that time reflects his struggle to find an identity. He told *Life* magazine that he didn't feel connected to Western culture, and so "I have got to stay on my own, get out from under induced values and discover who I am at the heart" (p. 59). Undoubtedly his art helped him understand this, for he successfully wove the black dialect, the black culture, and the black experience firmly together in his books.

His search for visual meaning can be seen in a chronological progression of his work as he moves through a series of experimentation with the elements of art. In *Stevie* and *Train Ride*, for example, color is the predominant element; there is little concern for representation, but we see how color can heighten the emotional impact of a story and how line can emphasize meaning and move the story forward.

With each succeeding book, however, we find subtle differences that, over the years, add up to dramatic stylistic changes. *All Us Come Cross the Water* by Lucille Clifton retains the brilliant colors of the earlier books, but now line and shape play more important roles. He carries this even further with *She Come Bringing Me That Little Baby Girl* by Eloise Greenfield (Figure 5.7). Here the lines break away from the figures, separating the pictorial space into interesting shapes and patterns and moving the eye across the page. In *Daddy Is a Monster . . . Sometimes*, vivid color is replaced by soft pastels. Now the main elements of the art are shape and value—the interplay of light and dark areas (Figure 5.8). Steptoe is still concerned with a decorative use of shapes, but these result from the interplay of light and dark.

This exploration of "the technical problems of dark and light" (Steptoe, 1988, p. 27) continues through several more books until, with *The Story of Jumping Mouse*, color is gone altogether and value is central. With this comes a much more representational portrayal, and we can see that Steptoe is a fine draftsman as well as an innovator. Steptoe reports that "getting a firm sure grip on black and white as a medium complemented my movement toward realism. I learned to develop a clarity of image, I am very happy about that" (Steptoe, 1988, p. 27). His subject matter was also

FIGURE 5.7
Steptoe uses color, line, and shape to create eye movement in Greenfield's *She Come Bringing Me That Little Baby Girl*.

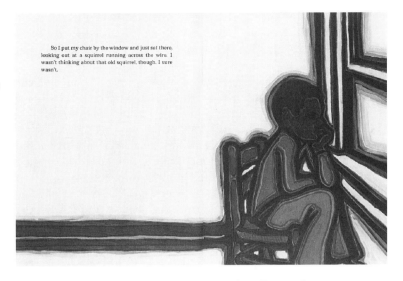

So I put my chair by the window and just sat there, looking out at a squirrel running across the wire. I wasn't thinking about that old squirrel, though. I sure wasn't.

Source: From SHE COME BRINGING ME THAT LITTLE BABY GIRL by Eloise Greenfield, illustrated by John Steptoe. Text copyright © 1974 by Eloise Greenfield. Illustrations copyright © 1974 by John Steptoe. Reprinted by permission of J. B. Lippincott Company.

FIGURE 5.8
In *Daddy Is a Monster . . . Sometimes*, Steptoe has become more concerned with relationships of dark and light.

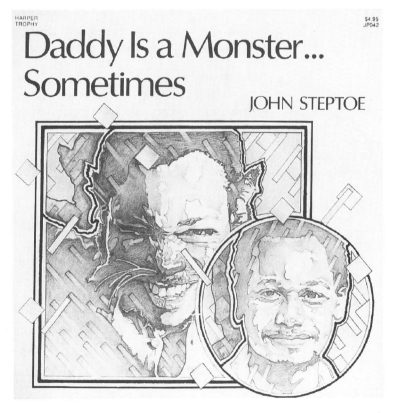

Source: From DADDY IS A MONSTER . . . SOMETIMES by John Steptoe. Copyright © 1980 by John Steptoe. Reprinted by permission of Harper & Row.

becoming less focused on his own culture. With *Mufaro's Beautiful Daughters*, he would reach his peak as an illustrator and reach out to his people's past.

With *Mufaro's Beautiful Daughters*, he applied a "knowledge of coloration to my new discoveries of black and white" (Steptoe, 1988, p. 27). The book, which Steptoe considered to be a variation of the Cinderella story, was his tribute to the civilizations in Africa that must have been the seat of all humanity. He was particularly struck by the ruins of a great civilization found in Zimbabwe, which European scientists had ignored for years. He thought about the magnificent city that must have existed there and the fact that recovered artifacts showed trade with Asia and within the African continent. He imagined a society much like our own in the way people and families related to one another.

> When we take away the thin layer of differences that twentieth century technology has made in people's lives, there's no reason to think that people of a thousand years ago behaved any differently toward one another than people do today. People love, laugh and quarrel; some are kind, and some are selfish and spoiled. (Steptoe, 1988, p. 27)

Mufaro's Beautiful Daughters, then, is a story of these contrasts, realized in the characters of two sisters, Nyasha and Manyara. Nyasha is as kind and loving as Manyara is bad tempered and selfish.

Steptoe's art is truly distinguished by the way he has visually represented this theme. For example, the overall color scheme of cool greens and blues evokes the lush flora of the African setting. Into each double-page spread, however, he adds a touch of contrast by using the color complements of oranges and reds. He sets up contrasting textures by creating the forms with painstaking crosshatching of tiny lines, overlaid at times with color washes. This rough feeling adds tension to the page, but it is balanced by the smooth, blank white areas of the page. His use of value, explored so thoroughly in *The Story of Jumping Mouse*, further extends the theme of contrasts between dark and light. It also lends a powerful sense of drama to the pages and dignity to the characters.

FIGURE 5.9
John Steptoe alternates perspectives to add contrast to *Mufaro's Beautiful Daughters*.

Source: Illustration from MUFARO'S BEAUTIFUL DAUGHTERS by John Steptoe. Copyright © 1987 by John Steptoe. Reprinted by permission of Lothrop, Lee and Shepard Books, a division of William Morrow & Co., Inc., with the approval of the estate of John Steptoe.

FIGURE 5.10
Details of African landscape and dress add authenticity to *Steptoe's Mufaro's Beautiful Daughters.*

Source: Illustration from MUFARO'S BEAUTIFUL DAUGHTERS by John Steptoe. Copyright © 1987 by John Steptoe. Reprinted by permission of Lothrop, Lee and Shepard Books, a division of William Morrow & Co., Inc., with the approval of the estate of John Steptoe..

The composition of each page has been carefully considered, and flowing forms lead the eye across the page. Alternating perspectives also lend variety to the total book design and reinforce the theme of contrasting viewpoints (Figure 5.9). Steptoe's meticulous research adds detailed authenticity to the pictures, especially in the final wedding scene with its embroidered wedding garments and other details.

The book, which took Steptoe 2½ years to complete, won the Boston Globe-Horn Book Award for Illustration in 1987 and the 1988 Caldecott Honor Medal, the only book named that year as an Honor Book. Steptoe admitted that while working on the book he felt that his "abilities as an artist were growing, and I began to realize that I was actually capable of creating images that I've wanted to see all my life" (Steptoe, 1988, p. 25). He also admitted, "Working on the book was a way to learn more about loving myself. One of the marvels of the book experience is that when it is finished others can join in that experience too" (p. 25).

The book has become a modern classic for all ages; it is a work of art that touches all readers deeply. *Mufaro's Beautiful Daughters* has realized John Steptoe's greatest hope, that the book is a statement "even greater than my discovery of reasons to be proud of African ancestors. I hope the book is also a statement of brotherhood in the wide world into which I was born" (Steptoe, 1988, p. 28).

Trina Schart Hyman

Studying the work of distinguished artists like Maurice Sendak, Tomie dePaola, and John Steptoe can be an enlightening and moving experience. No other illustrator imparts the sense of magic of Trina Schart Hyman.

The Brandywine Valley near Philadelphia has nurtured some of America's finest artists and illustrators: Howard Pyle, N. C. and Andrew Wyeth, Maxfield Parrish, Henry Pitz, and Trina Schart Hyman. Trina was born Diane Katrin Schart in 1939 and grew up Wyncote, Pennsylvania.

She believes she was born an artist, a person who sees things differently. Such vision does not make for an easy childhood, and she admits that she was "a weird little kid afraid of everything that moved or spoke—people, the stars, the wind" (Hyman, 1981, p. 9).

Her early years were influenced by these fears and colored by the stories her mother read to her. She particularly remembers *Little Red Riding Hood*. Not only did she learn to read as her mother read these favorite pages over and over to her, but for the next year she became Little Red Riding Hood, dressing up in a red cloak her mother made her and going off into the woods, with her dog as the wolf and her father as the woodsman. Years later she met that wolf again in a painting by Pieter Bruegel, which showed a man in red stockings clutching his hat, running from a hillside of sheep (Figure 5.11). She recalls "a dark tree in the extreme right of the painting and a bird perched on the only branch" (Hyman, 1981, p. 11). When she looked closer, she saw a wolf attacking the sheep. "He's really Little Red Riding Hood!" she realized (p. 11).

Connections like these surround Hyman, for this painting and her childhood experiences merged as she illustrated her own version of the story years later. She won the Caldecott Honor Medal for the book. Not only does she appear as Little Red Riding Hood, but her mother and grandmother are characters also. And in the forest stands a tall tree with a little bird perched in its single branch (Figure 5.12).

Before Hyman achieved this success, however, she had long years of hard work to come. Her school years were not particularly successful, but her childhood play was filled with fairy dolls and magic, and she never lost her love for stories or for art. She remembers being captivated by the illustrations of Jessie Wilcox Smith, a pupil of Howard Pyle, and at the age of 12 she decided to be an illustrator. After graduation, she took classes with Henry Pitz, who introduced her to the work of Arthur Rackham, Edmund Dulac, Howard Pyle, and N. C. Wyeth.

FIGURE 5.11
Pieter Bruegel's "The Unfaithful Shepard" reminded Trina Schart Hyman of *Little Red Riding Hood*.

Source: Reproduction from Bruegel, Pieter, the Elder, "The Unfaithful Shepard," The Philadelphia Museum of Art, The John E. Johnson Collection. Reprinted by permission.

FIGURE 5.12
Hyman's cover for *Little Red Riding Hood*
reflects childhood influences.

Source: From *Little Red Riding Hood*, retold and illustrated by Trina Schart Hyman. A Holiday House
Book. Copyright © 1983 by Trina Schart Hyman.

While she was living in Sweden with her former husband, Harris Hyman, she
published her first book for editor Astrid Lindgren. It wasn't until she and Harris
returned to Boston, however, that she began her career in earnest. After she illustrated a book of Irish fairy tales for the adult list at Little, Brown, children's book
editor Helen Jones gave her a book to do. Their relationship became one of the most
important in her professional and personal life.

In the early 1960s, divorced from Harris, Hyman took her young daughter
Katrin to live in Lyme, New Hampshire. She supported herself, Katrin, and an
assortment of dogs and cats with illustrating jobs and as the art director for *Cricket*
magazine. In 1973, however, she really came into her own with the publication of
her illustrated version of Howard Pyle's *King Stork*. With this book she found her
true spiritual home, the world of fairy tale, fantasy, and legend. Although she has
continued to illustrate book jackets and other types of stories, works like *Sleeping
Beauty, Snow White* (Grimm Bros.), and *The Fortune-Tellers* (Alexander) have been
among her most acclaimed. She has won numerous awards, including Caldecott
Honor Medals for *Little Red Riding Hood* (Grimm Bros.) and *Hershel and the
Hanukkah Goblin* (Kimmel). In 1985, she was awarded the Caldecott Medal for
Saint George and the Dragon (Hodges).

She brings an irreverent sense of humor to her work, as well as the sense of
angst that characterizes so many artists. She is not, in fact, an artist who draws for
children as much as she is an artist who sees life more clearly than most—especially
those hidden worlds of the psyche. Unfortunately, those afraid to face those hidden
worlds have continued to find objections to her work, and she has needed her sense
of humor to deal with critics who have complained about everything from the

FIGURE 5.13
Hyman pictured herself and her former husband as dwarfs to the right and left of her daughter as Snow White.

Source: From SNOW WHITE by Paul Heins. Text copyright © 1974 by Paul Heins; Illustrations copyright © 1974 by Trina Schart Hyman. By permission of Little, Brown and Company.

witch's erotic table in *King Stork* to the bottle of wine on the table in *Little Red Riding Hood* (White, 1983).

Friends, neighbors, and relatives are the models for many of her characters. Grandson Michou, for example, appears in *The Fortune-Tellers*. Daughter Katrin is *Snow White*, and she and ex-husband Harris appear as dwarfs in the same book (Figure 5.13). She appears in other books, as the scribe on the back cover of *St. George and the Dragon* and as the young wizard in *Magic in the Mist* (Kimmel). Because she sees herself as a vital part of these stories, she makes them come alive for the reader as well—for children and adults who still believe in magic.

Hyman works with brush and ink, colored pencils, or crayon. She works directly on watercolor board in pencil and then reworks the design in ink and acrylic washes. She puts in many hours of research before she begins her illustrations; the details she includes in each picture are historically and psychologically accurate. Almost all of the flowers in the borders in *Saint George and the Dragon* (Hodges), for example, are native to Great Britain (Figure 5.14).

Once the research is completed, Hyman lets the painting emerge from the surface of the illustration board rather than making numerous sketches and changes. She speaks of entering into her work as it emerges. "If I want to know what a place feels like or what the sky looks like after a certain patch of weather, I search deep inside my memory to find it, then put everything aside and go there, and then I try to find the right lines and colors to put it down" (Hyman, 1993, p. 192). She does not use devices like airbrushes or ruling pens, feeling that such tools would make her work look mechanical. Neither does she work from photographs, except for reference. She knows who her characters are and can maintain an image of them throughout the book. "If I ever had any doubt about who that peasant boy or knight or princess or dwarf should be—if I couldn't visualize them and put my whole conscious and unconscious self in their place as I was working on the story—then the

FIGURE 5.14
The key to border details in Hyman's *Saint George and the Dragon*

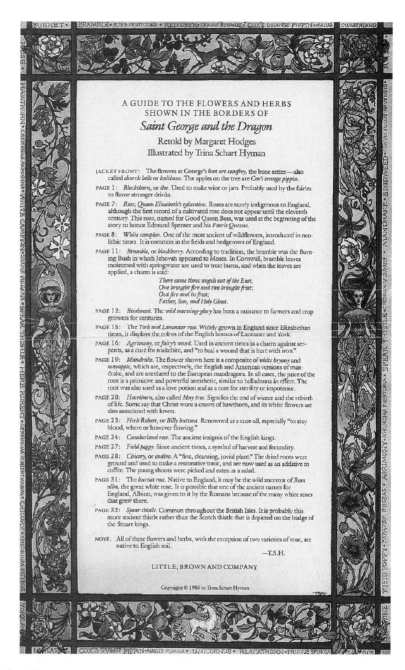

illustration was always in danger of falling apart" (Hyman, 1993, p. 191). This is certainly one of the reasons that her friends and family show up as characters in her books, but it is also why no one in the field can match the energy with which her characters live among the pages of her books.

In 1900, illustrator Howard Pyle described the aims of his teaching:

My final aim in teaching will not be essentially the production of illustrators of books but rather the production of painters of pictures. . . . I shall make it a requisite that the pupil whom I choose shall possess first of all imagination; second artistic ability; thirdly color and drawing. (Pitz, 1975, p. 67)

Hyman would unquestionably have been one of his choices. Her unique imagination, her facility with line, her handling of dramatic play of light and dark, her lively figures, and her strong sense of composition are reminiscent of the work of Pyle, Wyeth, Rackham, and Caldecott and hark further back to the illuminators of the Middle Ages. Indeed, one of her favorite books was Pyle's *The Wonder Clock*. *King Stork* was her tribute to him.

Although her style may owe much to these great masters of the book arts, however, her work remains a unique combination of her own inner vision and her superb craftsmanship, which has grown and strengthened over the years.

Even Hyman's early work shows evidence of the drawing ability valued by Pyle, especially the element of line. She has never been intimidated by this element of design; her lines are firm, strong, and vibrant. They curve and flow with a force that brings life to each picture and adds movement from page to page. For her, lines must have "that quality of human vulnerability that a hand-drawn and just slightly imperfect line will have" (Hyman, 1993, p. 193).

The use of value—the amount of light and dark in a picture—is her second strong point. Seeing life as a drama, she uses contrasting values to throw a spotlight on her characters and to increase the feeling that psychological secrets are hidden in the dark corners of the pages. *Snow White* is the darkest in value of all the fairy tales she has illustrated, reflecting her belief that the story was "heavy and psychologically dark and deep" (Hearn, 1979, p. 43). *Rapunzel* (Grimm Bros.) and *Hershel and the Hanukkah Goblins* (Kimmel) have darker values; works like *Little Red Riding Hood* (Grimm Bros.) and *The Fortune-Tellers* (Alexander) are much lighter in tone and theme. In fact, *The Fortune-Tellers* fairly glows with the intense brilliance of the African sun.

Over the years her facility with color has improved as she has experimented with expanding her palette. This is particularly apparent in *Saint George and the Dragon* (Hodges) and *The Fortune-Tellers*. Strong, contrasting values lend the stories drama, but the pages also sparkle with the kinds of colors that illuminated the best works of the Middle Ages.

The fact that so many of her books recall these earlier ages of picturebook illustration lends depth to Hyman's style, adds interest to the design of the page, and ties each book together. Her use of decorative borders grew out of an assignment to illustrate a book of Russian stories. Her research introduced her to Ivan Bilibin's work, who, she states, "used decorative borders to frame his illustrations the way most people use adjectives in their everyday speech only better" (Hyman, 1993, p. 189). In several of the books that followed, her borders took on an increasingly important role in visual storytelling, allowing her to embellish the main plot line with subtle details or to represent simultaneous action of the characters—something that is impossible to do with written text.

In the final scene of *Little Red Riding Hood*, for example, we see grandmother sharing a meal with Red Riding Hood in her kitchen while a small vignette pictures the woodsman heading home with the wolf pelt (Figure 5.15). In *Saint George and the Dragon*, the borders make reference to the setting and also illuminate lines from

FIGURE 5.15
Pictures in Hyman's *Little Red Riding Hood* depict simultaneous action.

Source: From *Little Red Riding Hood*, retold and illustrated by Trina Schart Hyman. A Holiday House Book. Copyright © 1983 by Trina Schart Hyman.

Edmund Spenser's *The Faerie Queene* (written in 1590), the source for Margaret Hodges' story. The lines aren't essential to the main plot, but references to the original poem highlight the literary and artistic history of the tale.

Hyman never lets borders become a "cute" device. Instead, she uses them to lend cultural or historical authenticity to the book as well as to unify the design. In *Little Red Riding Hood*, the folk art borders effectively made the break from the Germanic tales she had thus far illustrated and, as she intended, gave the book a "down-home New England tone" (White, 1983, p. 789). In *Saint George and the Dragon*, she views the scenes as though through a window, recalling conventions of early Christian and early Renaissance art. In *The Kitchen Knight* (Hodges), she used a framing device she had discovered in an Italian manuscript in which close-ups were embedded in frames within the larger painting (Figure 5.16).

Decorative borders also solved a design problem that faces many illustrators—unifying the printed text with the pictorial text. For example, the dark mood of *Snow White* is sometimes shattered by the abrupt and glaring placement of the type in white rectangles. In *Sleeping Beauty*, Hyman used lighter windows, arches, or sky to

FIGURE 5.16
Hyman includes framing devices from illuminated manuscripts in *The Kitchen Knight*.

Source: From *The Kitchen Knight*. Illustrations copyright © 1990 by Trina Schart Hyman. A Holiday House Book. All rights reserved.

carry the written text. By adopting borders in later works, she increased her ability to highlight many characters and themes while providing a unifying rhythm to text and pictures.

Her composition takes up the rhythm and further unifies the pages of her books. She is adept at placing a shape, twisting a tree trunk, or curving an arm to lead the eye across each double-page spread and on to the next. In *Snow White*, the branches of the trees on the title page convey movement and lead the eye from left to right, toward the title. In each double-page spread of *The Fortune-Tellers*, Hyman uses color, light, and the positions of her figures to bring the book to life (see color insert).

Hyman's point of view also gives her scenes movement and drama. The reader's eye moves back for a distance shot or in for a close-up. In *Sleeping Beauty*, after the evil spell has sent everyone to sleep for 100 years, she shows the castle from afar. On the following page she zooms in to view the full horror of the trapped skeletons of those who attempted to penetrate the barrier of thorns that has grown up around the castle. This in turn emphasizes the character of the prince who does manage to get through the obstruction.

As readers follow his passage through the castle, she moves the eye back to view the prince from afar, walking down deserted passageways. Here the rhythm of succeeding arches provides a visual echo to his lonely footsteps (Figure 5.17). When the prince finds the princess, he views her from the back of the picture. His face is lost in shadow, and hers is in close-up, a beautiful woman well worth the struggles that surround her.

These characters and the richly detailed settings they inhabit set Hyman's work apart. Like Jan Van Eyck and miniaturists of the late Gothic period, she fills her pictures with people and objects that invite us to read more into the story than might appear at first glance. And like all good storytellers, she creates characters, even minor ones, who are convincingly *human*.

FIGURE 5.17
The layout creates a visual rhythm in Hyman's *Sleeping Beauty*.

Source: From THE SLEEPING BEAUTY by Trina Schart Hyman. Copyright © 1977 by Trina Schart Hyman. By permission of Little, Brown and Company.

FIGURE 5.18
The stepmother is a fully realized character in Hyman's *Snow White*.

FIGURE 5.19
Hyman appears as the main character in Kimmel's *Magic in the Mist*.

Her heroines are earthy, worthy of the attention they receive or the jealousy they arouse. Others are fragile, deserving of sympathy and protection. Her heroes are strong and experienced but perhaps in need of a strong woman to help them cope with the intricacies of life.

More arresting, perhaps, are the minor characters and villains whose pictorial development allows the themes of the tales to be fully realized. In *Rapunzel*, for example, the witch seems to be the traditional old crone until we see her with the young Rapunzel, a lonely, sad old woman crying out for the love of this beautiful child. The wicked stepmother in *Snow White* is totally untraditional, gorgeously seductive, and driven to madness by the innocent loveliness of Snow White. Suddenly this familiar tale takes on new dimensions as the older woman is supplanted by a younger beauty (Figure 5.18).

The dwarf who accompanies the Lady Una (the story's heroine) and the Red Cross Knight in *Saint George and the Dragon* is among her most moving characters. He is true in spirit, patient, kind, and loved by animals and children. Forsaking glory, he stays in the background, performing the mundane, everyday chores so that his master may win riches and acclaim. He keeps a lonely vigil while his knight rides fighting or lies wounded. On the last page of the book, when he looks out at us from behind the frame, he seems to be making contact with the rest of us who are not brave enough to tackle dragons but are willing to serve those who do.

Hyman believes "that life is magical after all" (Hyman, 1981, p. 30). And what else could account for the prescient images in *Magic In the Mist*, a book she illustrated in 1975, that shows her in the guise of a troubled youngster staring at a tiny dragon sitting on the pages of a book. Ten years later she would win the Caldecott medal for distinguished illustration for a book about a dragon (Figure 5.19).

CONCLUSION

Because of the work of these artists and other fine illustrators, each new reading of a picturebook uncovers some new detail, and some new truth is discerned. My own world has been immeasurably enriched by the images these artists have given me. I can never look at a brick city wall with its layers of peeling paper and interesting textures without seeing the collages of Ezra Jack Keats. Each fall I'll wake up early to the first frost and find that the softened hues of a misty morning are colored with Tomie dePaola's palette. One winter evening, I'll look out the window to see the sky lit up with coral, aquamarine, and purple, and I'll think, "It's a Barbara Cooney sunset." On the wonderfully colorful streets of New York I'll watch the faces of the passersby, and I'll see the characters of Floyd Cooper, or Allen Say, or William Joyce. These artists have not taken away my imagination with their images; they have fed it.

"By virtue of our thoughts and imagination," argues Langer, "we have not only feelings but a life of feeling" (1953, p. 372). The energy of the artist's imagination as well as the energy of the book experience thus illuminates our view of ourselves and our feelings about our world.

CHAPTER

6

Style in Picturebooks:
A Theory of Criticism

The long tradition of the picturebook answers some essential human characteristic that over the centuries resulted from two urges: the artist's need to convey meaning through visual symbols and a cultural need to understand basic aspects of the individual and the race through image and myth. Over the years, the changing needs of society, as reflected in the culture of a given age, have determined the content of books and designated the audience. Technological advances have taken the medium from the wall of a cave and the floor of the desert to laser reproductions of original works on paper, bound between the covers of a book.

Moreover, just as the cave paintings of Lascaux, medieval illuminated manuscripts, and the dreamings of Australian aborigines are the province of art historians, today's picturebooks are art objects and should be subject to a similar visual criticism. A picturebook relies as much or more on visual meaning as it does on verbal meaning.

Understanding how meaning is made and determining the quality of the resulting aesthetic experience is a difficult task with any art object. With the picturebook, we are dealing at the very least with two different codes or systems of communication. This complicates a task that even within the realms of purely visual or purely verbal criticism is always a complex one.

Often scholars have studied the picturebook within the conventions of criticism of literature or art instead of dealing with the picturebook as a separate and unique entity. In this century, picturebooks generally have been classified as children's literature, and they frequently have been analyzed by those trained to critique literature rather than art (Sadler, 1992).

Theories of visual literacy have been developed; however, these often liken the art to verbal elements or treat reading pictures like reading words or reading signs (Storey, 1985). On the other hand, picturebook illustrations are sometimes categorized with terms more suitable to art history, such as *Impressionism*, *Expressionism*, or *Surrealism* (Cianciolo, 1990; Huck, Hepler, & Hickman, 1993). This suggests that styles of illustration are synonymous with styles of painting.

Useful theories regarding the art of the picturebook have developed out of the field of semiotic theory (the general study of signs). In this context, scholars have developed theories of the various relationships of pictures and text. (Moebius, 1986). Golden (1990), for example, proposes five different relationships between illustrations and text in picturebooks. In three of these relationships, the illustrations play a complementary, extending, or highlighting role, but if the text is read without the pictures, no essential meaning is lost. In the other two relationships, the illustrations either provide information crucial to the written text or clarify and go beyond information given in the words. In these last two, the pictures must be present if all information is to be obtained.

Nodelman (1988) suggests that the relationship between pictures and text is always an ironic one; that is, "the words tell us what the pictures do not show, and the pictures show us what the words do not tell us" (p. 222). He argues, for example, that

> When words and pictures combine, irony emerges from the way in which the incompleteness of each is revealed by the differing incompleteness of the other. The theoretically "fierce bad rabbit" in Beatrix Potter's book of that name looks soft and cuddly, anything but the evil creature that the text refers to. (p. 223)

A Journey Through Children's Literature Illustrations

As you look at the illustrations in this section, notice how the illustrators use the elements of line, color, shape, texture, and design to create memorable illustrations. Also notice how different artistic media and style influence the illustrations. When viewing the Cinderella comparisons, notice how the illustrators provide settings that seem appropriate for the cultural backgrounds.

The lines and movement provided by the wheat fields develop a feeling of the ocean that is important to the main character. Grandfather's Journey *is the winner of the 1994 Caldecott Medal. (Illustration from* Grandfather's Journey *by Allen Say. Copyright © 1993 by Allen Say. Reprinted by permission of Houghton Mifflin Co. All rights reserved.)*

Ehlert's collages create texture through the use of both natural and artificial materials. (Illustration from Red Leaf, Yellow Leaf, *copyright © 1991 by Lois Ehlert, reproduced by permission of Harcourt Brace & Company.)*

DePaola's admiration for folk art and folktales are reflected in his illustrations. (Illustration by Tomie dePaola reprinted by permission of G. P. Putnam's Sons from Strega Nona Meets Her Match, *copyright © 1993 by Tomie dePaola.)*

There once was a duck
who had the bad luck to live
with a lazy old farmer.
The duck did the work.
The farmer stayed
all day in bed.

Watercolors capture the humor and the irony in a tale in which the hard-working duck finally wins in a person-versus-person conflict. (Reproduced from Farmer Duck by Martin Waddell with the permission of Candlewick Press, Cambridge, MA. Illustration copyright © 1991 by Helen Oxenbury.)

Careful viewing shows that several plots are happening concurrently within these illustrations. (Illustration from Black and White by David Macaulay. Copyright © 1990 by David Macaulay. Reprinted by permission of Houghton Mifflin Co. All rights reserved.)

Detailed drawings place the setting for this tale in central Africa. (From The Fortune-Tellers by Lloyd Alexander, illustrated by Trina Schart Hyman. Copyright © 1992 by Trina Schart Hyman, illustrations. Used by permission of Dutton Children's Books, a division of Penguin Books USA Inc.)

The story elements, the characters, and the setting reflect a Chinese background in this Cinderella variant. (Illustration by Ed Young reprinted by permission of Philomel Books from Yeh-Shen: A Cinderella Story from China *retold by Ai-Ling Louie, illustrations © 1982 by Ed Young.)*

Pastel colors and soft, delicate lines create the feeling of a mythical kingdom in this French Cinderella. (Reprinted with the permission of Charles Scribner's Sons, an imprint of Macmillan Publishing Company from Cinderella *translated and illustrated by Marcia Brown. Copyright 1954 Marcia Brown; copyright renewed © 1982 Marcia Brown.)*

Both a Native-American setting and Native-American characters transform this Cinderella variant to an appropriate North American location. (Illustration by David Shannon reprinted by permission of G. P. Putnam's Sons from The Rough-Face Girl *by Rafe Martin, illustrations copyright © 1992 by David Shannon.)*

Photographs of dogs provide unique characters in this adaptation of Cinderella. (From Cinderella *by William Wegman. Text and photographs copyright © 1993 by William Wegman. Reprinted by permission of Hyperion Books for Children, a Walt Disney Company. All rights reserved.)*

An English setting and a strong heroine who relies on her own ingenuity are elements in this Cinderella variant. (Illustration from Princess Furball *by Charlotte Huck, illustrated by Anita Lobel. Illustration copyright © 1989 by Anita Lobel. By permission of Greenwillow Books, a division of William Morrow & Company, Inc.)*

Elements in this folktale show the influence of West Africa, the Caribbean, and the Sea Islands of South Carolina. (Reprinted with the permission of Four Winds Press, an imprint of Macmillan Publishing Company from Sukey and the Mermaid by Robert D. San Souci, illustrated by Brian Pinkney. Illustrations copyright © 1992 Brian Pinkney.)

Delicate illustrations highlighted with gold provide a setting for a story that encompasses both history and legend. (From Chingis Khan by Demi. Copyright © 1991 by Demi. Reprinted by permission of Henry Holt and Company, Inc.)

The illustrations extend this biography by providing details associated with the early Shakespearean theater. (Illustration from Bard of Avon by Diane Stanley and Peter Vennema, illustrated by Diane Stanley. Illustration Copyright © 1992 by Diane Stanley. By permission of Morrow Junior Books, a division of William Morrow & Co., Inc.)

f

Motifs from Irish folklore are found in the illustrations, completed in watercolors, and the text. (From The Children of Lir *by Sheila MacGill-Callahan, illustrated by Gennady Spirin. Copyright © 1993 by Gennady Spirin, pictures. Used by permission of Dial Books for Young Readers, a division of Penguin Books USA Inc.)*

Rich details similar to those found in the Book of Kells *create a historic mood for the text. (From* The Sailor Who Captured the Sea: A Story of the Book of Kells *by Deborah Nourse Lattimore. Copyright © 1991 by Deborah Nourse Lattimore. Used by permission of HarperCollins Publishers. All rights reserved.)*

The illustrations provide social commentary through headlines on paper worn by homeless children. (From We Are All in the Dumps with Jack and Guy *by Maurice Sendak. Copyright © 1993 by Maurice Sendak. Reprinted by permission of HarperCollins Publishers. All rights reserved.)*

Although an understanding of verbal/pictorial relationships might help us to do a close analysis of a particular picturebook, however, it does not necessarily give us a theory of criticism. The content of the pictures in *We Be Warm Till Springtime Comes* (Chaffin), which functions almost as a caption, is no less effective than the pictures in *Ms. Glee Was Waiting* (Hill), which are necessary to understanding the written text. I would argue with Langer that the fabric of *meaning* is the essence of any art form (Langer, 1942). Thus, a theory of visual criticism of picturebooks must explain how the art conveys meaning, rather than just categorizing the pictures according to periods of art history or identifying their relationship to text.

THE AESTHETIC NATURE OF THE PICTUREBOOK

According to Elliott Eisner the discipline of aesthetics "raises the question 'What do I know about art and what is my response to it?'" (Brandt, 1988, p. 7). Kaelin (1989) argues that aesthetics proper, then, "may be thought of as the discipline concerning itself with artistic communication—with the description of creativity of works of art, of artistic appreciation" (p. 710).

Thus, when considering any mode of communication—visual, verbal, or an interaction between the two—it is important to understand how meaning is expressed and understood. Although both language and visual art have a meaning-expressing potential, the two are not identical and cannot be matched at a word or sentence level. Furthermore, the result of the readers' engagement with visual and verbal texts may be very different. Nodelman (1988) suggests that the visual space "depicted in pictures implies *time* and that the temporal sequences depicted by words imply *space*" (p. 243). That is, words arranged and read in a linear, forward motion move us forward in time and must depict space by describing it in words. Pictures, which inhabit a spatial plane and are viewed at a single moment in time, must convey the passing of time. Gombrich (1982) argues that although both language and visual images can express, arouse, and describe, the visual image is most effective in evoking emotions. However, it is unable to match "the statement function of language" (p. 138).

On the other hand, when considering how meaning is expressed, verbal and visual art have much in common. Both the author and artist have elements that convey meaning. The author uses sounds and words, the phonetic and morphemic systems of language. The artist uses line, shape, color, value, and texture, the elements of art. Although language may engage the intellect in more precise meanings, it is also place-specific. It can only be understood by speakers (and readers) of that language. Art may more readily evoke our emotions, and its elements and symbols are more readily understood across cultures and places.

Both language and art, however, have syntactic and semantic properties. Hellman (1977), for example, explains that we recognize the syntactic properties of art, such as the organization of lines and color, as well as the semantic properties, in which lines and colors evoke metaphors such as quiet, warm, or angry. In addition, both authors and artists have principles of organization that they call *composition*. Aspects of composition like balance, rhythm, and pattern are common to both.

Finally, the word *style* is applied to the product created as a result of an author's or artist's choices of these elements and principles (Figure 6.1). The fact that the

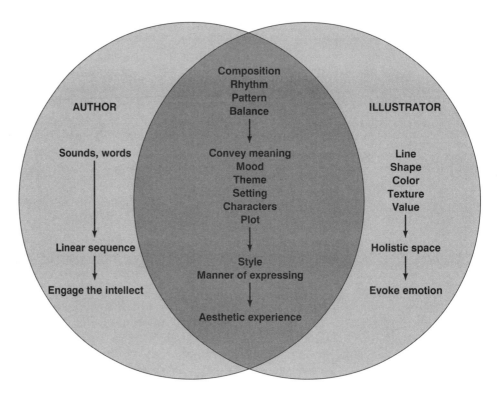

FIGURE 6.1
Similarities and differences in verbal and visual meaning of texts

concept of style is applied to both literature and art and that it is linked with the expression of meaning thus makes style a proper basis for a theory of visual criticism in picturebooks.

STYLE IN ART

Style, as the term is used in art, has been the subject of considerable debate, just as it has been in literary fields. The term *style* has been used to describe the work of individuals as well as that of cultures and eras. Novitz (1976) attempted to clarify the term by differentiating between pictorial styles, artistic styles, and personal styles. Pictorial styles, he explains, are distinguished by certain "umbrella conventions or widely accepted methods of depicting" (p. 336). This category would include the use of perspective or impressionistic perceptions. For example, artists of the early Renaissance began using recently discovered formulas of perspective; Impressionist painters were interested in the immediate image captured by the eye before the brain had time to clarify or define it.

Artistic styles involve changes in emphasis or in subject matter but not in overall methods of depicting—the Renaissance style as opposed to Mannerism or the movement from the religious or classical subject matter of the Renaissance to the homey interiors of Dutch genre painting.

Finally, individuals might work in the same pictorial and artistic styles but "idiosyncratic features" (Novitz, 1976, p. 331) would help distinguish one artist's picture from another—Michelangelo from Raphael or Monet from Pissarro (Figure 6.2).

A point of consensus in discussions of style in art seems to be the dual qualities of style. Wolfflin (1950) referred to "the double root of style" (p. 1). Drawing upon Goodman's (1976) work in the languages of art, Hellman (1977) discussed exemplified and expressed properties, likening them to syntactic and semantic systems of verbal language. Thus, any consideration of style must consider not only the formal objective properties of style but those subjective properties that lead to an interpretation of meaning.

Genova (1979) proposed a meaning-expressive model for style. She acknowledged a variety of sources for style, ranging from psychological to cultural and aes-

FIGURE 6.2
A comparison of stylistic features

> **PICTORIAL STYLES**
>
> Umbrella conventions—widely accepted methods of depicting
>
> Examples:
>
> The use of the scientific principles of perspective,
> which began to be used in the 1430s.
>
> The use of Impressionistic beliefs, which attempted to depict
> what the eye sees in the first moments before the brain has
> time to recognize and categorize what is seen.
>
> ---
>
> **ARTISTIC STYLES**
>
> Changes in emphasis or subject matter within the broader umbrella of conventions
>
> Examples:
>
> Renaissance (1400–1600) versus Mannerism (1500–1600)
>
> The Renaissance is characterized by a move toward realism,
> an emphasis on form and harmony. Mannerism used elongated
> figures, harsher color, and crowded canvas.
>
> Toward the end of this period subject matter changed from religious or classical
> subjects to genre paintings and homey, everyday interior scenes.
>
> ---
>
> **INDIVIDUAL STYLES**
>
> Idiosyncratic features of an artist's technique
>
> Examples:
>
> Recognizing a painting by Michelangelo or Raphael
>
> or by Monet or Renoir.

thetic ones, but she emphasized that style was the result of unconscious as well as conscious choices. Her crucial point, however, was that *style is symbolic of meaning.* The two are "inextricably interwoven; they reflect, express, and constitute each other" (Genova, 1979, p. 323).

Following these discussions, then, style might be defined most simply as a manner of expressing. The meaning of the word *express*—to make known, reveal, show—is in keeping with the dual nature of style. The word *manner* can encompass all the conscious as well as unconscious choices the artist embraces to "make known." Aspects of style such as formal elements, techniques, and pictorial conventions, then, are among the choices the artist makes to accomplish the primary purpose of expressing meaning.

STYLE IN PICTUREBOOKS

Although this discussion of theory of style is based on visual art, these concepts can be applied to the art of picturebooks with some modifications and additions. Both the painter and the illustrator choose elements of art, principles of composition, and historical and cultural conventions to express meaning. However, in executing a painting, an artist may choose to envision a story, capture a moment in history or time, explore an intellectual vision, or express some purely inner feeling, with little concern for how an audience will perceive the finished product. The illustrator, on the other hand, is bound to a specific idea or narrative and has some intent, at least, to convey a specific meaning to an audience. Moreover, the painter is concerned with a single image on one pictorial plane, but the illustrator is bound to a sequence of images, sometimes accompanied by words, sometimes not. Finally, although the painter is faced with choices of media (for example, oil or acrylic), the illustrator must consider original media as well as other technical choices inherent in the reproduction of the work within the covers of a book. These technical choices may also express meaning and add to or detract from the overall aesthetic experience.

EVALUATING PICTUREBOOKS

Marantz (1977) believes that "art objects are important because they have the potential for producing a transcendental experience, a state of mind where new and personal meanings can take shape" (p. 151). This, I believe, is the essence of the aesthetic experience possible as a result of a good picturebook.

When judging the quality of a picturebook, the critic must begin with the verbal text or, in the case of a concept book or wordless picturebook, with the book's idea or theme. This is, in most cases, where the artist begins. Even when artists are illustrating their own work, they usually compose the text first and then create the pictures.

Once we have some idea of the theme of the book, the motifs and moods, characters, setting, and events, we can evaluate how well the artist has chosen artistic elements, principles, and conventions to convey those meanings visually and how those artistic or stylistic choices have contributed to the overall aesthetic experience of the book. However, the written text and the overall design of the book are integral parts of the picturebook, and they must be evaluated along with the illustrations.

To a lesser extent, perhaps, the critic must also keep in mind the "implied reader" or viewer when evaluating the art of the picturebook. Iser (1978) explains that there is always a negotiation of insight between the author (artist) and reader (viewer). It is in this co-construction of meaning that the illustrator invites the reader to participate. Thus, in evaluating a picturebook we may also need to consider the age and experience of the child who is the implied reader.

First and foremost, however, we must consider the range of choices available to the artist for expressing meaning. These stylistic choices can be categorized by the elements and principles of art, the technical choices relating to book production, and the historical and cultural conventions of depicting. In considering the range of these choices, we must consider not only their formal properties but also the ways in which they can add to the intellectual understanding and emotional engagement with the book. Figure 6.3 provides an overview of criteria and categories of the artist's choices to convey meaning in picturebooks.

The Elements and Principles of Art

Line, shape, color, texture, and value are generally accepted as the basic elements with which the illustrator works. Principles of organization, or the ways in which the artist brings these elements together, can include compositional precepts such as eye movement, balance, rhythm, and pattern. (See Ovirk, Bone, Stinson, & Wigg, 1991, or Piper, 1981, for a useful overview of art fundamentals.)

Line is the most commonly found element in picturebooks, perhaps because, as MacCann and Richards (1973) suggest, it is the "traditional mode of graphic illustration" (p. 36). Lines have great expressive potential. They can convey repose when horizontal, stability when vertical, and movement when diagonal. Angular lines can create a feeling of excitement or tension; curving lines often express more rhythmic, peaceful qualities. The quality of line can be altered, so that thin lines may appear fragile and delicate, and thick lines can convey strength and weight.

The element of line is effectively used to express meaning in many picturebooks. In *Willie's Fire-Engine*, for example, Charles Keeping uses contrasting thicknesses to set up a tension between his characters and their circumstances. His main characters are children trapped in an urban ghetto with little hope of breaking out (Figure 6.4). Keeping draws them in thin, very delicate lines, suggesting fragility, but sets them in front of a black gate whose thick verticals resemble prison bars. The diagonals become slashes across the page, crossing out any chance of escape. These are echoed in the lighter diagonals to the upper right, which form repeated x's and add further tension to the scene.

A very different use of line is found in *The Napping House* (by Audrey Wood). Here, Don Wood uses the short, thick vertical lines of a picket fence to suggest stable tranquility. They are not frightening like Keeping's verticals because they are executed in softened shades of blue-white, and they are placed low on the page. By covering the top of the fence with rose bushes, Wood creates an outline that suggests the rhythmic snoring of the sleepers on the cover and the soft curves of their bodies, and he effectively leads the eye across the title and copyright pages. Without the curving line provided by the bushes, the picket fence would have ended in points, disturbing the quiet mood of the two pages (Figure 6.5).

FIGURE 6.3
Criteria for evaluating the art of the picturebook

DESIGN CHOICES

1. The elements of design (line, shape, color value, and texture) are chosen for their expressive qualities.
   - lines and shapes convey action, rhythm—they can be strong and solid or diminutive and quick
   - colors convey mood, emotions
   - value creates contrast, highly dramatic or soothing effects
   - texture conveys tension, adds interest or movement
   - space resulting from the use of line, shape, color, etc., provides tensions or interactions that heighten meaning
2. The principles of design or composition (balance, rhythm, repetition, variety in unity, eye movement) are chosen to tie individual pages into a complete whole that reinforces the overall meaning of the book.
   - layout and size of pictures carries the eye from page to page and creates a rhythm in keeping with the meaning of the book
   - pictures and printed text are well balanced and create a pleasing pattern
   - elements of design are used to create variety in unity

TECHNICAL CHOICES

1. Original media, end papers, paper stock, and typography are chosen to strengthen ideas or story.
   - choice of watercolor, acrylics, pencil, or print is in keeping with the mood of the story or concept

Source: Reprinted with permission from *Evaluating Children's Books: A Critical Look*. Edited by Betsy Hearne and Roger Sutton. Allerton Park Institute, Number 34. Urbana-Champaign, IL: Graduate School of Library and Information Science, p. 89. Copyright © 1993 The Board of Trustees of the University of Illinois.

When lines enclose space, like the bushes in *The Napping House*, they create shapes. As with line, the element of shape is also capable of expressing meaning. Rounded or curving shapes are called *biomorphic* because they resemble living organisms. The circle is a line endlessly meeting itself, and thus it symbolizes continuity and the eternal. Wood has used biomorphic shapes in *The Napping House* to convey a mood of tranquility and gentle humor as well as the renewal found in restful sleep. The repetition of circles, ovals, and half circles throughout the book echoes the rhythm established in the early pages and also evokes circadian rhythms of biological life. There is not a sharp or straight edge anywhere in the book to jar this effect; even the wooden furniture curves in defiance of reality (Figure 6.6).

Shapes with sharp edges and points, on the other hand, can convey excitement, action, tension, or even pain. Janina Domanska's use of abstract colorful shapes to retell *The Bremen Town Musicians* (Grimm Bros.) conveys the mournful quality of the animals' plight as each is threatened by illness or death. Later these shapes convinc-

- typeface is appropriate to type of book or story
- end papers prepare the reader by setting the mood, giving a preview, or complementing the illustrations
- the paper itself is in keeping with original media (acrylic on shiny paper, watercolor or pencil on a matte finish)

2. Pictorial content and the artist's point of view extends and enhances the story or concept.
   - choice of what to include in the picture is appropriate to the story and adds new dimensions, new or additional meanings
   - pictures add information and help us see ideas in new ways
   - close-ups, traditional perspective, worm's-eye view, or bird's-eye view are chosen to lend excitement, drama, and interest to the story

CHOICES OF HISTORICAL OR CULTURAL CONVENTIONS

1. Pictorial conventions are borrowed from styles of art throughout history to enhance and extend the meaning of the story or concept.
   - aspects of early Christian art, Renaissance painting, French Impressionist, etc. are used to convey mood and meaning

2. Pictorial conventions are borrowed from particular cultural groups to enhance meaning.
   - folk motifs or styles lend authenticity to tales, poems, or concepts related to particular cultures

ingly portray the nastiness of the robbers and the raucous victory of the animals as they trick these villains (see Figure 2.6, p. 26).

Mordicai Gerstein uses both geometric and biomorphic shapes in *The Mountains of Tibet*. To tell the life story of the Tibetan wood cutter, Gerstein places the pictures within squares, a perfect geometric shape, but, like life, a square has sharp edges and points. Here even the book itself is square rather than the usual rectangle. When the woodcutter dies, however, the square changes to a circle, the universal symbol of eternity. Then he is presented with choices for another life, all enclosed in circles. When he decides to return to the mountains of Tibet to live another life, he is reborn as a girl in a square-shaped picture. Gerstein artfully creates a metaphor for life and death that could never be expressed as powerfully with words alone (Figures 6.7 and 6.8).

The use of the element of shape can also create some interesting figure-ground relationships. Ann Jonas often works the background shapes in her two-dimensional pictorial spaces into major aspects of the design. This is particularly true in *Round Trip*, where the viewer must perceive the pure black and white shapes as either background or foreground and then switch when the book is turned over (Figure 6.9). The interchange between the two is the essence of visual play in the book.

FIGURE 6.4
Charles Keeping uses the
element of line to create tension in *Willie's Fire-Engine*.

The girl said, "Are you looking for Mick? I know where he is.
Come with me."

Source: From Keeping *Willie's Fire-Engine* (1980). Reprinted by permission of Oxford University
Press.

Molly Bang takes this interplay of background and foreground shapes even further in *The Grey Lady and the Strawberry Snatcher*. Here the reversal of traditional
shape or spatial relationships heightens the nightmare-like quality of the story. Moreover, the shapes formed by the larger areas of empty space set up lively tensions
between the two characters. (See Figures 3.2 and 3.3, pages 46–47.)

Color is one of the most expressive elements. Colors can convey temperature
(warm or cold) or emotion (red for anger or blue for melancholy). They are often
associated with personality traits (purple for royalty, pink for femininity) and as such
can lead to cultural stereotypes. In mainstream American culture, for example, the
hero has often been portrayed in white and the villain in black.

FIGURE 6.5
Don Wood's lines in *The Napping House* evoke stability and lead the eye across the page.

Source: Illustrations from THE NAPPING HOUSE by Audrey Wood, copyright © 1984 by Don Wood, reproduced by permission of Harcourt Brace & Company.

FIGURE 6.6
The shapes in *The Napping House* convey a restful mood.

Source: Illustrations from THE NAPPING HOUSE by Audrey Wood, copyright © 1984 by Don Wood, reproduced by permission of Harcourt Brace & Company.

FIGURE 6.7
Mordicai Gerstein uses
square shapes to surround
images of a woodcutter's life
in *The Mountains of Tibet.*

Source: From THE MOUNTAINS OF TIBET by Mordicai Gerstein. Copyright © 1987 by Mordicai Gerstein. Reprinted by permission of HarperCollins Publishers.

The intensity of a color (its brightness or dullness) as well as the ways in which colors are combined (color schemes) can also effect mood and evoke meaning. In *Bard of Avon: The Story of William Shakespeare*, Diane Stanley uses a full palette of colors but softens their intensity so that the overall tone suggests age. The muted paintings thus recall the sets of a theater seen through the gauzy curtain of time (see color insert).

The early pictures in *Willie's Fire-Engine* (Keeping) are dull brownish-grey, strengthening the dismal mood set up by Keeping's use of line. Later, however, as Willie's dream allows him to escape into the role of hero, Keeping shifts to bright reds and oranges. These colors not only literally represent the fire that Willie is rushing off to, but they also provide a glimpse of the heightened emotion of his inner feelings. Moreover, this color change occurs at the climax of the story, and thus the colors underscore this literary element like a crash of cymbals in the finale of a symphony.

FIGURE 6.8
Circles suggest eternity in
The Mountains of Tibet.

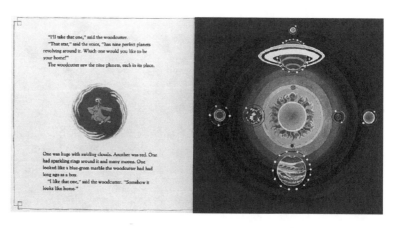

Source: From THE MOUNTAINS OF TIBET by Mordicai Gerstein. Copyright © 1987 by Mordicai Gerstein. Reprinted by permission of HarperCollins Publishers.

FIGURE 6.9
Ann Jonas manipulates fig-
ure-ground relationships in
Round Trip.

Source: Illustration from ROUND TRIP by Ann Jonas. Copyright © 1983 by Ann Jonas. Reprinted by
permission of Greenwillow Books, a division of William Morrow & Co., Inc.

In *The Napping House*, Wood begins the story with a monochromatic color
scheme (the use of single or closely related hues). The blues and purples of the early
pages are further softened by the addition of grey, which adds to the restful mood of
a gentle slumber. By the end of the book, however, when everyone is wakened by the
restless flea, the scheme has changed to complementary colors (using colors opposite
each other on the color wheel). The use of color complements not only makes each
color appear brighter, but it sends a burst of energy to the scene. Finally, on the endpapers at the back of the book, the grey has been removed to produce a bright and
cheerful robin's egg blue, as fully alive as a fresh spring morning.

In *The Napping House* many will recognize the similarity to Uri Shulevitz's
Dawn, which used a similar movement from monochromatic to complementary
scheme to great effect. In a later work, *Toddlecreek Post Office*, Shulevitz again manipulates color schemes effectively. The illustrations in this story about loss of community have an overall blue tone made possible by the specially tinted paper Shulevitz
used for the original art. The blue anticipates the sad climax from the first pages, yet
initially the inclusion of oranges and reds lends a sense of warmth to the scenes of
life that centers around a tiny village post office. When the post mistress who will
close down this rural outpost arrives, however, the warm colors are removed, leaving
cold, dark blues that chill our hearts.

Shulevitz's books also illustrate how contrast and mood can be manipulated in
another way, through the use of the element of value, the amount of light and dark
tones. Value is easiest to recognize when illustrations are executed in black and white,
but it is also a factor in full-color illustrations. When there is little contrast between
light and dark, the mood of the picture may be either serene or brooding. Note, for
example, Roger Duvoisin's illustrations in *Hide and Seek Fog* (Tresselt) or Paul Zelinsky's *Hansel and Gretel* (Grimm Bros.).

On the other hand, with strong contrast between light and dark the mood is
often one of excitement or high drama. When value is used to define shapes, they
take on a three-dimensional quality and become more lifelike. Lloyd Bloom's illustra-

tions for Lillie Chaffin's *We Be Warm Till Springtime Comes* show how strongly contrasting values not only breathe life into a picture but also can extend a message of warmth, even without color (see Figure 2.9, p. 29).

In his books, such as *Jumanji*, Chris Van Allsburg uses contrasting values to convey the feeling that the pictures might actually get up and move off the page. Because the reader's brain knows that the surface is two dimensional, however, this factor heightens the touch of mystery and the absurd that characterizes Van Allsburg's work.

John Steptoe created strong contrast between light and dark in *Mufaro's Beautiful Daughters*. This contrast echoes the theme of opposites, which is the essence of the story. Moreover, the contrasting values give the figures royal stature; in fact, in the first view of the Prince whom Nyasha will marry, he almost looks carved out of marble (Figure 6.10).

Steptoe also effectively uses the element of texture in *Mufaro's Beautiful Daughter*. Texture is less noticeable in picturebooks because it can only be implied on the two-dimensional surface of the book's page. Steptoe artfully extends his theme of contrast between the two sisters, and more subtly the contrast of id and ego within one personality, by executing the illustrations in crosshatching. This laborious use of tiny lines in opposition to each other, often in opposing colors, comprises all the drawings in the book and sets up a subtle feeling of movement or tension on each page. Moreover, Steptoe leaves areas of pure white on each double-page spread. The

FIGURE 6.10
John Steptoe's use of value lends depth and dignity to figures in *Mufaro's Beautiful Daughters*.

Source: Illustration from MUFARO'S BEAUTIFUL DAUGHTERS by John Steptoe. Copyright © 1987 by John Steptoe. By permission of Lothrop, Lee & Shepard Books, a division of William Morrow & Co., Inc., with the approval of the estate of John Steptoe.

theme of contrasts is further reinforced by the juxtaposition of the rough crosshatching and the shiny, smooth whiteness of the book's paper.

Like Steptoe, Charles Keeping uses the element of line to create texture. By including a variety of opposing linear patterns in illustrations for *Joseph's Yard* and *The Highwayman* (Noyes), Keeping communicates barely suppressed energy and heightens the emotional tension.

In other cases, texture can be achieved through the artist's choice of media for the original art. Collage can give a tactile quality to the pages of books like *Matthew's Dream* (Lionni) and *The Snowy Day* (Keats), while the scratchboard drawings by Brain Pinkney in *Sukey and the Mermaid* (Sans Souci) or the woodcut prints of Keizaburo Tejima in *Swan Sky* add sensory depth to the illustrations.

In good picturebooks like these, no single element exists apart from the others. Rather, the illustrator will use principles of composition to unify elements on each page and on each succeeding page. In arranging the elements on each page, including the printed type, the artist tries to obtain an effective balance between unity and variety and creates certain visual patterns that may be carried on from page to page. Illustrators try to ensure that the eye moves from one part of each double-page spread to another, both within the picture and between the picture and any printed text. This in turn sets up a subtle rhythm that can be carried throughout the book. All of these choices can further express the visual meanings expressed by the elements and contribute to a whole that is greater than the sum of its parts.

Charles Keeping has carefully considered these principles of design in *Willie's Fire-Engine*. In the early pages of the book, the dullness of Willie's life is echoed in the layout of the pictures on the first two double-page spreads. On the first left-hand pages, we see a far shot of Willie's city with a golden castle far in the distance, out of his reach. The facing page shows a close-up of Willie's tenement building. As we turn the page, we see a picture of Willie in his room. On the right, Willie is outdoors with the milkman, the only "hero" he knows. These four single pages set up a dull plodding echo that in their tones and use of line reflects the sameness of Willie's life. On the following pages, the two views are fragmented into four scenes, perhaps representing Willie's broken hopes.

When Willie meets a girl who will help him on his quest, however, Keeping begins to vary the shapes and number of vignettes on each double-page spread, increasing the tension and action just as the colors begin to brighten and the lines begin to flow. The design of the book increases the emotional intensity almost unbearably until finally the brilliant reds of the fire engine burst across a double-page spread (Figure 6.11). The scenes get smaller and more numerous as the denouement occurs. The colors remain intense, however, and even when we see on the last page that Willie has been dreaming, the changed colors and subjects of the pictures on his wall communicate hope and seem to indicate that his dreams may enhance his life.

In Verna Aardema's retelling of *Bringing the Rain to Kapiti Plain*, Beatriz Vidal used the principles of variety and unity to set up a visual pattern that echoes the verbal refrains, "This is the great Kapiti Plain, all fresh and green from the African rains." The clear poetic beat of this cumulative tale is echoed and enlivened by Vidal's design. Beginning on the title page, she uses the blocks of type as a visual element and alternates the placement of type and image from left to right. To enliven the symmetry of this pattern, however, she inserts a page where the shapes of cloud and earth cover the entire page. Variations on this pattern are carried out through the book, adding interest to text and image that might have become too static. In addi-

FIGURE 6.11
Charles Keeping's layout in
Willie's Fire-Engine height-
ens emotional suspense.

The streets thundered with the sound of hooves and wheels.
A smell of burning was on the air.

Source: From *Keeping Willie's Fire-Engine* (1980). Reprinted by permission of Oxford University
            Press.

tion, these strong visual rhythms recall the beats of an African drum and further
enhance the overall meaning and integrity of the book.

Grandfather's Journey by Allen Say shows how the artist's careful choices of the
elements and principles of design can deepen the power of a book's written message.
In the story, Say remembers his grandfather's journey between the countries of
America and Japan and the cultures of the West and East. The book also ties
together two generations; in the course of his narrative, Say comes to understand his
own story as well as his grandfather's.

The themes of the book, therefore, center on two places, two worlds, and two
people. Grandfather lived in both America and Japan, but he when he was in one
place he longed for the other. Say has similar feelings; in addition, he longs for this
man who is no longer a part of his life, except in his memory. This sense of attracting
and opposing forces is a subtle yet powerful underpinning of the story.

Say's illustrations convey these themes in complex and powerful ways. His
transparent watercolor paintings evoke the softened edges of memory appropriate
for recalling his grandfather's experiences. In places, the roughness of the paper used
in the original art is visible and contrasts with smooth washes of color. On some
pages, the colors are vibrant, and on others they are muted. Thus the elements of
texture and color represent a full range of life experiences and help us to understand
that if this man found satisfaction in his life, he also suffered.

Each illustration is carefully rendered and invites us to linger over details. Yet
the total design of the book ties the images together and extends the story's meaning. The cover shows Grandfather as a young man aboard a ship, captured for a
moment between two worlds. The title and the author's name are symmetrically balanced on the top and bottom of the picture and enclosed in a gold border that
frames the portrait. Here the pictorial image placed between the two lines of type
introduces us to the dual themes before we ever open the book.

We turn the cover to find soft brown endpapers that capture the feel of old photographs. This color is picked up on subsequent pages and suggests a family album. Yet the soft browns and greys of these pages are often balanced or opposed by a facing page that is brighter in color. The overall mood is therefore respectful rather than dull or sentimentally emotional.

The layout of each double-page spread is the same throughout the book; two pictures face each other with a brief line of type under each. This composition enhances the sense of respect and honor Say feels for his grandfather; there is great dignity conveyed through this visual arrangement. It also reinforces the themes of two worlds as it suggests a powerful connection between the two men.

Although the regularity of page layout unifies the book, the content of each picture is varied. On one page there may be a distant shot of some natural wonder while the facing page has a close-up of human beings. Details of Japanese life on one page may be balanced by figures in Western dress on the opposite page. By alternating viewpoints, contrasting the content in the pictures, and contrasting the color schemes, Say provides a counterbalance to the unified elements. This brings an important feeling of vitality to his story without losing the readers' regard for his subject.

The exception to the unified layout and to the variation in color and content is found at the beginning and ending of the story. The first illustration shows Grandfather in Japanese dress, posed as if for a formal portrait. It is placed on the left side of the two pages in a large rectangular frame. On the final left-hand page, the story finishes with this same picture, but now it is reduced in size and set within an oval frame. The art thus brings the story to a satisfying closure, suggesting an eternal and universal connection. Say's respect and love for his grandfather is clear from beginning to end, and our understanding of this poignant and very human experience is considerably deepened by his artistic choices. (See color insert.)

Technical Choices in Book Production

Although the illustrator's choices of the elements and principles of art can have the most profound effect on a book's aesthetic impact, aspects of book production can also convey subtle meanings and perhaps deepen that experience.

The cover provides the first inkling of the message to come and is an important invitation to enter the world of the book. Although most covers have title, author, and illustrator information along with the visual art, at least two books, Fred Marcellino's version of Perrault's *Puss in Boots* and Maurice Sendak's *We Are All in the Dumps with Jack and Guy*, have only a picture on their covers. The tale of *Puss in Boots* is so familiar that as soon as we see Marcellino's debonair cat in his elegant hat, we recognize the story. There is really no need for words. On the other hand, Sendak placed the title, *We Are All in the Dumps with Jack and Guy: Two Nursey Rhymes with Pictures*, on the back of the book because it was just too long and would have taken away from the visual impact and the quiet dignity of the cover illustration (which recalls Renaissance painter Andrea Mantegna's "Descent into Limbo"). This lends a unique emotional power to the book from the very start.

In *Red Leaf, Yellow Leaf*, Lois Ehlert creates a bright, inviting cover using shiny paper with one red leaf embossed, or raised, above the surface, adding tactile stimulation to the visual excitement. The endpapers are bright yellow leaves, created from pressed paper collage. In the center of the right-hand end paper, echoing the leaf on the cover but reversing its direction, a leaf shape is cut out, revealing the bright red of the following page. Thus, the endpapers, which are necessary in all books but are often left plain, can serve as important introductions to the story when the artist chooses to add something extra.

Paul Zelinsky created grandiose landscapes on the endpapers to provide the setting for his version of *Hansel and Gretel* (Grimm Bros.). These pictures pull the reader into his Renaissance setting immediately and then bring the story to closure. They provide a visual framing device that serves the same purpose as "once upon a time" and "they lived happily ever after," the classic signals of narrative structure.

The artist's choice of original media may also affect the mood and validity of the book's theme. Although a picturebook contains a reproduction of the artist's finished work and should be evaluated as such (just as we evaluate an etching or lithograph and not the original metal plate or stone), the quality of the original media often enhances or interferes with visual meaning. In *Rain Rain Rivers*, for example, Shulevitz's choice of transparent watercolor echoes the book's title and theme, and the white of the page shows through as if we were seeing light reflected in a rainy puddle.

Van Allsburg's choice of conte pencil for the original pictures in *Jumanji* reproduces well and combines with the choice of a matte, rather rough paper stock, to convey an air of mysterious smokiness. We almost feel as if the pencil dust might rub off on our fingers as we touch the page, just as the game comes to life for the children.

Illustrator Thomas Allen achieves a similar effect through his use of pastel chalk in nostalgic stories such as *Climbing Kansas Mountains* by George Shannon and *In Coal Country* by Judith Hendershot. In both books, the muted colors and hazy edges of figures and landscapes that are the result of the artist's medium evoke a lovely sense of memories softened by age. In addition, the dusty quality of the chalk reinforces the gritty setting of the coal mine with *In Coal Country*.

Molly Bang's inventive "found object" collages for *Red Dragonfly on My Shoulder* (Cassedy and Suetake) echo the underlying connections between the outer and inner worlds that are the essence of the haiku poetry she is interpreting. Huck, Hepler, and Hickman (1993) explain that in haiku, "a relationship between two parts is implied, either a similarity or a telling difference" (1993, p. 467). By using unusual combinations of everyday objects to illustrate the haiku poems of Kunihiro Suetake, Bang emphasizes these relationships in surprising ways.

Comparing two versions of the same tale shows how the choice of original media changes the meaning of a book. In the first edition of Jane Yolen's *Greyling*, a story set in and near the seas of Scotland, William Stobbs' use of transparent paint communicates the watery realm of the selkie, or seal, transformed into human form. The flowing brush strokes help to move the story along visually and heighten the stormy climax (Figure 6.12).

In the newer version of *Greyling*, David Ray has chosen acrylic paint, which he uses thickly, creating a texture that more closely resembles oil or oil pastels. Although this medium gives more solid form to the seal turned human and provides a different visual emphasis to the story, it renders the overall mood static. The watery forms, no longer fluid, seem changed into stone. For some readers, like me, the story loses its emotional impact.

FIGURE 6.12
Illustrations by (a) William
Stobbs and (b) David Ray
create different moods in
Greyling through their
choice of media.

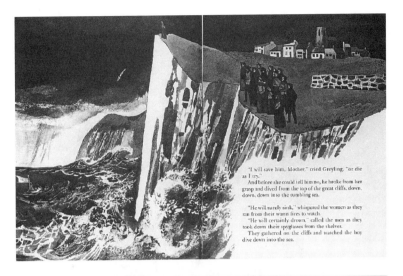

Source: From (a) GREYLING by Jane Yolen, illustrated by William Stobbs. Text copyright © 1968 by
Jane Yolen. Illustrations copyright © 1968 by William Stobbs. Reprinted by permission of
The World Publishing Company. (b)Illustration by David Ray reprinted by permission of
Philomel from GREYLING by Jane Yolen. Illustrations copyright © 1991 by David Ray.

Another technical decision that is unique to book production is the choice of typeface for the title and written text. The styles of typography and the white spaces between the letters are important to the visual effect of the book. Denise Fleming's choice of Helvetica (a clean, sans serif type) for *In the Tall, Tall Grass* echoes and balances the sharp edges of her cut-out shapes. In addition, the large letters, which are black on some pages and white on others, become part of the visual design of the page (Figure 6.13).

A more elaborate typeface was chosen for Sidjakov's illustrations in *Baboushka and the Three Kings* (Robbins) and becomes part of the linear design of the book, reflecting the pictorial forms and figures (Figure 6.14). Here the letter forms recall the Carolingian script used in illuminated manuscripts and suggest the geographical and historical roots of the story (see Figure 4.4, p. 76).

In Fred Marcellino's illustrations of *Puss in Boots* (Perrault), the typeface mirrors the ornate fussiness of a French court. The type is larger than is usual and is grey-green rather than black. Thus the letters help unite the visual design of the book by integrating the composition of each page and by tying in with the overall color scheme.

The artist's point of view can also extend or heighten the overall meaning of the book. In many books artists use point of view like the lens of a camera to zoom in on subjects at emotional moments, as does Charles Keeping in *Willie's Fire-Engine* or Donald Carrick in *Ben and the Porcupine* (see Figure 2.12, p. 33). Shulevitz moves the viewer from close-ups to long shots in *Dawn* to emphasize majestic views of the natural landscape.

To relieve the sameness of the repetition of the text and visual setting in *The Napping House*, Wood subtly moves the eye up the wall of the room so that eventually we are looking down on the scene from a bird's-eye view. Van Allsburg also changes perspective and point of view in *Jumanji* to add variety to the monotony of pictures always placed on the right-hand page.

The artist's choice of pictorial content can be essential to the book's overall meaning and may be the most important technical choice. Although many artists choose to represent or echo the verbal text of a book, the aesthetic experience is enhanced when the artist brings something extra to the scene. For example, in *Julius,*

FIGURE 6.13
Words become part of the visual art in Denise Fleming's *In the Tall, Tall Grass*.

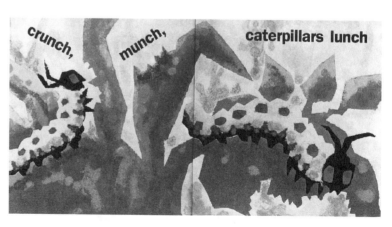

Source: From IN THE TALL, TALL GRASS by Denise Fleming. Copyright © 1991 by Denise Fleming. Reprinted by permission of Henry Holt and Company, Inc

FIGURE 6.14
Printed words reflect visual forms in Sidjakov's *Baboushka and the Three Kings*.

******** And it is said that every year, at the season when the birth of the Child was first heralded, Baboushka renews her search across that land with new hope.********

********* And it is said that every year little children await the coming of Baboushka. They find joy in the poor but precious gifts she leaves behind her in the silent night. *****

Source: From *Baboushka and the Three Kings* by Ruth Robbins, 1957.

The Baby of the World, Kevin Henkes' illustrations add to the sense of contrast between the parents' love for the new baby brother and sister Lilly's jealousy. The pictures contradict the objective tone of the words and reflect Lilly's intense emotional feelings while they add a strong note of humor to the story, acknowledging the young child's right to those feelings and accepting them with warmth rather than rejection (Figure 6.15).

In *Farmer Duck*, Helen Oxenbury's artwork brings Martin Waddell's brief, predictable text to life. "How goes the work?" asks the slovenly farmer, who sits in bed all day and eats chocolates while the poor duck gets ever more "sleepy and weepy and tired." Oxenbury's fully realized characters provide a visual punch for the repeated words and afford a satisfying experience for those of us who, like the duck, have ever felt overburdened with chores (see color insert).

Julie Vivas' interpretation of *The Nativity* lends a sense of warmth and wonder to a familiar yet often coldly formal verbal story. (The text is the King James version of the Christmas story.) The story is both human and personal as the characters are viewed through the naive but pure eyes of a child (Figure 6.16).

On the other hand, Trina Schart Hyman brings psychological darkness to her version of *Snow White* (Grimm Bros.) by showing the young and voluptuous stepmother's descent into madness. The familiar tale becomes an entirely new story through Hyman's pictorial choices, which include the objects in the rooms and the faces around the magic mirror (Figure 6.17).

Comparing Hyman's version of *Snow White* to Nancy Burkert's illustrations shows how pictorial content and point of view can yield very different meanings. For example, Hyman fully develops the character of the stepmother through the pictures, but Burkert never shows readers the stepmother's face. Moreover, Hyman's version immediately draws readers into the tale with dark flowing lines and shapes. In our first view of Snow White's mother, we are in the room with her as she pricks her finger, the red drops of blood visible on the snow on the window sill.

Burkert's version begins much more formally. Regular, geometric shapes on the endpapers communicate stately objectivity, as does the rectangular shape of the mirror placed squarely in the middle of the title page. In this version, we see Snow White's mother from outside the castle, and although she may have pricked her finger, we have no visual evidence of blood. Thus we are safely distanced from the emo-

FIGURE 6.15
Kevin Henkes adds humor to the illustrations in *Julius, The Baby of the World*.

Lilly spent more time than usual in the uncooperative chair.

Source: Illustration from JULIUS, THE BABY OF THE WORLD by Kevin Henkes. Copyright © 1990 by Kevin Henkes. By permission of Greenwillow Books, a division of William Morrow & Co., Inc.

tional intensity of the story. Unlike Hyman's version, which becomes a story of mother-daughter conflict resulting in the utter downfall of an evil person through her own failings, Burkert tells the story of an innocent child whose escape from evil is brought about by others. Both versions are powerful in their own ways, and both show how far beyond the verbal elements of text an artist can bring us. (See Figure 4.8, p. 80.)

FIGURE 6.16
Julie Vivas conveys a child's innocent understanding of the story of *The Nativity*.

Source: Illustration from THE NATIVITY, copyright © 1986 by Julie Vivas, reproduced by permission of Harcourt Brace & Company.

FIGURE 6.17
Trina Schart Hyman adds to the familiar story *Snow White* through her depiction of the stepmother.

Source: From SNOW WHITE by Paul Heins. Text copyright © 1974 by Paul Heins; Illustrations copyright © 1974 by Trina Schart Hyman. By permission of Little, Brown and Company.

Historical and Cultural Conventions

The last category of stylistic choices available to an artist concerns the pictorial conventions associated with particular times or peoples. If we recall Novitz's (1976) suggestion that certain pictorial conventions are accepted as procedures for depicting, we might regard these umbrella conventions, be they historical or cultural, as another range of choices open to the illustrator for expressing meaning.

For example, early Christian art is characterized by the need for a clear, uniform message to a mostly illiterate audience. This need for readily recognizable symbols and motifs transcended individualistic portrayals. Many illustrators have thus used these conventions to convey stories and songs associated with this broad time period. Janina Domanska echoes the stained glass windows of Romanesque churches to bring a Christmas carol, *Din Dan Don It's Christmas*, to book form. Deborah Nourse Lattimore includes decorative forms from Celtic art to tell *The Sailor that Captured the Sea: The Story of the Book of Kells* (see color insert). Juan Wijngaard, in *Sir Gawain and the Loathly Lady* (Hastings), and Trina Schart Hyman, in *Saint George and the Dragon* (Hodges), have both used illuminated manuscripts conventions from the 13th and 14th centuries. All these artists bring these books to life by associating the time of the original tales with the art of that period. These details can add a sense of wonder to our understanding of lives lived many centuries ago.

A broad range of historical conventions have been chosen effectively by other picturebook illustrators. Nancy Burkert draws on the stylized symbols of the late Gothic period to retell *Snow White and the Seven Dwarfs* (Grimm Bros.); Paul Zelinsky borrows from the Renaissance use of dramatic lighting and emphasis on form and space to retell *Hansel and Gretel* (Grimm Bros.).

Northern Renaissance painter Pieter Bruegel is well known for the storytelling qualities of his paintings, and conventions of his style can be found in the work of several illustrators. Sendak makes reference to Bruegel's "The Fall of Icarus" in *Outside Over There*, and Errol Le Cain paid homage to Bruegel's "Hunters in the Snow" in a scene in Andersen's *The Snow Queen*, a story that also has its roots in Northern Europe (Figure 6.18). Illustrator Gennady Spirin was trained in classical methods of painting in Russia and echoes the meticulous rendering associated with Bruegel and other Northern Renaissance artists in classic stories and folktales set in a similar time and place. *The Children of Lir*, by Sheila MacGill-Callahan, includes carefully painted details as well as grandiose landscapes typical of Renaissance painting and adds authenticity to our experience of the story (see color insert).

Artists of the 20th century have influenced many illustrators, and conventions of various modern schools can be found in picturebooks. Maurice Sendak's illustrations for Zolotow's *Mr. Rabbit and the Lovely Present* capture readers' interest with the light and color of Impressionist painters like Claude Monet. John Steptoe's early work reflects the intense, heightened colors used by Expressionist Marc Rouault, and Anthony Browne uses conventions of surrealism to convey his psychologically deep themes in *Changes* and other books (Figure 6.19).

Other artists may borrow conventions associated with particular cultures (Figure 6.20). Thus Paul Goble adapts the styles of the buffalo hide paintings of Northern Plains Indians to retell their legends and tales, such as *The Lost Children: The Boys Who Were Neglected* and *The Girl Who Loved Wild Horses*. Likewise, in their stories with Chinese or Asian settings or roots, Ed Young and Demi have effectively used techniques from Chinese art, which is characterized by the exploration of linear effects and the de-emphasis of realism. In *Yeh Shen: A Cinderella Story from China*, Young breaks the pictorial plane into panels reminiscent of Chinese scroll paintings. Demi's delicate figures and carefully rendered landscapes in *Chingis Khan* recall images from Chinese painting on silk and paper that date back a thousand years and more (see color insert).

In all these cases, the theme of the book, its setting in time and place, and its overall effect is strengthened by the artist's choice of certain historical or cultural conventions. We must judge the book, therefore, not as to whether the illustrations match the definition of a particular period or culture, but as to whether the artist has chosen elements that enhance and extend the meaning of the book for today's reader.

Finally, illustrators can flaunt the conventions of picturebook design to convey meaning, just as many of the best artists of the past pushed the defining constructs of their age. Such defiance of expectations can heighten the emotional response or lend a sense of the bizarre or the farcical to the picturebook experience. Certainly, in the later part of the 20th-century Maurice Sendak and Charles Keeping have helped redefine the picturebook and broadened its audience. In recent years, the happy partnership of author Jon Scieszka and illustrator Lane Smith has brought us books that have turned stories and picturebooks upside down—in some cases, literally upside down. In *The Stinky Cheese Man and Other Fairly Stupid Tales*, for example, they vary the size of the type, print it upside down, place the table of contents after the first story, and insert the endpapers in the middle of the book. Smiths' dark color tones and surreal images further extend the droll humor and sense of wackiness that brings readers of all ages back to the book again and again.

David Macaulay brings a similar sense of fun and play to *Black and White*, but he also demonstrates a deep understanding of the traditional elements of the picture-

FIGURE 6.18
Pieter Bruegel's (a)
"Hunters in the Snow"
influenced Eroll Le Cain's
illustrations for Andersen's
(b) *The Snow Queen*.

FIGURE 6.19
Anthony Browne's (a) *Changes* has similarities to Magritte's (b) "Time Transfixed."
Source: (a) From CHANGES by Anthony Browne. Copyright © 1991 by Anthony Browne. Reprinted
by permission of Alfred A. Knopf, Inc. (b) From *Magritte* by Bernard Noël. René Magritte,
Belgian, 1898–1967, Time Transfixed, oil on canvas, 1938, 146.1 × 97.5 cm, Joseph Winter-
botham Collection, 1970. 426. Photograph courtesy of the Art Institute of Chicago.

book, which he violates from the very beginning. The cover of the book has no picture, just the words *black and white* printed in blue and green. As we open the book
with the title still in our mind, the red endpapers suggest the old riddle—black and
white and red all over—and, sure enough a newspaper plays an important role in the
book. The title page design also disturbs the normal order, and a sign warns us that
there may be many stories within or just one.

The first double-page spread displays four pictures in four very different artistic
styles (see color insert). Here Macaulay tampers with the limits of a picturebook's
two-dimensional and linear nature. We don't need to read from left to right, nor are
we limited to one visual plot line as is usual. In the lower right picture, Macaulay
plays with figure-ground relationships, for as we look at the black and white cow, we
suddenly notice a laughing face. This manipulation of spatial expectations will even-

FIGURE 6.20
Conventions of Native American hide paintings like this Mandan bison robe are recalled
in many of Paul Goble's books.

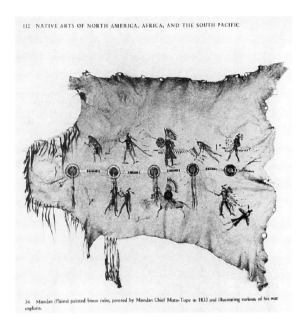

112 NATIVE ARTS OF NORTH AMERICA, AFRICA, AND THE SOUTH PACIFIC

34. Mandan (Plains) painted bison robe, painted by Mandan Chief Mato-Tope in 1833 and illustrating various of his war exploits.

Source: Reproduction courtesy of the Linden Museum, Stuttgart, Germany.

tually allow the separate stories to bleed into one large story on one double-page
spread before a final return to four separate images at the story's denouement. And,
just to intensify the book's many "secrets" and add to the fun, there are several visual
references to Macaulay's good friend Chris Van Allsburg.

This is certainly the kind of book that invites continued inspection and discussion. It could lead children to deepen their responses, intensify their connections,
and increase their understanding of the picturebook as an art object.

CONCLUSION

This chapter has presented a theory for exploring the potential of picturebooks. The
criteria proposed grows out of the understanding that the picturebook is a unique art
object, different from other visual art forms, and that they are based on criteria from
the field of aesthetics and art criticism that lend themselves to evaluating picturebooks. The theory grows out of a firm belief that we must understand how the illustrator chooses to convey meaning, and it seeks to explore the range of choices possible for illustrators of picturebooks in accomplishing that task.

These ideas are not presented here as a *formula* for evaluating picturebooks but
as a *beginning* point for exploring the possibilities that lie within their covers. Children can develop important understandings and deep emotional responses to picturebooks in the company of teachers and peers who have little training in art. However, teachers who want to extend those responses as fully as possible may find the
criteria discussed here and the activities that follow helpful in moving children
beyond visual literacy to realize the full aesthetic potential of the picturebook.

Kaelin (1989) has proposed that "Experience, reflection, criticism, renewed
experience, reflection and criticism describe the never-ending round of the philo-

sophical enterprise" (p. 3). As we have seen in children's responses to picturebooks, this philosophical process has the potential for moving the individual from an initial and private stage of experiencing, to meaning-making in the company of others, to an understanding of some real significance in the work of art. Langer (1953) has argued that the deepest aesthetic experience reveals our inner life as well as our outward existence. Thus, aesthetic understanding may result "in a richer, clearer, more enjoyable experience of the values to be found in living" (Kaelin, 1989, p. 3). I can ask nothing more from children who have explored picturebooks to their fullest potential.

PART

III

Picturebooks in the Classroom

CHAPTER

7

Classroom Connections

T he preceding chapters have provided descriptions of children's responses to picturebooks and information about the picturebook as an art object. This section presents practical classroom suggestions based on these previous concepts. The activities suggested here are possibilities for young children's exploration and opportunities for teacher's observations and research.

For older children, these activities may also provide opportunities for more formal inquiry about art history, artistic production, and aesthetic evaluation. As children reach the point where they begin to wonder about and consider the process of creating art as well as their own objective and subjective responses to works of art, teachers can support their questions with more formal instruction, with information, lessons, and techniques that could deepen their aesthetic understanding.

Thus, the following activities are presented for teachers of students of *all* ages. It is my hope that teachers will adapt these ideas to the age level that they teach and that they will use these suggestions as starting points, following the lead of children's interests and respecting their infinite meaning-making potential.

EXPLORING THE ART OF THE PICTUREBOOK

A unit on the art of the picturebook allows children to consider the art of book illustration and to focus on criteria for evaluating the picturebook as an aesthetic object. This could then be extended to understanding other art forms. The web in Figure 7.1 provides an overview of such a unit and can serve as an introduction to the teaching suggestions that follow. Each section of the web lists some of the related books and suggests questions that children may want to pursue further. (A bibliography of the books listed in the web can be found in Appendix A.)

To begin a study of the art in picturebooks, teachers might want to join forces with the art teacher to explore visual elements of design like line, shape, color, texture, and value and the principles of composition such as balance, rhythm, repetition, eye movement, variety, and unity. Even if without expert advice, however, teachers can join children in a study of books about the elements and principles of art. For help, there is no better place to begin than with illustrator Molly Bang's *Picture This: Perception and Composition* (1991). Using simple cut paper, abstract shapes, and only three colors, Bang explains how the art elements allow pictures to express meaning. The book is a wonderful resource for teachers or could be read by older children. Bang has used these ideas with upper elementary and middle school students who are writing and illustrating their own books, but the principles lend themselves to working with almost any age group.

There are also picture storybooks, concept books, and information books that help children understand concepts relating to the elements and principles of art. Although some these books speak specifically to matters of art appreciation, others, like Tana Hoban's *Shapes, Shapes, Shapes*, find and relate art elements to the everyday world as well as to the world of art. The following list suggests a variety of books on the subject, written for students.

THE ELEMENTS OF ART

Christiana, David. *Drawer in a Drawer*. New York: Farrar, Straus & Giroux, 1990.
˚Cole, Allison. *Color*. New York: Dorling Kindersley, 1993.
˚Cole, Allison. *Perspective*. New York: Dorling Kindersley, 1993.
Ehlert, Lois. *Color Farm*. New York: Lippincott, 1990.

EXPLORING MEDIA

Try original media used by illustrators.

Watercolor
Robert Andrew Parker (*Guess Who My Favorite Person Is?*)
Uri Shulevitz (*Dawn*)

Pastel Chalk
Thomas B. Allen (*Climbing Kansas Mountains*)

Acrylic
Barbara Cooney (*Ox-Cart Man*)

Air Brush
Donald Crews (*Freight Train*)

Collage
Lois Ehlert (*Red Leaf, Yellow Leaf*)
Suse MacDonald and Bill Oakes (*Once Upon Another*)

Etching
Arthur Geisert (*Oink Oink*)

Linoleum or Wood Block Print
Ashley Wolff (*A Year of Birds*)
Keizaburo Tejima (*Swan Sky*)

Scratchboard
Brian Pinkney (*Where Does the Trail Lead?* by B. Albert)

Batik
Patricia MacCarthy (*17 Kings and 43 Elephants*)
Harriet Peck Taylor (*Coyote Places the Stars*)

Photographs
Sarah Moon (*Little Red Riding Hood* by C. Perrault)
Patricia Mills (*Until the Cows Come Home*)
Ann Grifalconi (*Flyaway Girl*)
Dav Pilkey (*Dogzilla*)

Graphic (Drawing) Materials
Study the work of Chris Van Allsburg. What are the different drawing materials he has used in his books?

MAKING BOOKS

How a Book is Made
A Book Takes Root: The Making of a Picturebook
Simon's Book
Study the history and process of bookmaking and publishing.
Visit an art press, where type is set by hand, or a printing plant. How are the processes different? What are the steps that bookmaking entails?
The Art of the Handmade Book
Making Books
How to Make Pop-ups
Interview a printer or bookbinder.
Write and illustrate a book of your own.
Create a storyboard and book dummy before you do your final draft. Try different genres (ABC's, poetry) or formats (half page, pop-up)
Vicki Cobb's Papermaking Book and Kit
Paper Making Fun
Make your own paper.
Investigate other ways to make paper. Collect samples of specialty papers. Experiment with them as writing, drawing, painting, or printing surfaces.
The Practical Guide to Marbling Papers
Make marbleized covers or endpapers.
Try paste-paper covers, chalk-dust endpapers.

EXPLORING PICTUREBOOK DESIGN

The Mountains of Tibet
Mufaro's Beautiful Daughters
Look for the ways in which the artist uses elements and principles of design to tell the story or convey an idea.
The Napping House
Does the artist's use of the elements of art change throughout the book? How does this affect your enjoyment?
Sleeping Beauty
How do artists establish a visual rhythm or lead your eye across the page and on to the next?
Dawn
Ben and the Porcupine
Jumanji
How does the artist's point of view alter in these books? How does this add to the effect?
Snow White
Julius, Baby of the World
What details do artists add that provide new meaning to stories or ideas?

THE ART OF THE BOOK

Study the parts of a book. How do covers, dust jackets, and endpapers differ from book to book? Compare the hardback, paperback, and book club edition of the same book. Do you notice any differences?
What can you predict from endpapers? What do they tell about the story or idea?
How do endpapers relate to the story that follows?
Symbols—*Cinderella; We Are All in the Dumps with Jack and Guy*
Setting—*Hansel and Gretel* or *Rumplestilskin*
Designs—*Snow White and the Seven Dwarfs; The Fool of the World and The Flying Ship*
Saint George and the Dragon
In a Small, Small Pond
Make a list of other books with different typefaces. How can the typeface add to your enjoyment of the book?
The Mountains of Tibet
The Witch's Broom
Compare the size of books. How does the shape and size affect the meaning?
How can page layout and format differ? Do rough (matte) or shiny papers make a difference in the overall look of the book?
The Story of an English Village
Nuts to You; Color Zoo
The Very Hungry Caterpillar
How do artists make use of unusual formats like half pages or cutouts?

FIGURE 7.1
Exploring the art of the picturebook web

FOLKTALE COMPARISONS
Hansel and Gretel
Cinderella
The Bremen Town Musicians
Little Red Riding Hood
Compare different illustrated versions of the same folktale.
   Make a comparison chart of differences and liknesses.
How do the artist's choices affect the meaning of the story?
The Frog Prince
The Frog Prince Continued
Pondlarker
How do artists and writers collaborate to offer fresh
   versions of familiar tales?
A Story, a Story
Iktomi and the Boulder
Borreguita and the Coyote
The Boy of the Three-Year Nap
Do a cross-cultural comparison of motifs like the Trickster.
   Do the illustrators differ in the way they picture these
   stories? If so, how? Why?
Study folktales from around the world. How do artists
   make use of cultural conventions? How does this affect
   your enjoyment or understanding of the story?

ARTISTS AS MEANING MAKERS
How do artists communicate?
Shape Space
Drawer in a Drawer
Color Zoo
A Color Sampler
Is It Rough? Is It Smooth? Is It Shiny?
Study the elements of art. How do these elements make you feel?
List the different ways in which one of the elements can vary.
   Collect books that demonstrate these different uses. In your
   own art, try expressing different emotions using only one
   element.

Line and Shape
Why the Tides Ebb and Flow
The Grouchy Lady Bug
Your Own Best Secret Place

Color Intensity (Brightness)
When I Was Young in the Mountains
Waiting for Hannah

Color Scheme
I Have a Friend
Dawn

Texture
Red Leaf, Yellow Leaf
Two by Two

Value
Hansel and Gretel
Hide and Seek Fog

STUDYING ILLUSTRATORS
Donald Crews
Ann Jonas
James Stevenson
Barbara Cooney
What themes do you identify with these illustrators?
Study your favorite illustrators. Do their books seem to have
   similar themes or settings?
Can you find details or "secrets" that appear in many of their
   books?
Study the work of one illustrator over time.
How have the artist's pictures changed?
Do a research paper and find out more about the illustrator.
Write to his/her publisher for information.

EXPLORING THE ART OF THE PICTUREBOOK

THE ART OF THE WORD
Calligraphy: From Beginner to Expert
Learn the art of lettering, writing invitations, personal letters.
Compare typefaces in different picturebooks.
Illuminations
The Accidental Zucchini
Create an exhibit of alphabet books.
Choose a theme and create your own alphabet book.
Alphabet Art: Thirteen ABC's from Around the World
Alef-Bet: A Hebrew Alphabet
Ayokah and the Talking Leaves
Study changing forms of symbols in different languages. Write
   messages in different systems.
Make up your own alphabet. Teach it to someone else and write
   notes with it.
Roar and More
Short Cut
How do artists make use of words in their pictures? Make a list of
   books and other forms of communication where words are art.

FIGURE 7.1, *continued*

THE CALDECOTT MEDAL

Learn how the Caldecott Medal is awarded.

Develop your own criteria for awarding the Medal. Create your own class Caldecott committee and discuss and vote on the books you think should win for the present year.

Start a collection of past Caldecott winners and honor books. Has the art of the picturebook changed over the years? How?

THE BOOK ARTS OF THE MIDDLE AGES

The Book of Kells
The Golden Age
Study reproductions of early manuscripts.

Learn forms of Celtic decoration. Make your own decorated initial or draw borders for your pictures.

Sir Gawain and the Loathly Lady
Saint George and the Dragon
Merrily Ever After
How do illustrators use qualities of illuminated manuscripts to tell stories from that time period?

Pangor Ban
The Sailor Who Captured the Sea
Find out more about scribes and illuminators. What was their life in the Middle Ages like?

How were books part of daily life? Who had access to books?

The Man Who Loved Books
Gutenberg
Study bookmaking in the Middle Ages. How did Gutenberg's invention change the world?

PICTUREBOOKS FOR OLDER STUDENTS

Arithmetic; Dakota Dugout; The Day of Ahmed's Secret; A River Ran Wild
Use picturebooks across the curriculum. What criteria are important in picturebooks that present facts?

Hiroshima No Pika; Sadako, (nucular war, peace)
Fly Away Home; We Are All in the Dumps with Jack and Guy (homelessness)
Rose Blanche; Terrible Things (the Holocaust)
How are social issues and human rights addressed in picturebooks? Compare these books to informational texts. Do the picturebooks heighten the impact or make you feel differently?

Gorilla
Motel of the Mysteries
The Stinky Cheese Man and Other Fairly Stupid Tales
What makes a picturebook more suitable for older children and adults than for young children?

The Highwayman
Jason and the Golden Fleece.
Compare illustrated and non-illustrated versions of classic stories. Does the picturebook version contribute to your understanding in a different way?

Snow White
Prince Cinders
Baaa
Study literary elements through picturebooks. How does this help your understanding of your own reading and writing?

BEYOND THE CLASSROOM, INTO THE MUSEUM

The Art Lesson
From the Mixed-Up Files of Mrs. Basil E. Frankweiler
Read about characters like yourselves having adventures in the world of art.

Lives of the Artists
Choose an artist. Find out more about his or her life and work.

Stories in Art
The World of Water
Choose a theme and study paintings across historical periods. What differences do you find? Make a comparison chart.

Choose a landscape or still life. Do several versions, changing the style or medium you use for each. How do the changes affect your feelings? Which was the most difficult to do? The most fun?

Behind the Scenes: Painting
The Painter's Eye
The Key to Renaissance Art
Find out more about art in different periods of history.

Choose a century and study art forms across cultures. How are these forms alike? Different?

Visiting the Art Museum
Visit an art museum. Try some of the activities from this book. How is the art you see here different from what you see in picturebooks?

Ehlert, Lois. *Color Zoo*. New York: Lippincott, 1990.

Falwell, Cathryn. *Shape Space*. New York: Clarion, 1992.

Fisher, Leonard Everett. *Look Around: A Book About Shapes*. New York: Viking, 1986.

*Frayling, Christopher & Helen, & Ron Van der Meer. *The Art Pack*. New York: Knopf, 1992.

Hoban, Tana. *Dots, Spots, Speckles, and Stripes*. New York: Greenwillow Books, 1987.

Hoban, Tana. *Is It Red? Is It Yellow? Is It Blue?* New York: Greenwillow Books, 1978.

Hoban, Tana. *Is It Rough? Is It Smooth? Is It Shiny?* New York: Greenwillow Book, 1984.

Hoban, Tana. *Of Colors and Things* New York: Greenwillow Books, 1989.

Hoban, Tana. *Shapes, Shapes, Shapes*. New York: Greenwillow Books, 1986.

Jenkins, J. *Thinking About Colors*. New York: Dutton, 1992.

Jonas, Ann. *Color Dance*. New York: Greenwillow Books, 1989.

Juenesse, Gallinard, & Pascale de Bourgoing. *Colors*. Illustrated by P. M. Valet and Sylvaine Perols. New York: Scholastic, 1993.

Lionni, Leo. *Little Blue and Little Yellow*. New York: Astor, 1959.

Rosetti, Christina. *Color*. Illustrated by M. Teichman. New York: HarperCollins, 1992.

Serfozo, Mary. *Who Said Red?* Illustrated by K. Narahashi. New York: McElderry, 1988.

Walsh, Ellen S. *Mouse Paint*. San Diego: Harcourt Brace Jovanovich, 1988.

Westray, Kathleen. *A Color Sampler*. New York: Ticknor & Fields, 1993.

Yenawine, Phillip. *Colors*. New York: Delacorte, 1991.

Yenawine, Phillip. *Lines*. New York: Delacorte, 1991.

Yenawine, Phillip. *Shapes*. New York: Delacorte, 1991.

Chapter 6 discussed how picturebook illustrators make artistic choices that enhance the meaning of the story or idea they are trying to convey. Figure 7.2 includes a list of these choices and books that are especially good for opening discussion about the effective use of visual art elements relating to picturebook design. With books like these, teachers might simply ask children to consider how the artist's choices affect their own understanding and enjoyment of the book. Here questions like, "What are you thinking about as you're looking at this book?" or "How do these pictures make you feel?" may call forth many ideas. As they learn more about how the illustrator chooses among the elements of art and book design, children can add their own titles to the list.

EXPLORING AN ILLUSTRATOR'S WORK

Children who are involved in writer's workshops (Calkins, 1994) and who have begun to think about the choices they make in composing pieces of writing can extend those understandings to their own artwork as well as to the work of authors and illustrators. As they think about themselves as meaning makers, they can also study the meaning-making choices of all artists.

*Appropriate for older children

I. *DESIGN CHOICES*

   A. **Elements of design**

      1. **Line**

         a. Joan Chase Bowden/Marc Brown, *Why the Tides Ebb and Flow*

         b. Charles Keeping, *Willie's Fire-Engine*

         c. Charles Perrault/Marcia Brown, *Cinderella*

      2. **Shape**

         a. Grimm Bros./Janina Domanska, *The Bremen Town Musicians*

         b. Byrd Baylor/Peter Parnell, *Your Own Best Secret Place*

         c. Audrey Wood/Don Wood, *The Napping House*

      3. **Texture**

         a. Leo Lionni, *Matthew's Dream*

         b. Robert D. Sans Souci/Brian Pinkney, *Sukey and the Mermaid*

         c. Barbara Reid, *Two by Two*

      4. **Color**

         a. Uri Shulevitz, *Dawn, Toddle Creek Post Office*

         b. Eric Carle, *The Grouchy Ladybug*

         c. Marisabina Russo, *Waiting for Hannah*

         d. Keiko Narahashi, *I Have a Friend*

         e. Audrey Wood/Don Wood, *The Napping House*

      5. **Value**

         a. Alvin Tresselt/Roger Duvoisin, *Hide and Seek Fog*

         b. Lillie D. Chaffin/Lloyd Bloom, *We Be Warm Till Springtime Comes*

         c. Grimm Bros./Paul Zelinsky, *Hansel and Gretel*

   B. **Principles of design/Layout of the book**

      1. Raymond Briggs, *The Snowman*

      2. Charles Keeping, *Willie's Fire-Engine*

      3. Uri Shulevitz, *Dawn*

      4. Verna Aardema/Beatriz Vidal, *Bringing the Rain to Kapiti Plain*

II. *TECHNICAL CHOICES*

   A. **Original media**

      1. Uri Shulevitz, *Rain Rain Rivers* (water color)

FIGURE 7.2
Artistic choices in pictures

2. Arthur Geisert, *Oink Oink* (etching)

3. Barbara Cooney, *Miss Rumphius* (acrylic paint)

4. Ezra Jack Keats, *A Letter to Amy* (collage)

5. Gail Haley, *A Story, a Story* (wood block print)

6. Chris Van Allsburg, *Jumanji* (conte pencil and dust)

7. Judith Hendershot/Thomas Allen, *In Coal Country* (pastel chalk)

8. Thomas Locker, *Where the River Begins* (oil paint)

B. **End papers**

1. Arthur Ransome/Uri Shulevitz, *The Fool of the World and the Flying Ship*

2. Uri Shulevitz, *Dawn*

3. Grimm Bros./Nonnie Hogrogian, *Cinderella*

4. Grimm Bros./Paul Zelinsky, *Hansel and Gretel*

C. **Typography**

1. Ruth Robbins/Nicholas Sidjakov, *Baboushka and the Three Kings*

2. Lillie D. Chaffin/Lloyd Bloom, *We Be Warm Till Springtime Comes*

3. Maurice Sendak, *Outside Over There*

4. Eric Carle, *The Grouchy Ladybug*

5. Charles Perrault/Fred Marcellino, *Puss in Boots*

6. Demi, *Chingis Khan*

D. **Pictorial content**

1. Grimm Bros./Trina Schart Hyman, *Snow White*

2. Grimm Bros./Nancy Burkert, *Snow White and the Seven Dwarfs*

3. Kevin Henkes, *Julius, The Baby of the World*

4. Maurice Sendak, *We Are All in the Dumps with Jack and Guy*

5. Martin Waddell/Helen Oxenbury, *Farmer Duck*

E. **Point of view**

1. Chris Van Allsburg, *Jumanji*

2. Carol Carrick/Donald Carrick, *Ben and the Porcupine*

3. Audrey Wood/Don Wood, *The Napping House*

4. Jane Yolen/John Schoenherr, *Owl Moon*

FIGURE 7.2, *continued*

Studying the work of one illustrator can help children to find out more about the process of creation and to understand the meaning-making potential of the art in picturebooks. In addition to the books about illustrators listed in Chapter 5 (p. 98), there are many fine resources for finding out about illustrators. These can provide teachers with background information for planning a study; they are also possible resources for older children as part of their own research. *Book Links* and *Booklist* magazines, published by the American Library Association, regularly carry articles about authors and illustrators. *The New Advocate* and *The Horn Book Magazine* feature articles by and about illustrators, and profiles of illustrators often appear in journals like *Language Arts*. (For example, see Kiefer, 1987, for a *Language Arts* profile on Chris Van Allsburg.) In addition, in every July/August issue of *The Horn Book Magazine*, the Caldecott Award winner's acceptance speech is published, along with a brief biography of the artist. Series of books such as *Something About the Author* (Commire) and *Children's Literature Review* (Gerard) also provide information about illustrators.

For classroom study, teachers can highlight artists whose work clearly demonstrates the meaning-making potential of illustration. Teachers could begin by talking with children about choices they make in their own work and how that work changes over the course of several drafts. If children are creating portfolios (a term originally applied to the collection of an artist's work) as a means of assessment and are involved in self-evaluation, they can think about changes in their work over longer periods of time. Then they might develop important personal connections to the changing styles of artists like Marcia Brown, Trina Schart Hyman, Chris Van Allsburg, Charles Keeping, Arnold Lobel, David Macaulay, Helen Oxenbury, John Steptoe, Maurice Sendak, Diane Stanley, Uri Shulevitz, or Paul Zelinsky. These illustrators are among those whose work, I believe, has evolved in interesting ways over the years.

Another way to approach illustrator studies is to include the work of certain illustrators as subtopics within thematic units. For example, a theme of "journeys" could include books by Ann Jonas (*The Trek, Aardvarks, Disembark, Round Trip*) and Donald Crews (*Freight Train, Truck, Harbor*, etc.). Barbara Cooney's books, such as *Miss Rumphius, Island Boy, Hattie and the Wild Waves*, and *Ox-Cart Man* by Donald Hall, fit nicely with a theme of "changes." James Stevenson's books—among them, *Grandaddy's Place*, (Griffith) *Higher on the Door*, and *Say It* (Zolotow)—are appropriate for themes such as "families" or "growing up." Books by Patricia Polacco, such as *The Keeping Quilt, Thunder Cake*, and *Mrs. Katz and Tush*, work well in similar themes or in a study of "generations."

The work of many illustrators is so extensive that the whole class might be involved in a study of a single illustrator. Good prospects here include Aliki, Barbara Cooney, Leo and Diane Dillon, Steven Kellogg, James Marshall, Arnold Lobel, Alice and Martin Provensen, Peter Spier, William Steig, and Rosemary Wells. The Web in Figure 7.3 shows how such a study might evolve around the work of one of my favorites, Tomie dePaola. (A bibliography of books listed in the web can be found in Appendix B.)

EXPLORING MEDIA

Engaging children in artistic techniques available to illustrators can be a powerful learning tool for developing their own artistic skills as well as developing their eye for detail. Such experiences can also help children to look more carefully at the works of illustrators and other artists.

For most of these activities, readily available and inexpensive art materials will suffice. Most schools provide a budget for construction paper, white drawing paper, scissors, watercolor tins, tempera paint, pastel, oil pastels, and crayons. Or, instead of asking every child to bring a box of crayons, some teachers ask children to contribute

DePAOLA'S KITCHEN

Pancakes for Breakfast
Strega Nona
Jamie O'Rourke and the Big Potato
The Popcorn Book
Tony's Bread
Watch Out for Chicken Feet in Your Soup
Tom

Does dePaola love food? What do you think he eats every day? Make up a menu for a full day telling what you think dePaola would like to eat. Draw a picture of dePaola in his kitchen.

Try out the recipes in these books. Write a Tomie dePaola cookbook. Illustrate it.

Collect family recipes for chicken soup, popcorn, pasta, and pancakes. Are they different from dePaola's? Cook several recipes for the same food. Conduct a taste test. Compare the results.

Make braided bread dolls.

SPECIAL HOLIDAYS WITH DePAOLA

My First Passover
Petook: An Easter Story
Find out how these holidays are connected.

My First Hanukkah
An Early American Christmas
The Legend of the Poinsettia
The Family Christmas Tree Book
The Christmas Pageant
Create your own pageant to tell the stories of the holidays that are special to your classmates.

Jingle the Christmas Clown
The Legend of Old Befana
Merry Christmas Strega Nona
Read other holiday stories. Write one of your own.

DePAOLA'S RELIGIOUS HERITAGE

The Clown of God
The Lady of Guadalupe
Francis the Poor Man of Assisi
Noah and the Ark
Patrick, Saint of Ireland
Queen Esther
Tomie dePaola's Book of Bible Stories
Compare the book illustrations to religious art from these countries. Notice details like architecture, dress, and other symbols.

Learn about fresco paintings. What other techniques can be used to create art on large surfaces such as walls? Try a small relief sculpture mural using clay or papiér-maché.

DePAOLA'S FAMILY AND FRIENDS

Now One Foot, Now the Other
Nana Upstairs, Nana Downstairs
Tom
The Art Lesson
Write a biography of dePaola based on the information in these and some of his other books. Check your version against information in *Something About the Author* (Commire)

Oliver Button Is a Sissy
Nicholas Bentley Stoningpot III
Flicks
Haircuts for the Woolseys
What do you know about dePaola based on the kinds of stories he tells and the art he creates? What kind of friend would dePaola be?

Cookie's Week
The Kid's Cat Book
Bill and Pete
The Hunter and the Animals
I Love You Mouse
Is dePaola a friend to animals? Find evidence for or against.

What kind of animals might dePaola have for pets? How many might he have? Find places in his other books where he includes pictures of animals. How many different kinds do you find? Graph the results.

DePAOLA'S ART LESSON

The Art Lessons
What the Mailman Brought
Interview your art teacher. Find out how he or she thinks kids should learn to be artists. Do you have any special artists in your class? Find out more about them.

Bonjour Mr. Satie
The Clown of God
Find out about dePaola's training as an artist. How has he been influenced by artists of the past?

Do you have a favorite painter? What is it you like about his or her work?

COVERS AND QUILTS

The Mountains of Quilt
The Quilt Story
What shapes does dePaola use in these quilts? Use the same shapes to make new patterns. Can you find quilt patterns in any of his other books?

Charlie Needs a Cloak
The Walking Coat
Invite a weaver to class. Find out more about weaving and sewing. Make your own cloth on a simple loom. Use it to make a class quilt or a Tomie dePaola coat of many colors.

FIGURE 7.3
The books of Tomie dePaola

RHYMES, RIDDLES, AND POETRY

Hey Diddle Diddle

The Carsick Zebra and Other Animal Riddles

Oh Such Foolishness

Tomie dePaola's Mother Goose

Tomie dePaola's Favorite Nursery Tales

Choose some of your favorite riddles and rhymes to illustrate.

Make a collection of class riddles and rhymes.

The Comic Adventure of Old Mother Hubbard and Her Dog

What other nursery rhymes can you find hidden in this book?

Act out the story with puppets or on stage. Design and make the
scenery.

Mary Had a Little Lamb

Choose a favorite nursery rhyme. Illustrate it for a book of your own
or write a sequel.

Exploring the Books of Tomie dePaola

DePAOLA'S MONSTERS, DRAGONS, AND OTHER BEASTIES

Helga's Dowry

The Ghost with the Halloween Hiccups

Maggie and the Monster

The Good Giants and the Bad Puckwudgies

The Mysterious Giant of Barletta

Fin M'Coul: The Giant of Knockmany Hill

The Knight and the Dragon

Little Grunt and the Big Egg

How does dePaola visually create memorable characters?
Compare the characters in these stories. Rate their scariness on
a scale of 1 to 10.

DePAOLA'S MAGIC

Strega Nona

Big Anthony and the Magic Ring

Strega Nona's Magic Lessons

Strega Nona Meets Her Match

Merry Christmas Strega Nona

Make a comparison chart of characters in Strega Nona stories.
Compare things like personality, job, hobbies, physical
appearance, and where they live.

Interview classmates about their favorite Strega Nona story. What
are the reasons for their choices?

DePAOLA'S FOLKTALES

The Legend of the Bluebonnet

The Legend of the Indian Paintbrush

Jamie O'Rourke and the Big Potato: An Irish Folktale

Fin M'Coul: The Giant of Knockmany Hill

The Legend of Old Befana

The Cat on the Doverfel

The Legend of the Poinsettia

The Badger and the Magic Fan

Create a magic object museum. Collect objects from these and
other tales and display them.

STREGA NONA: EXTENDING THE BOOK

Read poems like Shel Silverstein's "Spaghetti," Eve Merriam's "A
Round," and Jack Prelutsky's "Spaghetti, Spaghetti."

Make and cook pasta from scratch. Measure the ingredients and
weigh the dough. Then measure the noodles and graph your
findings.

Write the recipe for making pasta.

Categorize different types of pasta according to size, color, and
shape. Choose a pasta and write a description. Display all types
of pasta and let other children match the written descriptions
with the correct pasta.

Have a pastry party. Plan the menu. Write invitations.

Write about the pasta party for the social column of the class
newspaper.

Listen to the musical scherzo by Paul Dukas called the "Sorcerer's
Apprentice." Choreograph the story of Strega Nona to this
music.

STREGA NONA: STUDY A BOOK IN DEPTH

Study dePaola's use of color and line. How does he use outline to
frame each picture? How does he place characters on the page?
What details does he include? What do you notice about the
layout?

Retell the story using stick puppets or a flannel board.

Make a "Strega Nona" board game that incorporates key events or
sequence. Write directions for play.

Make a "Strega Nona" mural or collage.

Choose character roles. Conduct an "interview" by asking
characters about their roles in the story.

Write a "help wanted" ad for Strega Nona or a "situation wanted"
ad for Big Anthony.

Write a front page headline for a newspaper, plus an article that
details the events in the story.

Read *Akimba and the Magic Cow: A Folk Tale from Africa; The
Magic Porridge Pot;* and *The Sorcerer's Apprentice.* Make a
comparison chart. Compare and contrast the books with *Strega
Nona.*

Materials needed:

Styrofoam trays

Tubes of water-based printing inks (acrylic or tempera paint can substitute)

Colored construction paper, white drawing paper, newsprint, or used duplicating paper

Drawing tools (ball-point pens, wooden orange sticks, scissors point, compass point, etc.)

Also recommended: Printing brayer and metal inking plates or glass for rolling ink

Optional: Soft-Kut printing blocks or block printing foam board is available through art supply
stores (See Appendix C)

A

Directions:

Cut Styrofoam tray so that it lays flat.

Plan a simple design and transfer it to Styrofoam, outlining the image with a ball-point pen or
scissors point.

Squeeze ink on metal or glass plate and roll it out with brayer until the surface of the brayer is
uniformly covered.

Roll brayer across the surface of the Styrofoam.

Place a sheet of paper on the Styrofoam and press or rub the back of the paper so that ink is
uniformly distributed. (See Figure A.)

FIGURE 7.4
Styrofoam prints

a set of pastels, colored pencils, oil pastels, or crayons to the class art corner. In addition, "found" materials—old wall paper books, magazines, sheets and other fabrics, dryer lint, and Styrofoam meat trays—can make interesting art materials. Look also for natural objects: natural fibers, grasses, seed pods, potatoes, leaves, and onions are among those treasures from nature that can be used for weavings, printing, and making natural dyes. Figures 7.4 and 7.5 provide two examples of projects that use inex-

Variations:
Contoured shapes can be cut out of the Styrofoam and printed. (See Figure B.)
When the first coat is dry, a second or third color can be added.

B

pensive materials to simulate more complicated techniques of block printing and air brush design.

At some point, however, children should try projects that require special supplies. Transparent watercolor, for example, should be experienced with cold pressed or rough watercolor paper to allow for full experimentation with the medium. In addition, good quality brushes can make a big difference in the outcome of the

Materials needed:

Recycled file folders
Colored construction paper, white drawing paper, newsprint, or used duplicating paper
Scissors
Pastel chalks

Directions:

Air brushes are tools used by commercial artists and illustrators to distribute paint evenly on a surface. A similar effect can be obtained by following these instructions:

1. Draw a simple contour shape on part of an old file folder.
2. Cut out the shape. Set the cut-out piece aside. The larger piece from which you cut the shape is the stencil.
3. Take a stick of pastel chalk and color hard around the edges of the stencil.
4. Place the stencil on a sheet of paper and with a finger tip rub the chalk lightly from the stencil to the paper underneath.
5. Repeat this step several times by moving the stencil slightly. (See figure)

Variations:

Use several colors beginning with the lightest in value (yellow before blue).
Flip the stencil over for a reverse image.
Use the cut out piece of file folder, rubbing the chalk outward on the paper, for a different effect.
Instead of pastel chalk, use tempera paint and sponges or the tip of a stiff brush to dab paint on the stencil.

FIGURE 7.5
Simulated air brush technique

artist's efforts. Materials like block-printing foam boards can be used by young children to simulate block-printing techniques, and older children will enjoy making linoleum or wood block prints with special cutting tools. If there is a school or district art teacher, this would be good opportunity for team planning and teaching, making use of art room equipment like ink brayers, linoleum blocks, and cutting tools. Many school districts have artist-in-residence programs, or parents who have professions or hobbies in visual arts or crafts might be enlisted to share professional or cultural experience. Teachers might also want to consider applying for small grants from their state arts and humanities council or local businesses to purchase special supplies.

Because children are curious about the original media used by illustrators and because they enjoy experimenting, Figure 7.6 suggests ways to explore picturebooks and media in the classroom. In addition, names of artists or art forms from historical and cultural milieus are suggested as a way to begin to extend children's aesthetic awareness beyond the classroom. Although most of the other materials and projects suggested in Figure 7.6 are likely to be familiar to teachers, art terms are further defined in the glossary at the end of this section. In addition, addresses for art suppliers are listed in Appendix C.

BOOKMAKING AND PUBLISHING

Many schools now regularly encourage children to publish books as a part of the writer's workshop approach. Although teachers will have discovered many simple bookmaking ideas that are sufficient for everyday publishing, they may want to devote a special unit to bookmaking once a year or so. Figures 7.7 and 7.8 provide directions for binding and making simple books. In addition, the following activities are suggested as an additional part of an in-depth study of bookmaking.

How a Book Is Made

A study of bookmaking could begin with two information books, Aliki's *How a Book Is Made* and Michael Kehoe's *A Book Takes Root: The Making of a Picture Book*. A visit to an art press, where type is set by hand, is another good introduction to bookmaking. Your local community may also have a printing plant or a book bindery that children could visit to see the steps of printing in action.

Audiovisual materials can give children access to experiences that may not be readily available in their community. "Reading Rainbow" (carried daily on most PBS television stations) has a segment titled "Simon's Book." Host LaVar Burton interviews illustrator Henrik Drescher, who gives tips for getting story ideas from doodles. Burton then visits a book bindery and follows the processes of production from making the color plates, to printing, to cutting and binding the book. The segment finishes with a short cartoon history of the book.

Weston Woods (see Appendix C) produces many excellent films, videos, and filmstrips on picturebooks. Their Signature Series includes inexpensive sound filmstrips on illustration that can set the stage for children as they plan their own bookmaking project. These are appropriate for all ages and include:

Cut-Paper Collage

Illustrator	Books to Explore
Eric Carle	*The Very Hungry Caterpillar*
Lois Ehlert	*Red Leaf, Yellow Leaf*
Denise Fleming	*In the Small, Small Pond*
Ezra Jack Keats	*The Snowy Day*
Leo Lionni	*Matthew's Dream*
Suse MacDonald & Bill Oakes	*Once Upon Another*
Patricia Mullins (G. Jorgensen, author)	*Crocodile Beat*
Ellen Walsh	*Mouse Paint*

Materials needed:	Use with:	Projects:
tissue paper	fabric	collage pictures
colored construction paper	white glue	mosaics
magazines	scissors	cut-paper pictures with
newspaper	crayons	crayon accents
wallpaper		
previously painted sheets of paper		

Connect to: Works by Picasso, Braque, Max Ernst, Hans Arp, Matisse

Collage Constructions (assemblage)

Illustrator	Books to Explore
Jennie Baker	*Where the Forest Meets the Sea*
Molly Bang (S. Cassedy & K. Suetake)	*Red Dragon Fly on My Shoulder*
Club de Madres Virgin del Carmen (A. Dorros)	*Tonight Is Carnival* (arpilleras or wall hangings)
Barbara Reid	*Two by Two*
Faith Ringold	*Tar Beach*

Materials needed:	Use with:	Projects:
paper, plasticine, or clay	paper or cardboard	murals
found objects	plywood or masonite	panels
natural materials	white glue	friezes
yarns, thread	burlap	pictures
embroidery needles	cloth	wall hangings
	rug backing	

Connect to: Folk art embroidery from Dahomey, Africa; Peru; Tibet, etc., Toltec or Mayan carvings; Relief sculpture of Donatello, Ghiberti; Constructions of Robert Rauschenberg, Louise Nevelson

FIGURE 7.6
Exploring media

160

Painting Techniques

Illustrator
Warwick Hutton (S. Cooper)
Ted Lewin (A.Scott)
Ted Rand (J. Aylesworth)

Robert Andrew Parker (B. Baylor)
Uri Shulevitz
Allen Say
Julie Vivas (S. Williams)
Diane Stanley & Peter Vennema
Marisabina Russo
Marcia Sewall
Floyd Cooper (E. Greenfield)
Thomas Locker
Peter Sis
Don Wood (A. Wood)
Paul Zelinsky (Grimm Bros.)
Barbara Cooney (D. Hall)
Leonard Everett Fisher
    (M. Livingston)
William Joyce

Books to Explore
The Selkie Girl (watercolor)
Cowboy Country (watercolor)
Country Crossing
    (sumibrush and ink and chalk)
Guess Who My Favorite Person Is? (watercolor)
Dawn (watercolor)
Grandfather's Journey (watercolor)
I Went Walking (watercolor)
Bard of Avon (gouache)
A Visit to Oma (gouache)
The Pilgrims of Plimoth (gouache)
Grandpa's Face (oil wash)
Where the River Begins (oil)
Komodo (oil)
The Napping House (oil on wood)
Rumplestiltskin (oil on paper)
Ox-Cart Man; *Miss Rumphius* (acrylic)
Sky Songs (acrylic)

A Day with Wilbur Robinson (acrylic)

Materials needed:	Use with:	Projects:
water color in cakes, tubes	watercolor paper, cold press or rough sable or sabeline brushes	landscapes portraits still life paintings handmade picturebook illustrations
gouache in tubes (tempera paint may substitute)	watercolor paper illustration board	
oil paint in tubes, thinned with turpentine if available	canvas, canvas board illustration board	
acrylic paint in tubes	illustration board masonite, canvas or fabric coated with gesso	

Connect to: Turner, Klee, Chinese paintings (watercolor, inks); Early Christian, Gothic, and Renaissance painting, Ben Shahn, Andrew Wyeth, Jacob Lawrence (tempera/gouache); Jan Van Eyck, Rubens, Caneletto, Gainsborough, Thomas Cole, Monet, Georgia O'Keeffe (oil); Post-1940s 20th century paintings (acrylic)

Resist Techniques:
Batik and Crayon Resist

Illustrator
Janina Domanska
Patricia MacCarthy (M. Mahy, author)
Harriet Peck Taylor
Marcia Sewall (R. Schotter)

Ed Young (L. Melmed)

Books to Explore
Din Dan Don It's Christmas
17 Kings and 42 Elephants
Coyote Places the Stars
Captain Snap and the
  Children of Vinegar Lane
The First Song Ever Sung

Materials needed:	Use with:	Projects:
white household candles or white crayon	cotton, silk fabric	banners
colored crayons	construction paper	wall hangings
tempera or watercolor paint	wax paper	scarves or shawls
white glue, rubber cement		collage
frisket		

Connect to: Indonesian, African fabric printing

Air Brush, Stencil, and Paper Cuts

Illustrator
Donald Crews
Leo & Diane Dillon (V. Aardema)

Aki Sogabe (R. Tiller)
Ed Young (R. Lewis; J. Yolen)

Books to Explore
Freight Train (air brush)
Why Mosquitoes Buzz in People's Ears
  (air brush)
Cinnamon, Mint and Mothballs (paper cuts)
All of You Was Singing (stencil);
The Emperor and the Kite (paper cuts)

Materials needed:	Use with:	Projects:
pastel chalk	construction paper	greeting cards
tempera paint	stencil paper	pictures
	sponges, toothbrushes, etc.	book illustrations
		endpapers
		wrapping paper

Connect to: Early American interior design; Advertising and poster art; Silk screen prints of Andy Warhol and others; Chinese, Japanese paper cuts; Matisse cut-outs

FIGURE 7.6, *continued*

Drawing Materials

Illustrator	Books to Explore
Thomas Allen (G. Shannon)	*Climbing Kansas Mountains* (charcoal and pastel)
Jim Arnosky	*Deer at the Brook* (colored pencils and watercolor)
Carole Byard (E. Greenfield)	*Africa Dreams* (charcoal, pastel, colored pencils)
Ann Grifalconi	*The Village of Round and Square Houses* (pastel, colored pencil)
Nancy Winslow Parker & Joan Richards Wright	*Frogs, Toads, Lizards, and Salamanders* (colored pencil, watercolor)
Brian Pinkney (B. Albert)	*Where Does the Trail Lead?* (scratchboard and oil pastel)
Marcia Sewall (R. Kennedy)	*Song of the Horse* (scratchboard)
Chris Van Allsburg	*The Garden of Abdul Gasazi* (carbon pencil), *Jumanji* (conte pencil and dust), *The Wreck of the Zephyr* (pastel), *Two Bad Ants* (pen and ink), *The Mysteries of Harris Burdick* (charcoal), *The Polar Express* (oil pastel), *The Stranger* (caran d'ache)
Ed Young (N. Larrick)	*Cats Are Cats* (pastel)

Materials needed:	Use with:	Projects:
crayons	colored construction paper	drawings
colored pencils	drawing paper	mixed media pictures
charcoal	pastel paper	sketch books
pastel	cloth	science projects
oil pastel	old sheets	poetry illustrations
conte pencils and crayons	scratchboard	story quilts
carbon pencils		
caran d'ache crayons		
scissors, compass point		

Connect to: Drawings by Rembrandt, Piranesi, Daumier, Ingres, Matisse, Picasso, David Hockney; pastels of Degas, Redon

Print Techniques

Illustrator	Books to Explore
Asley Bryan	*I'm Going to Sing* (woodblock)
David Frampton (C. Carrick)	*Whaling Days* (woodblock)
Arthur Geisert	*Oink Oink* (etching)
Carla Golembe (M. Gerson)	*Why the Sky Is Far Away* (monoprint)
Gail Haley	*Jack Jouett's Ride* (wood and linoleum block)
Keizaburo Tejima	*Swan Sky* (woodblock)
Ashley Wolff	*A Year of Birds* (linoleum block)

Materials needed:	Use with:	Projects:

water-based printing inks
tempera paint
brayers
sponges
potatoes and other
  natural objects
	rice paper and other
	  special papers
	newsprint
	construction paper
		book illustrations
		posters
		stationery and cards
		endpapers

Connect to: Japanese woodblock prints, African textiles, Dürer, Rembrandt, Blake

FIGURE 7.6, *continued*

1. Gerald McDermott, "Evolution of a Graphic Concept: *The Stonecutter*." McDermott tells of translating his film, *The Stonecutter*, to book form. He talks specifically about design and technical choices such as color, shape, layout, and type placement, and he shows how he developed the storyboard and book dummy. Changes he made between the dummy and final illustration provide a fascinating look at the process of meaning-making through art and can help children as they prepare to make their own books.

2. Steven Kellogg, "How a Picturebook Is Made with *The Island of the Skog*."

3. Gail E. Haley, "Wood and Linoleum Illustration with *Go Away Stay Away*"; "Creating *Jack and the Bean Tree*: Tradition and Technique"; and "Tracing a Legend: The Story of *The Green Man*."

The Art of the Handmade Book

Many communities have calligraphy guilds (see Appendix C) or art book associations whose members may be delighted to work with children. Often these artists are part of a district's artists in residence program. They will be able to help children with special projects such as paper making, paper marbling, block printing, and book binding. If you do not have access to such experts, however, the following "Books About Making Books," offers good resources. Vicki Cobb's *Paper Making Book and Kit*, for example, comes with paper maker's pulp, a bag of cotton pulp, and a wooden paper-making mold. Cobb gives clear directions and suggests additional materials, like dryer lint, for paper-making materials. A study of paper making could also lead children to find out about paper making in other cultures. The Japanese, for example, have carried decorative paper making to a high art, and samples can be obtained from art supply stores. Children might enjoy seeing samples of paper made from other cellulose-based materials such as rice paper or papyrus, as well as samples of vellum or parchment, which is made from animal skins.

BOOKS ABOUT MAKING BOOKS

Aliki. *How a Book Is Made*. New York: Thomas Y. Crowell, 1986
Brookfield, Karen. *Book*. Photographs by Laurence Pordes. New York: Knopf, 1993.

Cobb, Vicki. *Vicki Cobb's Paper Making Book and Kit*. New York: HarperCollins, 1993.

*Chambers, Anne. *The Practical Guide to Marbling Paper*. New York: Thames & Hudson, 1986.

*Dawson, Sophie. *The Art and Craft of Papermaking*. Philadelphia: Running Press, 1992.

Fennimore, Flora. *The Art of the Handmade Book*. Chicago: Chicago Review Press, 1992.

Fisher, Leonard Everett. *The Paper Makers*. New York: Godine, 1986.

Fleming, Denise. *Paper Making Fun*. New York: Henry Holt, 1994.

*Greenfeld, Howard. *Books: From Writer to Reader*. New York: Crown, 1988.

Irvine, Joan. *How to Make Pop-Ups*. New York: Greenwillow Books, 1991.

Irvine, Joan. *How to Make Super Pop-Ups*, New York: Greenwillow, 1993.

Johnson, Paul. *A Book of One's Own*. Portsmouth, NH: Heinemann, 1991.

Johnson, Paul. *Literacy Through the Book Arts* Portsmouth, NH: Heinemann, 1993.

Kehoe, Michael. *A Book Takes Root: The Making of a Picture Book*. Minneapolis, MN: Carolrhoda, 1993.

Weiss, Harvey. *How to Make Your Own Books*. New York: Thomas Y. Crowell, 1974.

Paper marbling, which dates back at least to 12th-century Japan, probably spread to Europe from Turkey in the 1600s. Although the process requires specialized materials such as Carragheen moss (a binder also used in ice cream), the effects are so beautiful that teachers may wish to take the trouble to experiment with paper marbling. Materials are available through art supply companies such as Dick Blick (see Appendix C). Blick also carries products such as an acrylic marbling kit by Delta/Shiva which make the process a bit easier. Figures 7.7 through 7.11 provide suggestions and directions for other book-related projects.

FOLKTALE COMPARISONS

Studying different illustrated versions of the same folktale can help children see how artists make choices to convey meaning and how various choices can enhance and extend different parts of the story. Children will also enjoy seeing how authors and illustrators have transformed traditional tales into modern-day versions, sequels, regional versions, and reversals. Here, they can consider how the illustrator's imagination helps create something entirely new and unexpected. This, in turn, may encourage children to create their own version of a traditional tale (see color insert).

In addition to comparing folktales with similar origins, children may want to take one character, such as the trickster, or one motif, such as wishes, and follow these across cultures. Such comparisons provide interesting understandings about story patterns that exist in many cultures. Comparing the art in these tales can often provide details about a culture or information about cultural methods of depicting. Children should be encouraged to make connections between the art in the stories and the art and artifacts known to be associated with a given culture.

*Appropriate for older children

Materials:
Cardboard or old file folders (the back of legal pads make good book covers)
White drawing paper or construction paper
Endpapers—Contrasting color of construction paper, marbleized paper
Dry mount tissue (available in photo supply or art supply stores) or Elmer's Glue-All™
Fabric, wrapping paper, paste paper for cover
Needle and thread
Scissors

Directions:
Directions given are for a book that measures approximately 8½" high X 6½" wide closed
with 16 pages (open it will measure 8½" by 13"). The size of the book and the number of
pages can vary. If Elmer's Glue-All is used instead of dry mount tissue, use a piece of
cardboard to spread it uniformly on the book surfaces.

1. Create a storyboard for a 16-page book. Cut 4 sheets of notebook paper for a dummy.
   Fold these in half, number them, and sketch in the art work from the storyboard. This will
   insure that the layout of the book has been correctly planned.

2. Measure 4 sheets of book paper and 2 sheets of endpaper 8" high by 12" wide and cut.
   Note that *2 sheets* of
   endpaper are required
   for the finished book.

3. Place the 2 sheets of
   endpaper on the
   bottom or outside of the
   book paper and use the
   bookbinding stitch
   (Figure 7.10) to stitch
   the pages together.
   (See Figure A.)

4. When the pages and
   endpapers are bound
   together, create the art
   work and write the text
   as planned on the
   storyboard. Set aside.

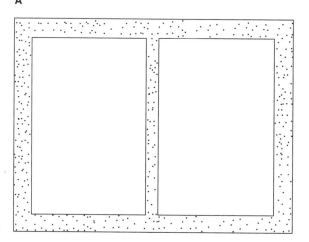

A

B

5. Cut 2 sheets of
   cardboard for cover
   approximately 8½" X
   6".

6. Cut 4 sheets of dry
   mount tissue the same
   size as the covers (8½"
   X 6").

7. Cut cover fabric or
   paper at least 12½" X
   17". (It is better to cut
   the cover fabric too
   large than too small.)

8. Lay the cover fabric *face
   down* on work surface.
   Take 2 sheets of dry
   mount tissue and place them under the cover boards. Place these on the cover fabric so
   that the dry mount is sandwiched between the cover boards and the cover fabric. Leave

FIGURE 7.7
Making a simple bound book

a ¹/₂" space between the two cover boards. (This will allow the finished book to open and close easily.) The cover fabric should extend about 2" beyond the cover boards. (See Figure B.)

9. With a dry iron on the wool setting, press until the dry mount tissue adheres to the cover fabric. You may need to turn the cover over and press from the other side.

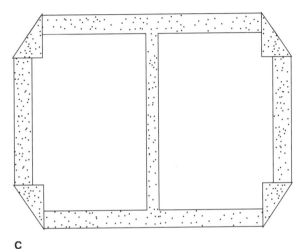

C

10. With the fabric on the bottom and the cardboard facing up, fold the corners of the fabric cover to form triangles, (See Figure C.)

11. Tack the corners down with glue and fold the remaining fabric over the cover cardboard. Tack with glue.

12. Turn the cover face up and attach a contrasting strip of fabric, bookbinding tape, or Scotch Brand plastic tape over the spine and at least 2" into the inside cover on top and bottom.

13. With the inside of the book and the cardboard cover facing you, place a sheet of dry mount tissue on the left hand (or inside front) cardboard cover.

14. Take the bound, illustrated book and place the underneath of the bottom endpaper on the dry mount tissue. Press until it adheres. (See Figure D.)

D

15. Do the same with the right hand (or back) cover. The book should now close without gapping, and the inside edges of the cover paper should be hidden by the endpapers.

Materials:
Embroidery needle
Heavy-duty thread or dental floss (can be of a contrasting color)

Directions:

1. Fold the signature (the two sheets of endpaper and the book pages) in half. With the needle, punch three holes in the fold. The middle hole should be in the middle of the fold and the other two should be about a half inch to an inch from each end.

2. Thread the needle and knot one end of the thread, leaving a tail about one inch long past the knot.

3. Hold the book open and sew with the needle and thread through the center hole. Go to one of the outer holes and bring the needle through to the inside of the book. On the inside of the book, take the needle and thread past the center hole to the other end hole and pass the needle through. (See Figure A.)

4. Sew with the needle and thread through the center hole once again. You should finish on the inside of the book.

5. Take the two ends of the thread, keeping the thread that runs the length of the book in between them, and tie a square knot (left over right; right over left). Leave a tail of at least $1/8$ of an inch. If you choose, you can leave the tail longer as a decorative touch.

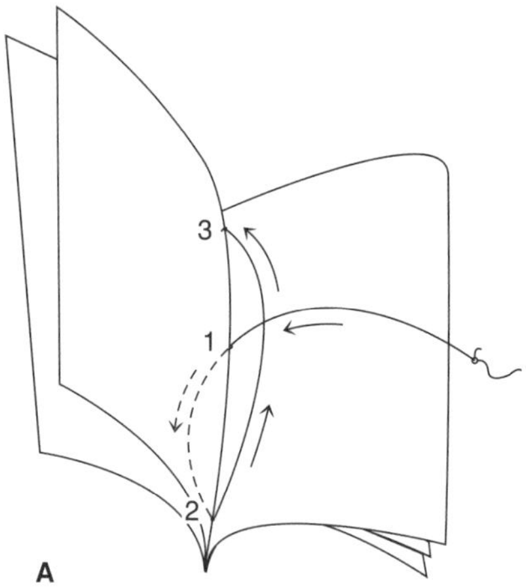

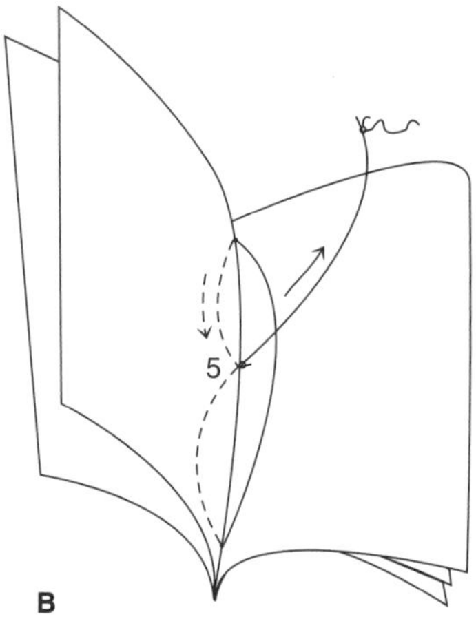

FIGURE 7.8
The bookbinding stitch

This kind of careful looking and attention to detail is an important part of the research conducted by many illustrators before they begin their artwork. Studying the books of illustrators like Deborah Nourse Lattimore, whose training qualifies her as a historian as well as an illustrator, can help children to understand that art can be an important primary source as well as something beautiful to look at. A list of Lattimore's books follows. In addition the bibliographies in Figures 7.12 and 7.13 suggest folktales that may be used to compare and contrast illustrated versions of a familiar tale, patterns that cut across many cultures, and books that represent an illustrator's use of historical and cultural details in illustration.

Materials:

Drawing paper, construction paper (needs to be fairly strong)

Acrylic or tempera paints

Wide brushes, serrated plastic ice scrapers, combs, and other implements to create patterns in paste.

Paste

Paste Recipe:

This can be prepared ahead of time and kept sealed in a refrigerator for about a week.

4 tablespoons white all-purpose flour

3 tablespoons rice flour

½ teaspoon glycerin

1 teaspoon green tincture soap

3 cups boiling water

tap water as needed

double boiler

strainers

wire whisk

Directions for Paste:

1. Sift flours together. Add tap water slowly and mix with a fork until the consistency is like heavy cream (with no lumps).

FIGURE 7.9
Paste paper covers

THE WORKS OF DEBORAH NOURSE LATTIMORE: CULTURAL DETAILS IN THE ART OF FOLKTALES

The Dragon's Robe. Deborah Nourse Lattimore. New York: HarperCollins, 1990.

The Flame of Peace: A Tale of the Aztecs. Deborah Nourse Lattimore. New York: HarperCollins, 1987.

The Prince and the Golden Axe: A Minoan Tale. Deborah Nourse Lattimore. New York: HarperCollins, 1988.

Punga, Goddess of Ugly. San Diego: Harcourt Brace Jovanovich, 1993.

The Sailor Who Captured the Sea: The Story of the Book of Kells. Deborah Nourse Lattimore. New York: HarperCollins, 1991.

Why There Is No Arguing in Heaven: A Mayan Myth. Deborah Nourse Lattimore. New York: HarperCollins, 1989.

The Winged Cat: A Tale of Ancient Egypt. Deborah Nourse Lattimore. New York: HarperCollins, 1992.

Zekmet the Stone Carver: A Tale of Ancient Egypt. Mary Stolz. Illustrated by Deborah Nourse Lattimore. San Diego: Harcourt Brace Jovanovich, 1988.

2. Heat the double boiler. Remove the hot top and add the flour mixture to it. Slowly add 1 cup boiling water, stirring constantly.

3. Place the mixture back on the double boiler, continue stirring, and add the second cup of boiling water. Let cook for 5 minutes, stirring constantly.

4. Add the third cup of boiling water and cook for a few more minutes.

5. Remove from heat and pour through the strainer to remove lumps.

6. Add glycerin and soap. Mix slowly with the wire whisk. Don't stir too quickly or air bubbles will form.

7. Let cool. Refrigerate in a sealed container.

8. To add color, pour some paste into a strainer and hold over a glass jar or other container. Add paint, then more paste and push through the strainer with a stiff brush. (Expect colors to be soft hues, not intense colors.)

Directions for Paste Paper:

1. Fill a tray or pan with warm tap water.

2. Dip the paper through the tray, wetting it thoroughly.

3. Lay one corner of the paper on a smooth, non-absorbent surface (glass or Formica).

4. Gradually lay the paper down, using a paper towel to work out any bubbles. Wipe off excess moisture.

5. Spread the paste on the paper. The colors will act much the same as finger paint and designs can be worked into the paste with stiff brushes or other implements. Two colors can be laid side by side and blended together.

6. Remove and let dry on newspaper, then use for book covers.

FIGURE 7.9, *continued*

HOLDING A MOCK CALDECOTT AWARD

Every January or early February, the Caldecott Award is awarded to "the artist of the most distinguished American picture book for children published in the United States during the preceding year" (Association for Library Service to Children, 1980, p. 3). This is a good time to alert children to the process of presenting the award, to help them to understand that there are criteria upon which works of art can be judged, and to involve them in their own Caldecott Award experience. The following list provides additional references about the award.

*INFORMATION ABOUT THE CALDECOTT AWARD**

Association of Library Services to Children. (1991). *The Newbery and Caldecott Awards: A guide to medal and honor books.* Chicago: American Library Association.

Kingman, L. (Ed.). (1965). *Newbery and Caldecott Medal books, 1956–1965.* Boston: Horn Book.

Kingman, L. (Ed.). (1975). *Newbery and Caldecott Medal books, 1966–1975.* Boston: Horn Book.

*List continues on page 177.

Materials:

An oblong pan of water (kitty litter trays make good containers for this activity and
   paper marbling)

Construction paper (the paper should have a somewhat absorbent rough texture)

Pastel chalk or sidewalk chalk (large single sticks, available in art supply stores,
   provide the richest color and the greatest amount of chalk dust)

Kitchen knife or scissors

Directions:

1. Using the kitchen knife, scrape the chalk over the pan of water in random
   spots. A second or third color can be added.

2. Place a sheet of paper gently on the surface of the water, tapping it lightly to
   remove any air bubbles.

3. Remove the paper carefully and let it dry. When dry, the chalk dust will be
   bound to the paper in a delicate attractive design.

4. Repeat the process on the reverse side for the sheet of endpaper that is not
   glued to the cover board.

FIGURE 7.10
Chalk dust endpapers

Materials:

Large container

Scrap paper (old newspaper, computer paper)

¼ cup bleach

Sponge

Toweling

Wooden frame covered with nylon or wire screen (small mesh)

Kitchen blender

2 pieces of wooden board or masonite

Weights

Directions:

1. Tear paper into tiny pieces and add to container full of water (bleach will make
   paper whiter).

2. Soak overnight.

3. Add a little water to the blender. Set blender to liquefy. Drop in soaked paper a
   little at a time. (Short pulses on the blender may be more effective than running blender continuously.)

4. Pour mixture over screen, distributing it evenly. Let water drain off.

5. Roll pulp onto towel and press with another towel or sponge to remove water.

6. Place pulp between two boards and put weights on top.

7. Let dry.

FIGURE 7.11
Handmade paper

Baba Yaga

Baba Yaga. Katya Arnold. New York: North South Books, 1993.

Baba Yaga. Retold by Eric Kimmel. Illustrated by Megan Lloyd. New York: Holiday House, 1991.

*Babushka Baba Yaga. Patricia Polacco. New York: Philomel, 1993.

Beauty and the Beast

Beauty and the Beast. Mme. de Beaumont. Illustrated by Jan Brett. Boston: Houghton Mifflin, 1989.

Beauty and the Beast. Mme. de Beaumont. Illustrated by Mordecai Gerstein. New York: Dutton, 1989.

Beauty and the Beast. Mme. de Beaumont. Illustrated by Michael Hague. New York: Holt, 1988.

Beauty and the Beast. Mme. de Beaumont. Illustrated by Warwick Hutton. New York: Atheneum, 1985.

The Bremen Town Musicians

The Bremen Town Musicians. Grimm Bros. Illustrated by Donna Diamond. New York: Delacorte, 1981.

The Bremen Town Musicians. Grimm Bros. Illustrated by Ilse Plume. New York: Doubleday, 1980.

The Bremen Town Musicians. Grimm Bros. Translated by Elizabeth Shub. Illustrated by Janina Domanska. New York: Greenwillow Books, 1980.

The Bremen Town Musicians. Grimm Bros. Illustrated by Janet Stevens. New York: Holiday House, 1992.

The Bremen Town Musicians. Retold and illustrated by Hans Wilhelm. New York: Scholastic, 1992.

The Traveling Musicians of Bremen. Retold by P. K. Page. Illustrated by Kady MacDonald Denton. Boston: Little, Brown, 1991.

East of the Sun and West of the Moon

East of the Sun and West of the Moon. Michael & Kathleen Hague. Illustrated by Michael Hague. San Diego: Harcourt Brace Jovanovich, 1980.

East o' the Sun and West o' the Moon. George Dasent. Illustrated by Gillian Barlow. New York: Philomel, 1988.

East o' the Sun and West o' the Moon. P. J. Lynch. Cambridge, MA: Candlewick Press, 1992.

East of the Sun and West of the Moon. D. J. MacHale. Illustrated by Vivienne Flesher. Rowayton, CT: Rabbit Ears Press, 1992 .

The Frog Prince

*Emily and the Enchanted Frog. Helen V. Griffith. Illustrated by Susan Conde Lamb. New York: Greenwillow Books, 1989.

*A Frog Prince. Alix Berenzy. New York: Holt, 1989.

The Frog Prince. Jan Ormerod & David Lloyd. Illustrated by Jan Ormerod. New York: Lothrop, 1990.

The Frog Prince. Retold by Edith H. Tarcov. Illustrated by James Marshall. New York: Scholastic, 1974.

The Frog Princess. Retold by Elizabeth Isele. Illustrated by Michael Hague. New York: Thomas Y. Crowell, 1984.

*The Frog Prince Continued. Jon Scieszka. Illustrated by Steve Johnson. New York: Viking, 1991.

*Pondlarker. Fred Gwynne. New York: Simon & Schuster, 1990.

The Princess and the Frog. Rachel Isadora. New York: Greenwillow Books,1989.

*The Princess and the Frog. A. Vesey. Boston: Atlantic Monthly, 1985.

*The Princess and the Froggie. Harve & Kaethe Zemach. Illustated by Margo Zemach. New York: Farrar, Straus & Giroux, 1975.

*Princess Smartypants. Babette Cole. New York: Putnam, 1986.

FIGURE 7.12
Comparing illustrations in folktales

Goldilocks and the Three Bears

Goldilocks and the Three Bears. James Marshall. New York: Dial, 1988.

Goldilocks and the Three Bears. Lorinda Bryan Cauley. New York: Putnam, 1981.

Goldilocks and the Three Bears. Janet Stevens. New York: Holiday House, 1986.

Deep in the Forest. Brinton Turkle. New York: Dutton, 1976.

The Three Bears. Paul Galdone. New York: Clarion, 1985.

Hansel and Gretel

Hansel and Gretel. Grimm Bros. Illustrated by Lisbeth Zwerger. New York: Morrow, 1979.

Hansel and Gretel. Grimm Bros. Illustrated by Antonella Bottiger-Savelli. New York: Oxford, 1981.

Hansel and Gretel. Grimm Bros. Illustrated by Anthony Browne. New York: Knopf, 1988.

Hansel and Gretel. Grimm Bros. Illustrated by Paul Galdone. New York: McGraw-Hill, 1982.

Hansel and Gretel. Grimm Bros. Retold by Rika Lesser. Illustrated by Paul Zelinsky. New York: Dodd Mead, 1984.

Hansel and Gretel. Grimm Bros. Translated by Elizabeth Crawford. Illustrated by Lizbeth Zwerger. New York: Morrow, 1979.

Jack and the Beanstalk

The History of Mother Twaddle and the Marvelous Achievement of Her Son Jack. Paul Galdone. New York: Clarion, 1979.

*Jack and the Bean Tree. Retold and illustrated by Gail Haley. New York: Crown, 1986.

Jack and the Beanstalk. Lorinda Bryan Cauley. New York: Putnam, 1983.

Jack and the Beanstalk. Alan Garner. Illustrated by Julek Heller. New York: Doubleday, 1992.

Jack and the Beanstalk. Retold and illustrated by John Howe. Boston: Little, Brown, 1989.

Jack and the Beanstalk. Joseph Jacobs. Illustrated by Margery Gill. New York: Walck, 1975.

Jack and the Beanstalk. Retold and illustrated by Steven Kellogg. New York: Morrow, 1991.

Jack and the Beanstalk. Illustrated by William Waisner. New York: Scholastic, 1965.

*Jack and the Wonder Beans. James Still. Illustrated by Margot Tomas. New York: Putnam, 1977.

*Jim and the Beanstalk. Raymond Briggs. New York: Coward McCann, 1970.

*Jack the Giant Chaser. Kenn & Joanne Compton. New York: Holiday House, 1993.

Little Red Riding Hood

Little Red Cap. Grimm Bros. Translated by E. Crawford. Illustrated by Lisbeth Zwerger. New York: William Morrow, 1983.

Little Riding Hood. Retold and illustrated by Trina Schart Hyman. New York: Holiday House, 1983.

Little Red Riding Hood. Paul Galdone. New York: McGraw-Hill, 1974.

Little Red Riding Hood. Charles Perrault. Illustrated by Beni Montresor. New York: Doubleday, 1991.

Little Red Riding Hood. Charles Perrault. Photographs by Sarah Moon. Mankato, MN: Creative Education, 1983.

Lon Po Po: A Red Riding Hood Story from China. Ed Young. New York: Philomel, 1989.

Red Riding Hood. Retold and illustrated by Christopher Cody. New York: Dutton, 1991.

Red Riding Hood. Retold and illustrated by James Marshall. New York: Dial, 1987.

*Ruby. Michael Emberly. Boston: Little, Brown, 1990.

Puss in Boots

Puss in Boots. Translated by Malcom Arthur. Illustrated by Fred Marcellino. New York: Farrar, Straus & Giroux, 1990.

Puss in Boots. Lorinda Bryan Cauley. San Diego: Harcourt Brace Jovanovich, 1986.

Puss in Boots. Paul Galdone. New York: Clarion, 1976.

Puss in Boots. John Goodall. New York: McElderry, 1990.

Puss in Boots. Retold by Lincoln Kirstein. Illustrated by Alain Vaïs. Boston: Little, Brown, 1992.

Rapunzel

Rapunzel. Retold by Barbara Rogasky. Illustrated by Trina Schart Hyman. New York: Holiday House, 1982.

Rapunzel. Retold and illustrated by Jutra Ash. New York: Holt, Rinehart & Winston, 1982.

Petrosinella. Giamba Hista Basile. Illustrated by Diane Stanley. New York: Frederick Warne, 1981.

Rumpelstiltskin

Duffy and the Devil. Harve Zemach. Illustrated by Margot Zemach. New York: Farrar, Straus & Giroux, 1973.

Rumpelstiltskin. Retold and illustrated by Paul Galdone. New York: Clarion, 1985.

Rumpelstiltskin. Grimm Bros. Illustrated by Donna Diamond. New York: Holiday House, 1983.

Rumpelstiltskin. Grimm Bros. Illustrated by John Wallner. Englewood Cliffs, NJ: Prentice-Hall, 1984.

Rumpelstiltskin. Grimm Bros. Illustrated by William Stobbs. New York: Walck, 1970.

Rumpelstiltskin. Retold and illustrated by Jonathon Langley. New York: Harper-Collins, 1991.

Rumpelstiltskin. Grimm Bros. Illustrated by Paul Zelinsky. New York: Dutton, 1986.

Tom Tit Tot. Evaline Ness. New York: Scribner, 1965.

Snow White and the Seven Dwarfs

Snow White. Grimm Bros. Illustrated by Trina Schart Hyman. Boston: Little, Brown, 1974.

Snow White. Retold by Josephine Poole. Illustrated by Angela Barrett. New York: Knopf, 1991.

Snow White and the Seven Dwarfs. Retold by Froya Littledale. Illustrated by Susan Jeffers. New York: Four Winds, 1980.

Snow White and the Seven Dwarfs. Grimm Bros. Illustrated by Nancy Burkert. New York: Farrar, Straus & Giroux, 1972.

The Three Little Pigs

The Three Little Pigs. Paul Galdone. New York: Clarion, 1979.

The Three Little Pigs. James Marshall. New York: Dial, 1989.

The Three Little Pigs and the Big Bad Wolf. Glen Rounds. New York: Holiday House, 1992.

*The Three Little Pigs and the Fox. William Hooks. Illustrated by S.D. Schindler. New York: Macmillan, 1989.

The Three Little Wolves and the Big Bad Pig. Eugene Tivizas. Illustrated by Helen Oxenbury. New York: McElderry, 1993.

*The True Story of The Three Little Pigs. Jon Scieszka. Illustrated by Lane Smith. New York: Viking, 1989.

FIGURE 7.12, *continued*

Cinderella Theme

Cinderella. Retold and illustrated by David Delamare. New York: Green Tiger, 1993.

Cinderella. Grimm Bros. Illustrated by Nonny Hogrogian. New York: Greenwillow Books, 1981.

Cinderella. Retold by Barbara Karlin. Illustrated by James Marshall. Boston: Little, Brown, 1989.

Cinderella. Charles Perrault. Illustrated by Marcia Brown. New York: Charles Scribner's Sons, 1954.

The Egyptian Cinderella. Shirley Climo. Illustrated by Ruth Heller. New York: Thomas Y. Crowell, 1989.

The Korean Cinderella. Shirley Climo. Illustrated by Ruth Heller. New York: HarperCollins, 1993.

Lovely Vasilisa. Retold by Barbara Cohen. Illustrated by Anatoly Ivanor. New York: Atheneum, 1980.

Moss Gown. William H. Hooks. Illustrated by Donald Carrick. New York: Clarion, 1987.

Mufaro's Beautiful Daughter. John Steptoe. New York: Lothrop, 1987.

Princess Furball. Charlotte Huck. Illustrated by Anita Lobel. New York: Greenwillow Books, 1989.

The Rough Faced Girl. Rafe Martin. Illustrated by David Shannon. New York: Putnam, 1992.

Vasilisa the Beautiful. Elizabeth Winthrop. Illustrated by Alexander Koshkin. New York: HarperCollins, 1991.

Vasilisa the Beautiful. T. P. Whitney. Illustrated by Nonny Hogrogian. New York: Macmillan, 1970.

Yeh-Shen (A Chinese Cinderella). Retold by Ai-Ling Louie. Illustrated by Ed Young. New York: Philomel, 1982.

Gingerbread Boy Theme

The Bun: A Tale from Russia. Marcia Brown. San Diego: Harcourt Brace, 1972.

The Fine Round Cake. Adapted by Arnica Esterl. Illustrated by Andrej Dugin & Olga Dugina. New York: Four Winds, 1991.

The Gingerbread Boy. Scott Cook. New York: Knopf, 1987.

Journey Cake Ho! Ruth Sawyer. Illustrated by Robert McCloskey. New York: Viking, 1953.

The Pancake Boy. Lorinda Bryan Cauley. New York: Putnam, 1988.

No Room Theme

Could Anything Be Worse? Marilyn Hirsch. New York: Holiday House, 1974.

The Cow in the Kitchen. Evelyn Johnson. Illustrated by Anthony Rao. Honesdale, PA: Bell, 1991.

It Could Always Be Worse. Margot Zemach. New York: Farrar, Straus & Giroux, 1976.

Too Much Noise. Ann McGovern. Illustrated by Simms Taback. New York: Scholastic, 1967.

The Wise Man of the Mountain. Eilis Dillon. Illustrated by Gaynor Chapman. New York: Atheneum, 1969.

Stone Soup Theme

Burgoo Stew. Susan Patron. Illustrated by Mike Shenon. New York: Orchard, 1991.

Nail Soup. Harve Zemach. Adapted from Nils Kjurklo. Illustrated by Margo Zemach. New York: Follett, 1964.

Stone Soup. Ann McGovern. Illustrated by Nola Langer. New York: Scholastic, 1968.

Stone Soup. Marcia Brown. New York: Scribner, 1947.

The Soup Stone. Retold and illlustrated by Iris VanRynbach. New York: Greenwillow Books, 1988.

FIGURE 7.13
Comparing characters and motifs across cultures

Three Wishes Theme

The Fisherman and the Grateful Turtle. Urashimo Taro. Retold by Essei Okawa. Illustrated by Koichi Murakami. Union City, CA: Heian International, 1985.

The Fisherman and his Wife. Grimm Bros. Retold by John Stewig. Illustrated by Margot Tomes. New York: Holiday House, 1988.

The Fisherman and his Wife. Grimm Bros. Illustrated by Monika Laimgruber. New York: Greenwillow Books, 1978.

The Fool and the Fish. Alexander Afanasyev. Illustrated by Gennady Spirin. New York: Dial, 1990.

Momtaro, The Peach Boy. Linda Shute. New York: Lothrop, 1986.

The Old Woman Who Lived in a Vinegar Bottle. Rumer Godden. Illustrated by Mairi Hedderwick. New York: Viking, 1972.

The Seven Ravens. Grimm Bros. Translated by Elizabeth D. Crawford. Illustrated by Lizbeth Zwerger. New York: Morrow, 1981.

The Stonecutter: A Japanese Folktale. Gerald McDermott. New York: Penguin, 1975.

The Three Wishes. Margot Zemach. New York: Farrar, Straus & Giroux, 1986.

Transformation Theme

The Boy Who Lived with the Seals. Rafe Martin. Illustrated by David Shannon. New York: Putnam, 1993.

The Children of Lir. Sheila MacGill-Callahan. Illustrated by Gennady Spirin. New York: Dial, 1993.

The Crane Wife. Sumiko Yagawa. Translated by Katherine Paterson. Illustrated by Suekichi Akaba. New York: William Morrow, 1981.

The Donkey Prince. Retold by M. Jean Craig. Illustrated by Barbara Cooney. New York: Doubleday, 1977.

Greyling. Jane Yolen. Illustrated by David Ray. New York: Philomel, 1991.

The Hedgehog Boy: A Latvian Tale. Jane Langton. Illustrated by Ilse Plume. New York: Harper& Row, 1985.

The Little Snow Girl. Carol Croll. New York: Putnam, 1989.

The Orphan Boy. Tolowa Mollel. Illustrated by Paul Morin. New York: Clarion, 1991.

The Seal Mother. Mordecai Gerstein. New York: Dial, 1986.

The Selkie Girl. Susan Cooper. Illustrated by Warwick Hutton. New York: Macmillan, 1986.

The Snow Child. Retold by Freya Littledale. Illustrated by Barbara Lavallee. New York: Scholastic, 1989.

The Story of Jumping Mouse: A Native American Legend. John Steptoe. New York: Morrow, 1984.

Tam Lin. Jane Yolen. Illustrated by Charles Mikolaycak. San Diego: Harcourt Brace Jovanovich, 1990.

Trickster Theme

Borrequita and the Coyote. Verna Aardema. Illustrated by Petra Mathers. New York: Knopf, 1991.

Ther Boy of the Three-Year Nap. Diane Snyder. Illustrated by Allen Say. Boston: Houghton Mifflin, 1988.

Clever Tom and the Leprechaun. Linda Shute. New York: Lothrop, 1988.

Iktomi and the Boulder: A Plains Indian Story. Paul Goble. New York: Orchard, 1988.

Rabbit Makes a Monkey of Lion. Verna Aardema. Illustrated by Jerry Pinkney. New York: Dial, 1989.

A Story, a Story. Gail Haley. New York: Atheneum, 1970.

Wiley and the Hairy Man. Molly Bang. New York: Macmillan, 1976.

FIGURE 7.13, *continued*

Kingman, L. (ed.). (1986). *Newbery and Caldecott Medal books, 1976–1985*. Boston: Horn Book.

Lacy, L. E. (1986). *Art and design in children's books: An analysis of Caldecott Award winning illustrations*. Chicago: American Library Association.

Miller, B. M. (1957). *Caldecott Medal books: 1938–1957*. Boston: Horn Book.

Peltola, B. J. (1988) Choosing the Caldecott Medal winners. *Journal of Youth Services to Libraries, 1* (2), 155.

The Randolph Caldecott Award (named in honor of illustrator Randolph Caldecott) was established by the American Library Association at the urging of Frederick Gershon Melcher. First awarded to Dorothy P. Lathrop in 1938 for *Animals of the Bible, A Picture Book*, the medal has a scene from Caldecott's *The Diverting History of John Gilpin* on the face and a scene from Caldecott's illustration of the nursery rhyme "Four and Twenty Blackbirds" on the reverse (Immroth, 1991).

Until 1979, one committee selected both the Newbery and Caldecott awards, but in 1980 two committees were formed—one to select each set of awards.

Committee members are also members of the American Library Association and its division, the Association for Library Service to Children (ALSC). There are 15 members on each committee; seven members and the chair are elected by the members of ALSC, and seven members are appointed by the ALSC vice president/president-elect. Committee members who agree to serve need to have access to newly published books and must be able to attend two meetings: the ALA annual conference in the summer and the ALA's midwinter meeting when final deliberations take place. Furthermore, no committee member can have a conflict of interest with possible nominees.

The terms of the Caldecott Award follow:

1. The medal shall be awarded annually to the artist of the most distinguished American picture book for children published in the United States during the preceding year. There are no limitations as to the character of the picture book except that the illustrations be original work. Honor books may be named. These books are also to be truly distinguished.

2. The Award is restricted to artists who are citizens or residents of the United States (ALSC, 1980, p. 3).

The Award committee manual defines a picturebook for children as "one that essentially provides the child with a visual experience" (ALSC, 1980, p. 3) and considers the term *children* to include an audience up to and including age 14.

The process of deciding on the Award begins in January of the year preceding the Award, when new books begin to appear. My own committee work thus began in January of 1987, considering books published in 1987 for the 1988 Award.

The committee's deliberations are initially a broadening rather than a narrowing process. During the first 9 months of the year, as they look at the many books that are published, members nominate titles and send these to the chair, who circulates a list to the entire committee. In addition, the ALSC membership is encouraged to submit titles to the committee.

At the summer conference, the committee meets mainly to review procedures, although some discussion of books may take place. Then in the fall, two preliminary ballots are taken. In October each committee member chooses three books that he or she considers particularly noteworthy and writes a brief rationale for each. Another ballot is taken in December. The resulting lists are circulated to the entire committee, giving members a chance to reread books as well as to begin to articulate a rationale for their top choices.

At the midwinter meeting, all books that have been suggested or nominated during the year are shipped to the meeting site, and the committee prepares for three days of intense, closed-door deliberations. Although procedures are standard, the substance of these meetings is kept confidential.

The first order of business at this meeting is to appoint a secretary, who records procedural decisions, and three tellers, who tabulate ballots and tallies. Committee members then decide how the books will be discussed and how books will be eliminated from consideration. Some committees discuss the entire list of suggested books first and then move to those nominated in the two preliminary ballots; others consider nominated books first. Whatever the process, all books nominated or suggested during the year must be discussed. Once a book is eliminated from consideration, it cannot be reinstated. Therefore the committee carefully deliberates about each book on the table. Since there may be as many as 200 to 300 books under consideration this is quite a lengthy process.

When the committee decides that all books have been fully discussed, they move to a ballot. The balloting procedure has been decided previously and can be by a show of hands or by some other method. One way to handle the balloting may be to give each committee member a piece of paper and to ask them to list their top three choices, numbering them from one to three. These ballots are then collected by the tellers, who give each first-place title four points, each second-place title three points, and each third-place title two points. To win, a book must have at least eight first-place votes and must be at least eight points ahead of the next highest title.

This method ensures that the winner is the clear choice of many committee members. It also means that consensus is not always possible on the first ballot. Thus, some award sessions may go long into the night. Once a winner is chosen, the chair asks the committee if it wishes to name honor books. If so, then another ballot is taken, and the committee can decide to name one or more books as honor winners. When these books are announced to the public, they are listed in alphabetical order; they are not considered "runners up" but are considered worthy of the term *distinguished illustration*.

THE ART OF THE WORD

In many cultures and in many historical periods, writing has been considered an important art form apart from its utilitarian uses. Chinese and Arabic decorative forms and painting, for example, grew out of an intense interest in writing. Prior to the invention of movable type, writing was dependent on the skilled hand of scribes as well as on their instruments, and painting and writing were on a par as artistic techniques.

According to Gaur (1992), writing systems can be categorized as thought writing, which conveys a thought directly, or sound writing, which translates ideas into the sounds of a particular word or sentence and then represents these sounds with symbols. From these two main categories come ideographic writing systems (logographic, word, and concept scripts) and phonetic systems (alphabetic, consonantal, and syllabic scripts), as well as those systems that mix features of both. Gaur lists over 160 alphabets and many variations of these systems that developed worldwide over the centuries.

Asian artists used (and still use) brushes and ink to recreate their extensive alphabets; the Chinese system of writing, for example, contains over 50,000 signs. Our own alphabet probably developed from the cuneiform and hieroglyphic systems of Sumeria and Egypt. For these scripts, scribes used reed pens rather than brushes made of animal fibers, and these instruments likely influenced the way the letter forms evolved. Cursive letter forms derived from hieroglyphics have been dated to 2500 B.C. They probably evolved because it was easier and faster to form letters this way with the pen-brushes used as writing instruments.

The Roman alphabet that we use today was adapted from the Greek and was used for inscriptions in stone as well as for handwriting. Initially our alphabet had only capital letters, called *majuscule*. Lower-case letters evolved in the Middle Ages and were called *miniscule*. Our present day terms, *upper-* and *lower-case letters*, developed because type setters arranged majuscule letters on the top of their trays and miniscule letters on the bottom (Avrin, 1991).

With Gutenberg's invention of movable type, letters were cast in metal in small blocks. The printer's collection of type, which included both upper- and lower-case letters, numbers, and other symbols in varying sizes, was called a *font*. The font used by Gutenberg was the Gothic or Black-Letter style, and although it resembled the handwritten scripts of many medieval manuscripts, it was difficult to read. Eventually Roman typefaces were imported to England, and type designers such as William Caslon, John Baskerville, and Hermann Zapf expanded the range of letter forms available today (Olmert, 1992). Although modern printing has now moved beyond hand-set type, traditional fonts are now found in computer and electronic printing, and new typefaces continue to be developed. Mass production, however, has not eliminated our appreciation for the hand-lettered form or the hand-printed book, and calligraphy societies and small presses can be found around the country. (See Appendix C.)

As part of a study of the art of the picturebook, children could explore the many fonts that appear in their picturebooks, perhaps making a chart of features of the different fonts that they find. This could lead to the discovery of general categories such as serif and sans serif letters or roman and italic letters. They might also consider if and how the font used in a particular book complements the style of the illustrations. If children have access to a computer, they can experiment with different fonts and decide which fonts are best for the different types of writing they include in their own writing portfolios.

Once children have enough small motor control, they could also be encouraged to try their hand at calligraphy. With the availability of chisel-tip markers, this style of writing is not the chore or the mess that it was with metal-tip pens and India ink. Such explorations also place the traditional school subject of handwriting in a much more authentic context. Calligraphy kits or lettering books like *Speedball Textbook* (Fink), show step-by-step procedures for many classic fonts. Figure 7.14 gives directions for creating the italic alphabet in calligraphy, and the following list contains books about the art of lettering.

FIGURE 7.14
The italic alphabet
Source: Drawing courtesy of Dan Darigan.

THE ART OF LETTERING

Baron, Nancy. *Getting Started in Calligraphy*. Sterling, 1979.

Bostick, William A. *Calligraphy for Kids*. Franklin, MN: La Stampa Calligrafa, 1991.

Bulloch, Ivan & James, Diane. *The Letter Book*. Photographs by Toby Maudsley. New York: Simon & Schuster, 1990.

Carter, Patricia. *Illuminated Calligraphy*. Turnbridge Wells, England: Search Press, 1991.

Carter, Patricia. *Illuminated Calligraphy, Borders and Letters*. Woodstock, NY: Arthur Schwartz, 1992.

Drogin, Marc. *Medieval Calligraphy: Its History and Technique*. New York: Dover Publications, 1980.

Fink, Joanne C. *Speedball Textbook* (22nd ed.). Philadelphia, PA: Hunt Manufacturing, 1991.

Graham, David. *Color Calligraphy*. Turnbridge Wells, England: Search Press, 1991.

Grillis, Peter. *The Calligraphy Book*. New York: Scholastic, 1990.

Spellman, Linda. *Castles, Codes, Calligraphy*. Santa Barbara, CA: Learning Works, 1984.

Wilson, Diana Hardy. *The Encyclopedia of Calligraphy Techniques*. Philadelphia, PA: Running Press, 1990.

Young, Caroline. *Calligraphy from Beginner to Expert*. Illustrated by Chris Lyon & Paul Sullivan. Calligraphy by Susan Hufton. Tulsa, OK: EDC Publishing, 1990.

A study of the history of writing and the forms used by different cultures might also be undertaken. Teachers can begin with a study of alphabet art and create a class exhibit of alphabet books. For example, Jonathon Hunt's book, *Illuminations*, is an alphabet book used to convey information about the Middle Ages and connects nicely to the "art of the picturebook" theme. Children can then create their own alphabet books, using a theme to unify each book, or they might want to design illuminated initials for their names. The following alphabet books can give students some ideas.

THE ART OF ABC

Adkins, Jan. *Letterbox: The Art and History of Letters*. New York: Walker, 1980.

Azarian, Mary. *A Farmer's Alphabet*. New York: David Godine, 1981.

Bernhard, Durga. *Alphabeasts*. New York: Holiday House, 1993.

Ehlert, Lois. *Eating the Alphabet*. San Diego: Harcourt Brace Jovanovich, 1989.

Fisher, Leonard Everett. *ABC Exhibit*. New York: Macmillan, 1991.

Fisher, Leonard Everett. *Alphabet Art: Thirteen ABC's from Around the World*. New York: Four Winds, 1978.

Grover, Max. *The Accidental Zucchini: An Unexpected Alphabet*. San Diego: Browndeer/Harcourt Brace, 1993.

Hoban, Tana. *A, B, See!* New York: Greenwillow Books, 1982.

Hoban, Tana. *26 Letters and 99 Cents*. New York: Greenwillow Books, 1987.

Hunt, Jonathon. *Illuminations*. New York: Bradbury, 1989.

Lobel, Anita. *Allison's Alphabet*. New York: Greenwillow Books, 1990.

Lobel, Arnold. *On Market Street*. Illustrated by Anita Lobel. New York: Greenwillow Books, 1981.

MacDonald, Suse. *Alphabatics*. New York: Bradbury, 1986.

Martin, Bill Jr., & Archambault, John. *Chicka Chicka Boom Boom*. Illustrated by Lois Ehlert. New York: Simon & Schuster, 1989.

Micklethwait, Lucy. *I Spy: An Alphabet in Art*. New York: Greenwillow Books, 1992.

Neumeier, Marty, & Glaser, Byron. *Action Alphabet*. New York: Greenwillow Books, 1985.

Provensen, Alice, & Provensen, Martin. *A Peaceable Kingdom: The Shaker Abecedarius*. New York: Viking, 1978.

Rubin, Cynthia. *ABC Americana*. New York: Greenwillow Books, 1981.

Sullivan, Charles. *Alphabet Animals*. New York: Rizzoli, 1991.

Van Allsburg, Chris. *The Z Was Zapped: A Play in Twenty-Six Acts*. Boston: Houghton Mifflin, 1987.

Wells, Ruth. *A to Zen: A Book of Japanese Culture*. Illustrated by Yoshi. Saxonville, MA: Picture Book Studio, 1992.

Leonard Everett Fisher's *Alphabet Art: Thirteen ABC's from Around the World* makes a good introduction to a study of written forms in other cultures. Children might enjoy translating their own messages into other written systems such as hieroglyphics or Native American pictographs. Deborah Nourse Lattimore's books such as *Why There Is No Arguing in Heaven: A Mayan Myth* or *The Winged Cat: A Tale of Ancient Egypt* use these scripts in the illustrations. Children might also want to learn more about Sequoya, the Cherokee leader who invented a system of writing for his people, and to consider how different systems are used throughout the world to represent ideas. Other books about writing across cultures are listed below.

WRITING ACROSS CULTURES

Edwards, Margaret. *Alef-Bet: A Hebrew Alphabet*. New York: Lothrop, 1992.

Hackwell, John W. *Signs Letters Words, Archeology Discovers Writing*. New York: Scribners, 1987.

Lattimore, Deborah Nourse. *Why There Is No Arguing in Heaven: A Mayan Myth*. New York: HarperCollins, 1989.

Lattimore, Deborah Nourse. *The Winged Cat: A Tale of Ancient Egypt*. New York: HarperCollins, 1992.

Manniche, Lise. *The Prince Who Knew His Fate*. New York: Philomel, 1981.

Roehrig, Catharine. *Fun with Hieroglyphs*. (boxed kit). New York: Viking/Metropolitan Museum of Art, 1990

Roop, Peter, & Roop, Connie. *Ahyoka and the Talking Leaves*. Illustrated by Y. Miyake. New York: Lothrop, 1992.

Rossini, Stephanie. *Egyptian Hieroglyphics: How to Read and Write Them*. New York: Dover, 1989.

Wells, Ruth. *A to Zen: A Book of Japanese Culture*. Illustrated by Yoshi. Saxonville, MA: Picture Book Studio, 1992.

In many books the illustrator incorporates the printed word as part of the visual art. For example, Robert Froman's book, *Seeing Things: A Book of Poems*, is a collection of concrete poems, where the words become both the art *and* the poem. Suse MacDonald's *Alphabatics* is an alphabet book that takes a bright, bold letter form and, in several twists, turns it into a picture of the thing the letter represents. (For example, an *A* turned on its side and then upside down becomes an ark.) Donald Crews incorporates words in the pictures in many of his books, such as *Short Cut*, *Light*, and *Rain*. For example, the rain on the endpapers of *Rain* is created from the letters r-a-i-n printed over and over on a diagonal.

Studying the art of the printed word can provide young children with a context for developing concepts about print. Books like Donald Crew's *Short Cut, Light*, and *Rain*; Karla Kuskin's *Roar and More*; or Bill Martin and John Archambault's *Chicka Chicka Boom Boom* can help children focus on letter forms, letter sound relationships, and words, as they enjoy the aesthetic qualities of art and literature. In the following books, words are a major feature of the art.

THE ART OF THE WORD FOR YOUNGER CHILDREN

Brown, Craig. *City Sounds*. New York: Greenwillow Books, 1992.

Crews, Donald. *Flying*. New York: Greenwillow Books, 1986.

Crews, Donald. *Freight Train*. New York: Greenwillow Books, 1978.

Crews, Donald. *Light*. New York: Greenwillow Books, 1981.

Crews, Donald. *Rain*. New York: Greenwillow Books, 1978.

Crews, Donald. *Short Cut*. New York: Greenwillow Books, 1993.

Dodds, Dayle Ann. *Wheel Away!* Illustrated by Thatcher Hurd. New York: HarperCollins, 1989.

Duff, Maggie. *Rum, Pum, Pum*. New York: Macmillan, 1978.

Duffy, Dee Dee. *Barnyard Tracks*. Illustrated by Janet Marshall. Honesdale, PA: Boyds Mills, 1992.

Ehlert, Lois. *Feathers for Lunch*. San Diego: Harcourt Brace Jovanovich, 1990.

Ehlert, Lois. *Red Leaf, Yellow Leaf*. San Diego: Harcourt Brace Jovanovich, 1992.

Falwell, Cathryn. *Clowning Around*. New York: Orchard, 1991.

Fleming, Denise. *In a Small, Small Pond*. New York: Holt, 1993.

Fleming, Denise. *In the Tall, Tall Grass*. New York: Holt, 1991.

Frank, John. *Odds 'n' Ends Alvy*. Illustrated by G. Brian Karas. New York: Four Winds, 1993.

Froman, Robert. *Seeing Things: A Book of Poems*. Lettering by Ray Barber. New York: HarperCollins, 1974.

Hill, Eric. *Where's Spot?* New York: Putnam, 1980.

Hines, Anna Grossnickle. *Rumble Thumble Boom*. New York: Greenwillow Books, 1992.

Hoban, Tana. *I Read Signs*. New York: Greenwillow Books, 1983.

Jorgensen, Gail. *Crocodile Beat*. Illustrated by Patricia C. Mullins. New York: Bradbury, 1989.

Kuskin, Karla. *Roar and More*. New York: HarperCollins, 1990.

Lillie, Patricia. *When the Rooster Crowed*. Illustrated by Nancy Winslow Parker. New York: Greenwillow Books, 1991.

Most, Bernard. *The Cow That Went Oink*. San Diego: Harcourt Brace Jovanovich, 1990.

Whybrow, Ian. *Quacky Quack-Quack!* Illustrated by Russell Ayto. New York: Four Winds, 1991.

PICTUREBOOKS FOR OLDER STUDENTS

Earlier in this century, picturebooks were the province of the very young. Today, however, more and more artists seem to be attracted to the field of book illustration, and they are finding it a rich field for experimentation. In addition, many adults and almost all children have been raised with television, and these audiences are, perhaps, more open to visual stimuli.

Whatever the cause, the audience for picturebooks has clearly expanded, and many picturebooks can be enjoyed by older children and young adults. These books cover a range of genres and subject matter. Many authors and illustrators, for example, find the visual aspect of the picturebook lends impact to stories about such topics as war or homelessness. Others find that the two forms of communication possible in picturebooks, the verbal and the visual, increase the shock value of such traditionally literary qualities as irony or satire.

The many picturebooks and information books that deal with historical, cultural, scientific, and mathematical topics lend themselves to inclusion across the curriculum, across the grades, and throughout the year. Appendix D lists a few of the many fine picturebooks that are appropriate for older audiences.

Teachers might also want to develop special units of study on the art of the picturebook for older students. Many high school teachers now offer courses on picturebooks to teenagers. Asking what makes a picturebook appropriate for a "child" might start an interesting debate as well as introduce older students to the variety of topics and styles found within the genre.

Older students who are interested in peace and social and human rights issues will find that books like *Fly Away Home* (Bunting) and *We Are All in the Dumps with Jack and Guy* (Sendak) (which deal with homelessness), *Rose Blanche* (Gallaz & Innocenti) and *Terrible Things* (Bunting) (the Holocaust), and *Hiroshima No Pika* (Maruki) and *Sadako* (Coerr) (the effects of the atom bomb) convey an impact not possible through written reports.

Older students could also compare versions of illustrated and non-illustrated works such as Alfred Noyes' *The Highwayman*, Robert Service's *The Cremation of Sam McGee*, or Leonard Everett Fisher's *Jason and the Golden Fleece*. They can consider how their response to the literature differs when there are pictures.

Finally, picturebooks make good vehicles for helping students better understand literary elements as well as the elements of art. Just as graphic organizers can aid reading comprehension, the visual art in books can illuminate such devices as character development, elaboration, mood, point of view, irony, and satire. Susan Benedict and Lenore Carlisle (1992) have edited a collection on using picturebooks with older students titled *Beyond Words: Picture Books for Older Readers and Writers*. Susan Hall's (1990) *Using Picture Story Books to Teach Literary Devices* provides an extensive list of ideas and books that support students' understanding of elements of literature. Figure 7.15 highlights just of few of the books that can heighten children's understanding of literary elements as well as their knowledge of art elements.

THE BOOK ARTS OF THE MIDDLE AGES

The hand-painted and hand-lettered book (manuscript) reached its peak in the Middle Ages, the years between 500 and 1500 A.D. This time period has long fascinated children and adults. For example, members of the Society for Creative Anachronism learn the arts and crafts of the Middle Ages and regularly participate in medieval jousts and fairs. This time period is well represented in children's literature through historical fiction, information books, and picturebooks that retell stories from the Middle Ages. The wealth of resources about the period make it suitable for a unit of study all its own. As part of a study of the art of the picturebook, however, teachers might choose to focus only on the book arts of the Middle Ages.

The books in the following list, therefore, provide strong connections to the art of the book. For example, the historical fiction listed includes scribes and monasteries. The main character in Mary Stolz's *Pangur Ban* is a young peasant boy who longs to learn the art of illumination. He is admitted to the monastery and is instrumental in saving one of the manuscripts from a Viking raid. The artistic conventions of the illuminated manuscripts appear in many of the picturebook versions of stories from that era, such as Selena Hastings' *Sir Gawain and the Loathly Lady*. Fantasy lovers will enjoy Ann Curry's *The Book of Brendan*, in which the characters in illumi-

Characterization   Characters have many facets, and their strengths and weaknesses are portrayed. They grow or deteriorate over the course of the story.

> Grimm Bros. *Rapunzel.* Retold by Barbara Rogasky. Illustrated by Trina Schart Hyman. New York: Holiday House, 1982.
>
> Grimm Bros. *Snow White.* Retold by Paul Heins. Illustrated by Trina Schart Hyman. Boston: Little, Brown, 1974.
>
> Waddell, Martin. *Farmer Duck.* Illustrated by Helen Oxenbury. Cambridge, MA: Candelwick, 1992.

Climax   The point in the story where the outcome is decided; the moment of greatest tension.

> Crews, Donald. *Shortcut.* New York: Greenwillow Books, 1993.
>
> Noyes, Alfred. *The Highwayman.* Illustrated by Charles Keeping. New York: Oxford University Press, 1981.

Elaboration and Detail   Details add unique qualities to characters, setting, and plot, and they deepen our understanding and appreciation of the story.

> Grimm Bros. *Snow White.* Retold by Paul Heins. Illustrated by Trina Schart Hyman, Boston: Little, Brown, 1974.
>
> Kellogg, Steven. *Paul Bunyan.* New York: Morrow, 1984.
>
> Lear, Edward. *The Owl and the Pussycat.* Illustrated by Jan Brett. New York: Putnam, 1991.
>
> Sendak, Maurice. *Outside Over There.* New York: Harper & Row, 1981.
>
> Sendak, Maurice. *We Are All in the Dumps with Jack and Guy.* New York: HarperCollins, 1993.

Foreshadowing   Helps the reader to anticipate coming events.

> Brett, Jan. *Annie and the Wild Animals.* Boston: Houghton Mifflin, 1985.
>
> Briggs, Raymond. *The Snowman.* New York: Random House, 1978.
>
> Brown, Ruth. *The Big Sneeze.* New York: Lothrop, 1985.
>
> Hill, Donna. *Ms. Glee Was Waiting.* Illustrated by Diane Dawson. New York: Atheneum, 1978.

Irony   The situation in which actions or words are the opposite of what we expect or what they appear to be.

> Briggs, Raymond. *Father Christmas Goes on Holiday.* New York: Puffin, 1977.
>
> Burningham, John. *Come Away from the Water Shirley.* New York: Harper & Row, 1977.

FIGURE 7.15
Teaching literary forms through picturebooks

Tone or Mood   The implied feeling or attitude of the author.

 Bunting, Eve. *The Man Who Could Call Down Owls.* Illustrated by Charles Mikolaycak. New York: Macmillan, 1984.

 Gallaz, Christophe, & Innocenti, Roberto. *Rose Blanche.* Illustrated by Roberto Innocenti. Mankato, MN: Creative Education, 1985.

 Rylant, Cynthia. *The Relatives Came.* Illustrated by Stephen Gammell. New York: Bradbury, 1985.

 Shulevitz, Uri. *Dawn.* New York: Farrar, Straus & Giroux, 1974.

 Shulevitz, Uri. *Toddlecreek Post Office.* New York: Farrar, Straus & Giroux, 1990.

Parody   The humorous imitation of a well-known work or form.

 Cole, Babette. *Prince Cinders.* New York: Putnam, 1987.

 Cole, Babette. *Princess Smartypants.* New York: Putnam, 1986.

 French, Fiona. *Snow White in New York.* New York: Oxford, 1986.

 Macaulay, David. *Motel of the Mysteries.* Boston: Houghton Mifflin, 1980.

Point of view   The perspective taken by the author in telling the story.

 Scieszka, Jon. *The True Story of the Three Little Pigs.* Illustrated by Lane Smith. New York: Viking, 1989.

 Willis, Nancy. *Earthlets as Explained by Professor Xargle.* Illustrated by Tony Ross. New York: Dutton, 1989.

Satire   Criticism of societal or human weaknesses, often through exaggeration.

 Briggs, Raymond. *Fungus the Bogeyman.* New York: Puffin, 1977.

 Briggs, Raymond. *When the Wind Blows.* New York: Schocken, 1982.

 Macaulay, David. *Baaa.* Boston: Houghton Mifflin, 1985.

FIGURE 7.15, *continued*

nated manuscripts come to life to help two children perform a difficult task that calls for the help of King Arthur, Guinevere, and Merlin.

  Information books and biographies also use the arts of the Middle Ages through written facts and pictorial connections. For example, *Merrily Ever After* by Joe Lasker is an information book created in the style of the medieval "Book of Hours." Trina Schart Hyman's illustrations for Jean Fritz's fictionalized biography of St. Columbia, *The Man Who Loved Books*, borrow elements from the style of the Bayeaux Tapestry, another important story-telling art of the Middle Ages. Finally, Leonard Everett Fisher's biography of *Gutenberg* could bring closure to the study of the art of the hand-made book and lead into a history of bookmaking in modern times.

THE BOOK ARTS OF THE MIDDLE AGES

Aliki. *A Medieval Feast.* New York: Thomas Y. Crowell, 1983.

Anno, Mitsumasa. *Anno's Medieval World.* Adapted from the translation by Ursula Synge. New York: Philomel, 1980.

Burkert, Nancy Ekholm. *Valentine and Orsin*. New York: Farrar, Straus & Giroux, 1989.

Chaucer, Geoffrey. *Canterbury Tales*. Selected and adapted by Barbara Cohen. Illustrated by Trina Shart Hyman. New York: Lothrop, 1988.

˙Curry, Ann. *The Book of Brendan*. New York: Holiday House, 1989.

˙de Angeli, Marguerite. *The Door in the Wall*. New York: Doubleday, 1949.

Fritz, Jean. *The Man Who Loved Books*. Illustrated by Trina Shart Hyman. New York: Putnam, 1981.

Hastings, Selena. *Sir Gawain and the Green Knight*. Illustrated by Juan Wijngaard. New York: Lothrop, 1981.

Hastings, Selena. *Sir Gawain and the Loathly Lady*. Illustrated by Juan Wijngaard. New York: Lothrop, 1985.

Hodges, Margaret. *The Kitchen Knight*. Illustrated by Trina Schart Hyman. New York: Holiday House, 1990.

Hodges, Margaret. *Saint George and the Dragon*. Illustrated by Trina Schart Hyman. Boston: Little, Brown, 1984.

Hunt, Jonathon. *Illuminations*. New York: Bradbury, 1989.

Lasker, Joe. *Merrily Ever After*. New York: Macmillan, 1976.

Lattimore, Deborah Nourse. *The Sailor Who Captured the Sea: The Story of the Book of Kells*. New York: HarperCollins, 1991.

Macaulay, David. *Castle*. Boston: Houghton Mifflin, 1977.

Macaulay, David. *Cathedral: The Story of Its Construction*. Boston: Houghton Mifflin, 1973.

˙Picard, Barbara Leonie. *One Is One*. New York: Holt, 1966.

˙Stolz, Mary. *Pangur Ban*. New York: Harper & Row, 1988.

˙Sutcliff, Rosemary. *The Witch's Brat*. New York: Walck, 1970.

Students may also enjoy trying their hand at the types of borders and initials found in books of the Middle Ages. *The Book of Kells* and *The Book of Lindisfarne* are among the most beautiful of the medieval manuscripts and represent the Celtic style of illumination. Although animals, plants, and figures were present in these decorations, geometric ornaments give the books their unique qualities. Modern versions that include reproductions of the original manuscripts are available (*The Lindisfarne Gospels* by Blackhouse and *The Book of Kells* by Brown).

Although these designs were based on precise mathematical principles, they can easily be adapted by those who have the patience. Students might want to incorporate spirals and chains into a design for their own initials or as borders for picturebooks or other art. Figures 7.16 and 7.17 provide instructions for creating spirals and simple chains. More information on Celtic design can be found in Eva Wilson's (1983) *Celtic and Early Medieval Designs from Britain*. Students will also enjoy seeing Deborah Nourse Lattimore's recreation of these designs in *The Sailor Who Captured the Sea: The Story of the Book of Kells* (see color insert).

BEYOND THE CLASSROOM, INTO THE MUSEUM

The preceding activities offer children opportunities to explore the aesthetic potential of picturebooks. Understanding this one art form can, I believe, help children clarify their experience with other art forms. Since illustrators are part of the wider field of

---

˙Appropriate for older children

1. Spirals are variations drawn upon the basic geometric form of the circle. To draw a spiral, begin with a circle lightly drawn in pencil. At some point on the circle draw a tail that arcs out from the surface of the circle much the way a satellite might leave the earth's surface (Figure A). At the point where the tail leaves the surface of the circle there is a break, and the line of circumferance is drawn inward toward the center of the circle. With a single tail the line continues inward around the circle until it reaches the center (Figure B).

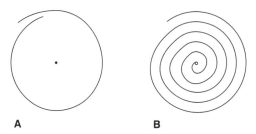

    A   B

2. If there are two tails there are two breaks. The lines are also drawn inward, eventually joining at an S curve through the point of the circle (Figures C and D).

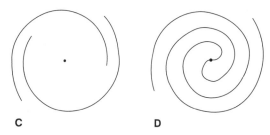

    C   D

3. The same is true with three or four tails. Note that with this many lines it is best to draw a little of each line, following inside the circumference of the circle until the three (or four) lines are close to the center. Then join each to the center point with a curving line. (Figures E, F, and G show a three-tail spiral.)

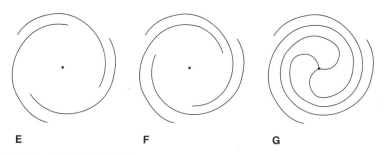

    E   F   G

FIGURE 7.16
Drawing Celtic spirals

4. These patterns can be worked together in various ways, either in a formal design as in Figures H, I, and J or simply to fill spaces within initial letters or designs. Further study of the pages of *The Book of Kells* or *The Book of Lindisfarne* (or Lattimore's *The Sailor Who Captured the Sea*) will show how spirals and chains were used to decorate Celtic manuscripts.

H

I

J

1. Like spirals, Celtic chains are also worked on geometric figures, this time on squares. Figure A shows the basic plan for drawing chains. First, using a pencil, place a dot in the four corners of square. Continue making these dots on additional squares to cover a larger area. (In this case, graph paper was used as a starting point.) Then place a dot in the center of each of these squares. These dots form a second set of squares that are diagonal to the first set.
2. Once you have the patterns of dots, draw lines *in between* these dots to form chains. The resulting pattern is similar to the lattice work formed in folding beach chairs. Note that the lines are not drawn from dot to dot but *inside* the dots (Figure B).

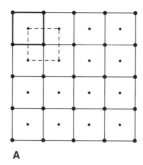 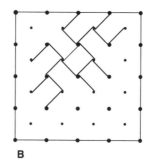

A **B**

3. When the lines or chains reach the perimeter of the figure they curve around to join to the chain below or above. At the corners of they form a U shape (Figure C).

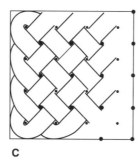

C

Once the chains are drawn in pencil, go over the lines with a darker pen and color in the space so the dots are hidden (Figure D).

D

FIGURE 7.17
Drawing Celtic chains

4. Variations can be worked by drawing straight lines within the larger rectangular shapes or by shaping the outer perimeter to fit letters, shapes, corners, or other parts of the design (Figures E and F).

E

F

visual art, it is thus natural to help children make connections between the art of the printed page and the art on museum walls or other public places. Too often, however, museums are forbidding places where children march through halls rather than engage with art.

One way to ensure that the museum is a place of wonder rather than ennui is to introduce children to the art in museums through stories. Often, the unfamiliar becomes familiar through story, and we learn "the facts" by connecting to fiction.

Stories can introduce children to characters like themselves who love to create art, as in Tomie dePaola's *The Art Lesson*. Or, they may learn about artists of the past through historical fiction such as Elizabeth Borton de Trevino's story of Velasquez, told through the eyes of his black assistant, in *I, Juan de Pareja*. Other works of fiction introduce children to the sometimes forbidding Metropolitan Museum of Art in New York City, such as the engaging story *From the Mixed-Up Files of Mrs. Basil E. Frankweiler* by E. L. Konigsburg. Thus, when art is used as a theme in books, children's feelings are engaged as well as their intellects. The following list includes picturebooks and novels that have art as a central focus.

ART AS A THEME IN BOOKS

Picturebooks

Agee, Jon. *The Incredible Painting of Felix Clousseau*. New York: Farrar, Straus & Giroux, 1988.

Alcorn, J. *Rembrandt's Beret: Or the Painter's Crown*. New York: Tambourine, 1991.

Carle, Eric. *Draw Me A Star*. New York: Philomel, 1992.

Cohen, Miriam. *No Good in Art*. Illustrated by Lillian Hoban. New York: Greenwillow Books, 1980.

Collins, P. L. *I Am an Artist*. Brookfield, CT: Millbrook, 1992.

Cooney, Barbara. *Hattie and the Wild Waves*. New York: Viking, 1990.

Craven, Carol. *What the Mailman Brought*. Illustrated by Tomie dePaola. New York: Putnam, 1987.

dePaola, Tomie. *The Art Lesson*. New York: Putnam, 1988.

dePaola, Tomie. *Bonjour, Mr. Satie*. New York: Putnam, 1991.

Demi. *The Artist and the Architect*. New York: Henry Holt, 1991.

Edwards, M. *A Baker's Portrait*. New York: Lothrop, 1991.

Ernst, L. *Hamilton's Art Show*. New York: Lothrop, 1986.

Johnson, R. *Kenji and the Magic Geese*. Illustrated by J. Tseng. New York: Simon & Schuster, 1992.

Lionni, Leo. *Matthew's Dream*. New York: Knopf, 1991.

Mathers, Petra. *Victor and Christable*. New York: Knopf, 1993.

McCully, Emily A. *Speak Up Blanche*. New York: HarperCollins, 1991.

Rylant, Cynthia. *All I See*. Illustrated by Peter Catalanotto. New York: Orchard Books, 1988.

Schick, Eleanor. *Art Lessons*. New York: Greenwillow Books, 1987.

Simmons, Posie. *Lulu and the Flying Babies*. London: Jonathon Cape, 1988.

Velthuijs, M. *Crocodile's Masterpiece*. New York: Farrar, Straus & Giroux, 1992.

Wadell, Martin. *Alice the Artist*. Illustrated by J. Langley. New York: Dutton, 1988.

Wolkstein, Diane. *Little Mouse's Painting*. Illustrated by M. Begin. New York: William Morrow, 1992.

Novels

Clarke, J. *Riffraff*. New York: Henry Holt, 1992.

de Trevino, Elizabeth B. *I, Juan de Pareja*. New York: Farrar, Straus & Giroux, 1965.

Dubelaar, T. *Looking for Vincent*. New York: Checkerboard, 1992.

Fenner, Carol. *Randall's Wall*. New York: Margaret McElderry, 1991.

Henkes, Kevin. *Words of Stone*. New York: Greenwillow Books, 1992.

Konigsburg, E. L. *From the Mixed-Up Files of Mrs. Basil E. Frankweiler*. New York: Atheneum, 1967.

Konigsburg, E. L. *The Second Mrs. Giaconda*. New York: Atheneum, 1975.

MacLachlan, Patricia. *Journey*. New York: Delacorte, 1991.

Nunes, Louis. B. *My Friend the Painter*. San Diego: Harcourt Bruce Jovanovich, 1991.

Oneal, Zibby. *In Summer Light*. New York: Viking, 1985.

Paterson, Katherine. *Bridge to Terabithia*. New York: HarperCollins, 1979.

Paulsen, Gary. *The Monument*. New York: Delacorte, 1991.

Peck, Richard. *The Unfinished Portrait of Jessica*. New York: Delacorte, 1991.

Picard, Barbara Leonie. *One Is One*. New York: Henry Holt, 1966.

Plummer, L. *My Name Is Sus5an Smith: The 5 Is Silent*. New York: Delacorte, 1991.

Pullman, Phillip. *The Broken Bridge*. New York: Knopf, 1992.

Sutcliff, Rosemary. *Sun Horse, Moon Horse*. New York: Dutton, 1978.

Another way to connect children to the art in museums is through picture-books. Illustrators often call upon strong historical or cultural roots to painting and other art forms. Discovering those roots can be both rewarding and illuminating for children. As discussed in Chapter 6, many illustrators adapt general "umbrella" or artistic conventions of depicting from various periods of history or from cultural groups from which stories have originated. These conventions deepen our pleasure and understanding of the picturebook. Examples are listed below.

ILLUSTRATORS' USE OF HISTORICAL AND CULTURAL CONVENTIONS

I. HISTORICAL MOVEMENTS

A. EARLY CHRISTIAN ART/NEAR EASTERN ART—a clear, uniform message was desired. Dramatic form was subdued for repetition of motifs and conventional symbols. This style can be found in Middle Eastern and Russian art today.
1. "Book of Kells"
   a. Margaret Hodges/Chris Conover, *The Little Humpbacked Horse*
   b. Deborah Nourse Lattimore, *The Sailor Who Captured the Sea*
2. Persian Miniatures
   a. P. L. Travers/Leo & Diane Dillon, *Two Pairs of Shoes*
   b. Sally Scott, *The Magic Horse*
   c. Walter McVitty/Margaret Early, *Ali Baba and the Forty Thieves*
   d. Diane Stanley, *Fortune*
3. Stained Glass Windows
   a. Janina Domanska, *Din Dan Don It's Christmas*

B. GOTHIC—style that began with architecture and sculpture; showed a movement toward a more natural, although still decorative, depiction of religious subjects.
   1. Giotto, "Marriage of the Virgin"
      a. Tomie dePaola, *The Clown of God*
C. LATE GOTHIC—movement away from stylized two-dimensional art, toward a renewed interest in realism. Symbolism survives but in an increasingly realistic form.
   1. Jan Van Eyck, "The Marriage of Giovanni Arnolfini"
      a. Grimm Bros./Nancy Eckholm Burkert, *Snow White and the Seven Dwarfs, Valentine and Orson*
D. RENAISSANCE—move toward realism; an emphasis on forms, proportioning of space, and dramatic lighting.
   1. Pieter Bruegel, "The Harvesters"
      a. Sheila MacGill-Callahan/Gennady Spirin, *The Children of Lir*
      b. Grimm Bros./Paul Zelinsky, *Hansel and Gretel, Rumplestiltskin*
E. BAROQUE ART—a move away from classicism to a more grandiose, richly ornamented style. Genre painting increased viewer's feeling of intimacy with the subject matter.
   1. Rembrandt, "Self Portrait"
   2. Vermeer, "View of Delft"
      a. Maxine Kumin/Arnold Lobel, *The Microscope*
F. ROCOCO ART—centered in France with a move to genre scenes or mythology set in idealized park settings. Characterized by highly decorated, almost fussy use of curving lines, flowing forms, and lightened colors.
   1. Fragonard, "The Swing"
      a. Margaret Early, *Sleeping Beauty*
      b. Lincoln Kirstein/Alain Vaës, *Puss in Boots*
G. ROMANTICISM—late-18th to mid-19th century movement influenced by the romantic literature of Goethe and Byron. Nostalgic identification with nature and the past. Belief in the sanctity of childhood. Often focused on melancholy, emotional subjects.
   1. Caspar David Friedrich, "Moonrise at Sea," "Morning Fog in the Mountains"
      a. Chris Van Allsburg, *The Wreck of the Zephyr, The Polar Express*
   2. Philip Otto Runge, "The Hulsenbeckschen Children"
      a. Maurice Sendak, *Outside Over There*
H. HUDSON RIVER SCHOOL—mid-19th century group of American landscape painters who were interested in the glories of nature. Their work was influenced by the moral and literary ideas of the times.
   1. Thomas Cole, "Sunny Morning on the Hudson River"
      a. Thomas Locker, *Where the River Begins*
I. IMPRESSIONISM—concerned with a momentary and spontaneous view of a scene; characterized by broken color, softened contours.
   1. Claude Monet, "Woman Seated Under the Willows"
      a. Charlotte Zolotow/Maurice Sendak, *Mr. Rabbit and the Lovely Present*
   2. Sisley, "Wheatfields Near Argentenil"
      a. John Burningham, *Would You Rather*

J. 20TH CENTURY ART—characterized by rapidly changing, often simultaneous movements, as painting moved away from the realistic representation of the world to the depiction of intellectual and emotional ideas of the artist's inner world. Some of these movements include:

  1. EXPRESSIONISM—emotionally rooted, intense themes, characterized by brilliant, shocking colors and rough rapid brushwork.
    a. Rouault, "The Old King"
      i. John Steptoe, *Stevie*
    b. Kokoshka, "Bunch of Autumn Flowers"
      i. Charles Keeping, *Joseph's Yard*
  2. SURREALISM—acknowledged the irrational and the power of imagination. Mixed a realistic style with bizarre, dislocated imagery.
    a. Magritte, "Time Transfixed"
      i. Anthony Browne, *Changes*
    b. Salvador Dali, "The Persistence of Memory"
      i. Molly Bang, *The Grey Lady and the Strawberry Snatcher*
  3. COMIC ART—characterized by economy of form and humorous reference.
    a. Ronald Searle, "The Fat Cat"
      i. Jack Kent, *The Fat Cat: A Danish Folktale*

II. *CULTURAL CONVENTIONS*

A. NAIVE ART—A broad category which refers most often to arts of rural or tribal societies, characterized by simplified forms and/or bright colors, childlike perspective.

  1. Henri Rousseau, "The Equitorial Jungle"
    a. Maurice Sendak, *Where the Wild Things Are*
  2. African figures, Bakota area, Gabon
    a. Gail Haley, *A Story, a Story*
    b. Lorenz Graham/Leo & Diane Dillon, *Song of the Boat*
  3. Zo Tom, "Running From an Enemy: A Kiowa Brave Chasing a Navajo" (Northern Plains Native American, buffalo-hide paintings)
    a. Paul Goble, *The Girl Who Loved Wild Horses*
    b. Nancy Van Laan/Beatriz Vidal, *Buffalo Dance*
  4. Navajo sand paintings
    a. Virginia Sneve/Stephen Gammell, *Dancing Teepees*
  5. Apache hide paintings
    a. Tryntje Seymour/Apache Artists, *The Gift of Changing Woman*
  6. Seifert, "Res. of Mr. E. R. Jones" (early American limner painter)
    a. Mitsumasa Anno, *Anno's Counting Book*
    b. Donald Hall/Barbara Cooney, *Ox-Cart Man*
    c. Reeve Lindbergh/Kathy Jakobsen, *Johnny Appleseed*
    d. Frané Lessac, *My Little Island*
    e. Mary Ann Hoberman/Malcah Zeldis, *A Fine Fat Pig*

B. FOLK ART—term applied to crafts (more often than to painting) that use traditional designs. Often produced in rural communities.

  1. Harriet Powers, story quilts; Dahomey, Tibetan, Indian, Central and South American embroideries
    a. Mary E. Lyons, *Stitching Stars: The Story Quilts of Harriet Powers*

        b. Mordicai Gerstein, *The Mountains of Tibet*
        c. Arthur Dorros/Elisa Kleven, *Abuela,* Elisa Kleven, *The Lion and the Little Red Bird*
        d. Arthur Dorros, *Tonight Is Carnivale*
  C. ASIAN ART—method of painting using silk, fine papers, and inks that promoted exploration of linear and spatial effects. The style is rooted in calligraphy and involves controlled handling of the brush.
    1. Wang Hui (1680), "Fisherman's Huts and Clearing Skies in Autumn"
        a. Hans Christian Andersen/Nancy Burkert, *The Nightingale*
        b. Feenie Ziner/Ed Young, *Cricket Boy*
        c. Mercer Mayer, *Everyone Knows What a Dragon Looks Like*
        d. Demi, *The Empty Pot, Chingis Khan*
    2. Japanese Woodblock prints of the 17th through 19th centuries were characterized by flattened forms, large areas of color, and decorative tensions created by use of line and shape.
        a. Hokusai, "The Eight Fold Bridge"
        b. Hiroshige, "Fan Print"
            i. Katherine Paterson/Leo & Diane Dillon, *The Tale of the Mandarin Ducks*
            ii. Diane Snyder/Allen Say, *The Boy of the Three-Year Nap*

At other times, illustrators make visual references to specific works of art or to famous artists. Often, their references are as playful as they are profound. Whatever the illustrator's impetus, the connections between picturebook art and other art forms can be fun for children to explore, another aspect of finding "secrets" in books. For ideas, see the following list of illustrators and their ties to well known painters and paintings.

ILLUSTRATORS' REFERENCES TO SPECIFIC PAINTERS AND PAINTINGS

Mitsumasa Anno
    Anno's Alphabet—works of M. C. Escher
    Anno's Journey—Van Gogh, "Bridge at Arles"; Seurat, "The Bathers," "Sunday Afternoon on La Grand Jatte"; Millet, "The Gleaners," "The Angelus"
    Anno's Britain—John Constable, "The Hay Wain"
Raymond Briggs
    Fee Fi Fo Fum—Velasquez, "The Infanta Margarita"
Leo & Diane Dillon (Nancy Willard, author)
    Pish, Posh, Said Hieronymous Bosch—J. Bosch, "The Garden of Earthly Delights"
Janina Domanska
    What Do You See, If All the Seas Were One Sea—Paul Klee, "Sinbad the Sailor"
Ron Himler (Byrd Baylor, author)
    The Best Town in the World—Thomas Eakins, "Swimming Hole"
Errol Le Cain (Hans Christian Andersen, author)
    The Snow Queen—Pieter Bruegel, "Hunters in the Snow"
Charles Keeping
    Willie's Fire-Engine—Chuck Close (photo realist), "Self Portrait"
Petra Mathers
    Victor and Christabel—Vittore Carpaccio's "Saint Ursula's Dream"

Tord Nygren
   The Red Thread—works of Picasso, Renoir, Leonardo DaVinci, Modigliani, Van Gogh, and others
Dav Pilkey
   When Cats Dream—James Whistler, "The Artist's Mother"
   When Cats Dream—works of Marc Chagall
Maurice Sendak
   Outside Over There—Phillip Otto Runge, "The Hulsenbeckscher Children"
   We Are All in the Dumps with Jack and Guy—Andrea Mantegna, "Descent into Limbo"
Chris Van Allsburg
   Wreck of the Zephyr—Winslow Homer, "Inside the Bar, Tynemouth"

It can be a worthwhile experience for children to view original works of art, whether in the museum or in some other public place. For example, if children have only seen reproductions of paintings in books, when they see the real art they may notice the difference in color and texture in the original works that cannot be captured in a reproduction. Moreover, they may be surprised at how greatly the size of the original differs from the reproduction they have seen. Works by abstract artist Mark Rothko, for example, are monumental; a work titled "Four Darks in Red" measures approximately 9 by 10 feet. This large size can have a great impact on how the viewer responds to the work and can never be experienced through reproductions.

Art teachers and museum education departments can help teachers and children make further connections between the art of the picturebook and the art in the wider world. If there is no easy access to museums, there are many sources for reproductions of paintings that could bring the museum within classroom walls. Many teachers collect fine art calendars when they go on sale every January and haunt garage sales or second-hand book stores for old art history books. Several publishers of art education materials have series that include reproductions or overhead transparencies of paintings, sculpture, and other art forms. Large national museums carry reproductions and slides in their gift shops, and teachers can order these by mail. As CD ROM becomes more available to classrooms, children will have access to entire museum collections. (See Appendix C for addresses of sources for such materials.)

Finally, there are many fine information books about art history and art appreciation. Many of these books are organized around a theme, such as "the sea," "cities," or "families," that fit nicely within an integrated curriculum. There are also many excellent biographies of artists, and several series of biographies focus on African-American or woman artists who have traditionally been outside the mainstream of Western tradition.

BOOKS ABOUT ART APPRECIATION

The Artists

Bjork, C. *Linnea in Monet's Garden*. Illustrated by L. Anderson. New York: R & S, 1985.
Harris, N. *Leonardo and the Renaissance*. Chicago: Franklin Watts/Bookwright, 1987.

Everett, G. *Li'l Sis and Uncle Willie: A Story Based on the Life and Paintings of William H. Johnson*. New York: Rizzoli, 1992.

Freedman, Russell. *An Indian Winter*. Paintings and photographs by K. Bodmer. New York: Holiday House, 1992.

Goffstein, M. B. *Lives of the Artists*. New York: HarperCollins, 1983.

Greenfeld, H. *Leonardo da Vinci*. New York: Abrams, 1990.

Kastner, J. *John James Audubon*. New York: Abrams, 1992.

Niemark, A. E. *Diego Rivera: Artist of the People*. New York: HarperCollins, 1992.

Provensen, Alice, & Provensen, Martin. *Leonardo Da Vinci*. New York: Viking, 1984.

Ventura, Piero. *Great Painters*. New York: Putnam, 1984.

Zhensun, Z., & Low, A. *A Young Painter: The Life and Paintings of Wang Yani—China's Extraordinary Young Artist*. New York: Scholastic, 1991.

Series Books

Art for Children

Raboff, Ernest. *Henri Matisse*. New York: Lippincott, 1988. Also *Renoir, DaVinci, Rembrandt, Van Gogh*, and others.

African-American Artists and Artisans

Lyons, Mary E. *Starting Home: The Story of Horace Pippin, Painter*. Scribner, 1993. Also *Stitching Stars: The Story Quilts of Harriet Powers*.

Come Look with Me

Blizzard, Gladys S. *Enjoying Art with Children*. Charlottesville, VA: Thamasson Grant, 1992. Also *Animals in Art, World of Play, Exploring Landscape Art*.

First Impressions

Meyer, Susan E. *Mary Cassatt*. New York: Abrams, 1990.

Waldron, Ann. *Claude Monet*. New York: Abrams, 1991. Also *Francisco Goya, Andrew Wyeth, Leonardo DaVinci*.

Introducing the Artist

Heslewood, Julie. *Introducing Picasso*. Boston: Little, Brown, 1993.

Richmond, Robin. *Introducing Michelangelo*. Boston: Little, Brown, 1992.

Portraits of Woman Artists for Children

Turner, Robyn Montana. *Faith Ringold*. Boston: Little, Brown, 1993. Also *Georgia O'Keeffe, Rosa Bonheur, Mary Cassatt*, and *Frieda Kahlo*.

Metropolitan Museum Series

Mühlberger, Richard. *What Makes a Bruegel a Bruegel?* New York: Metropolitan Museum of Art, 1993. Also similar books on Degas, Van Gogh, Raphael, Rembrandt, and Van Gogh.

A Weekend with the Artist

Bonafoux, Pascal. *A Weekend with Rembrandt*. New York: Rizzoli, 1992.

Rodari, Florian. *A Weekend with Picasso*. New York: Rizzoli, 1991.

Skira-Venturi, Rosabianca. *A Weekend with Renoir*. New York: Rizzoli, 1991.

Skira-Venturi, Rosabianca *A Weekend with Degas*. New York: Rizzoli, 1992.

Art History

Arenas, J. F. *The Key to Renaissance Art*. Minneapolis, MN: Lerner, 1990.

Brown, Laurene K., & Brown, Marc. *Visiting the Art Museum*. New York: Dutton, 1986.

Davidson, Rosemary. *Take a Look: An Introduction to the Experience of Art*. New York: Viking, 1993.

Greenburg, J., & Jordan, S. *The Painter's Eye: Learning to Look at Contemporary American Art*. New York: Delacorte, 1991.

Highwater, J. *Many Smokes, Many Moons: A Chronology of American Indian History Through Indian Art*. New York: Lippincott, 1978.

Issacson, Philip M. *A Short Walk Around the Pyramids and Through the World of Art*. New York: Knopf, 1993.

Janson, H. W., & Janson, A. F. *History of Art for Young People*. New York: Abrams, 1987.

Knox, Bob. *The Great Art Adventure*. New York: Rizzoli, 1993.

Pekarik, A. *Behind the Scenes: Painting*. New York: Hyperion, 1992.

Pekarik, A. *Behind the Scenes: Sculpture*. New York: Hyperion, 1992.

Richardson, Joy. *Inside the Museum*. New York: Abrams, 1993.

Sullivan, Charles (ed.). *Imaginary Gardens: American Poetry and Art for Young People*. New York: Abrams, 1989.

Sullivan, Charles (ed.). *Children of Promise: African-American Literature and Art for Young People*. New York: Abrams, 1991.

Woolf, Felicity. *Picture This: A First Introduction to Paintings*. New York: Doubleday, 1990.

Woolf, Felicity, *Picture This: An Introduction to Twentieth Century Art*. New York: Doubleday, 1993.

Series Books

The DK Art School

Smith, Ray. *An Introduction to Watercolor*. New York: Dorling Kindersly, 1993. Also *An Introduction to Acrylics, An Introduction to Oil Painting, An Introduction to Pastel*.

Eyewitness Art

Welton, Jude. *Impressionism*. New York: Dorling Kindersly, 1993. Also *Monet, Manet, Gauguin, Goya, Van Gogh, Post Impressionism, Color, Perspective*, and *Watercolor*.

Looking at Paintings

Roalf, Peggy. *Cats*. New York: Hyperion, 1992. Also *Dancers, Families, Horses, Landscapes, Seascapes, Dogs, Music, Circus, Self Portraits, Flowers*, and *Children*.

Millbrook Arts Library

Peppin, Andrea. *Nature in Art*. Brookfield, CT: Millbrook Press, 1992.

Williams, Helen. *Stories in Art*. Brookfield, CT: Millbrook Press, 1992. Also *People in Art, Places in Art*.

Museum of Modern Art

Yenawine, Phillip. *People*. New York: Delacorte, 1993. Also *Stories, Color, Line, Shape*, and *Places*.

The World of Art

Richardson, Wendy and Jack. *The World of Water*. Chicago: Children's Press, 1991. Also *Animals, Cities, Entertainers, Families*, and *The Natural World*.

These books should be part of the classroom or school library. By helping children make these connections, we can extend their aesthetic understanding of the picturebook as well as expand their ability to think and feel deeply about all art.

APPENDIX

Exploring the Art of the Picturebook

17 Kings and 43 Elephants. Margaret Mahy. Illustrated by Patricia MacCarthy. New York: Dial, 1987.

The Accidental Zucchini: An Unexpected Alphabet Book. Max Grover. San Diego: Browndeer/Harcourt, 1993.

Alef-Bet: A Hebrew Alphabet. Margaret Edwards. New York: Lothrop, 1992.

Alphabet Art: Thirteen ABC's From Around the World. Leonard Everett Fisher. New York: Four Winds, 1978.

Arithmetic. Carl Sandburg. Illustrated by Ted Rand. Harcourt Brace Jovanovich, 1993.

The Art Lesson. Tomie dePaola. New York: Putnam, 1988.

The Art of the Handmade Book. Flora Fennimore. Chicago: Chicago Review Press, 1992.

Ahyoka and the Talking Leaves. Peter and Connie Roop. Illustrated by Y. Miyake. New York: Lothrop, 1992.

Baaa. David Macaulay. Boston: Houghton Mifflin, 1985.

Behind the Scenes: Painting. A. Pekarik. New York: Hyperion, 1992.

Ben and the Porcupine. Carol Carrick. Illustrated by Donald Carrick. New York: Clarion Books, 1981.

The Book of Kells. Peter Brown. New York: Thames & Hudson, 1989.

A Book Takes Root: The Making of a Picture Book. Michael Kehoe. Minneapolis, MN: Carolrhoda, 1993.

Borrequita and the Coyote. Verna Aardema. Illustrated by Petra Mathers. New York: Knopf, 1991.

The Boy of the Three-Year Nap. Diane Snyder. Illustrated by Allen Say. Boston: Houghton Mifflin, 1988.

The Bremen Town Musicians. Grimm Bros. Illustrated by Ilse Plume. New York: Doubleday, 1980.

Calligraphy: From Beginner to Expert. Caroline Young. Illustrated by Chris Lyon and Paul Sullivan. Tulsa, OK: EDC Pub., 1990.

Cinderella. Grimm Bros. Illustrated by Nonnie Hogrogian. New York: Greenwillow Books, 1981.

Climbing Kansas Mountains. George Shannon. Illustrated by Thomas Allen. New York: Bradbury, 1993.

A Color Sampler. Kathleen Westray. New York: Ticknor & Fields, 1993.

Color Zoo. Lois Ehlert. New York: Lippincott, 1990.

Coyote Places the Stars. Harriet Peck Taylor. New York: Bradbury, 1993.

Dakota Dugout. Ann Turner. Illustrated by Ron Himler. New York: Macmillan, 1985.

Dawn. Uri Shulevitz. New York: Farrar, Straus & Giroux, 1974.

The Day of Ahmed's Secret. Heide, Florence Parry, & Judith Heide Gilliland. Illustrated by Ted Lewin. New York: Lothrop, 1990.

Dogzilla. Dav Pilkey. San Diego, CA: Harcourt Brace Jovanovich, 1993.

Drawer in a Drawer. David Christiana. New York: Farrar, Straus & Giroux, 1990.

Fly Away Home. Eve Bunting. Illustrated by Ron Himler. New York: Clarion, 1991.

The Fool of the World and the Flying Ship. Arthur Ransome. Illustrated by Uri Shulevitz. New York: Farrar, Straus & Giroux, 1968.

Freight Train. Donald Crews. New York: Greenwillow Books, 1978.

The Frog Prince Continued. Jon Scieszka. Illustrated by Steve Johnson. New York: Viking, 1991.

The Frog Prince. Jan Ormerod and David Lloyd. Illustrated by Jan Ormerod. New York: Lothrop, 1990.

From the Mixed-Up Files of Mrs. Basil E. Frankweiler. E. L. Konigsburg. New York: Atheneum, 1967.

The Golden Age: Manuscript Painting at the Time of Jean, Duke of Berry. Marcel Thomas. New York: George Braziller, 1979.

Gorilla. Anthony Browne. New York: Franklin Watts, 1983.

The Grouchy Ladybug. Eric Carle. New York: Thomas Y. Crowell, 1977.

Guess Who My Favorite Person Is? Byrd Baylor. Illustrated by Robert Andrew Parker. Scribner, 1992.

Gutenberg. Leonard Everett Fisher. New York: Macmillan, 1993.

Hansel and Gretel. Grimm Bros. Retold by Rika Lesser. Illustrated by Paul Zelinsky. New York: Dodd Mead, 1984.

Hide and Seek Fog. Alvin Tresselt. Illustrated by Roger Duvoisin. New York: Lothrop, 1965.

The Highwayman. Alfred Noyes. Illustrated by Charles Keeping. New York: Oxford University, 1981.

Hiroshima No Pika. Toshi Maruki. New York: Lothrop, 1980.

How a Book Is Made. Aliki. New York: Thomas Y. Crowell, 1986.

How to Make Pop-Ups. Joan Irvine. New York: Greenwillow Books, 1991.

I Have a Friend. Keiko Narahashi. New York: McElderry, 1987.

Iktomi and the Boulder: A Plains Indian Story. Paul Goble. New York: Orchard, 1988.

Illuminations. Peter Hunt. New York: Bradbury, 1989.

In a Small, Small Pond. Denise Fleming. New York: Holt, 1993.

Is It Rough? Is It Smooth? Is It Shiny? Tana Hoban. New York: Greenwillow Books, 1984.

Jason and the Golden Fleece. Leonard Everett Fisher. New York: Holiday House, 1990.

Julius, The Baby of the World. Kevin Henkes. New York: Greenwillow Books, 1991.

Jumanji. Chris Van Allsburg. Boston: Houghton Mifflin, 1981.

The Key to Renaissance Art. J. Arenas. Minneapolis: Lerner, 1990.

Little Red Riding Hood. Charles Perrault. Photographs by Sarah Moon. Mankato, MN: Creative Education, 1986.

Lives of the Artists. M. B. Goffstein. New York: Harper & Row, 1983.

The Man Who Loved Books. Jean Fritz. Illustrated by Trina Schart Hyman. New York: Putnam, 1981.

Merrily Ever After. Joe Lasker. New York: Macmillan, 1976.

Motel of the Mysteries. David Macauley. Boston: Houghton Mifflin, 1980.

The Mountains of Tibet. Mordicai Gerstein. New York: Harper & Row, 1987.

Mufaro's Beautiful Daughters. John Steptoe. New York: Lothrop, 1987.

The Napping House. Audrey Wood. Illustrated by Don Wood. San Diego: Harcourt Brace Jovanovich, 1984.

Nuts to You. Lois Ehlert. San Diego: Harcourt Brace Jovanovich, 1993.

Oink Oink. Arthur Geisert. Boston: Houghton Mifflin, 1993.

Once Upon Another. Suse MacDonald and Bill Oakes. New York: Dial, 1990.

Ox-Cart Man. Donald Hall. Illustrated by Barbara Cooney. New York: Viking, 1979.

The Painter's Eye: Learning to Look at Contemporary American Art. Jan Greenburg and S. Jordan. New York: Delacorte, 1991.

Pangor Ban. Mary Stolz New York: Harper & Row, 1988.

Paper Making Fun. Denise Fleming. New York: Henry Holt, 1994.

Pondlarker. Fred Gwynne. New York: Simon & Schuster, 1990.

The Practical Guide to Marbling Paper. Anne Chambers. New York: Thames and Hudson, 1986.

Prince Cinders. Babette Cole. New York: Putnam, 1987.

Red Leaf, Yellow Leaf. Lois Ehlert. San Diego: Harcourt Brace Jovanovich, 1992.

A River Ran Wild. Lyn Cherry. San Diego: Harcourt Brace Jovanovich, 1992.

Roar and More. Karla Kuskin. New York: HarperCollins, 1990.

Rose Blanche. Christophe Gallaz & Robert Innocenti. Mankato, MN: Creative Education, 1985.

Rumplestiltskin. Grimm Bros. Illustrated by Paul Zelinsky. New York: Dutton, 1986.

Sadako. Eleanor Coerr. Illustrated by Ed Young. New York: Putnam, 1993.

The Sailor Who Captured the Sea: The Story of the Book of Kells. Deborah Nourse Lattimore. New York: HarperCollins, 1991.

Saint George and the Dragon. Margaret Hodges. Illustrated by Trina Shart Hyman. Boston: Little, Brown, 1984.

Shape Space. Cathryn Falwell. New York: Clarion, 1992.

Shortcut. Donald Crews. New York: Greenwillow Books, 1992.

Sir Gawain and the Loathly Lady. Selena Hastings. Illustrated by Juan Wijngaard. New York: Lothrop, 1985.

Sleeping Beauty. Charles Perrault. Illustrated by Trina Schart Hyman. Boston: Little, Brown, 1974.

Snow White and the Seven Dwarfs. Grimm Bros. Illustrated by Nancy Burkert. New York: Farrar, Straus & Giroux, 1972.

Snow White. Grimm Bros. Retold by Paul Heins. Illustrated by Trina Schart Hyman. Boston: Little, Brown, 1974.

The Stinky Cheese Man and Other Fairly Stupid Tales. Jon Scieszka. Illustrated by Lane Smith. New York: Viking, 1992.

Stories in Art. Helen Williams. Brookfield, CT: Millbrook, 1992.

The Story of an English Village. John Goodall. New York: Atheneum, 1979.

A Story, a Story. Gail Haley. New York: Atheneum, 1970.

Swan Sky. Keizaburo Tejima. New York: Philomel, 1988.

Terrible Things: An Allegory of the Holocaust. Eve Bunting. Illustrated by Stephen Gammell. New York: Harper & Row, 1989.

Two by Two. Barbara Reid. New York: Scholastic, 1993.

Until the Cows Come Home. Patricia Mills. New York: North South, 1993.

The Very Hungry Caterpillar. Eric Carle. New York: Philomel, 1969.

Vicki Cobb's Paper Making Book and Kit Vicki Cobb. New York: HarperCollins, 1993

Visiting the Art Museum. Laurene K. Brown. Illustrated by Marc Brown. New York: Dutton, 1986.

Waiting for Hannah. Marisabina Russo. New York: Greenwillow Books, 1989.

We Are All in the Dumps with Jack and Guy: Two Nursery Rhymes with Pictures. Maurice Sendak. New York: HarperCollins, 1993.

When I Was Young in the Mountains. Cynthia Rylant. Illustrated by Diane Goode. New York: Dutton, 1982.

Where Does the Trail Lead? Burton Albert. Illustrated by Brian Pinkney. New York: Simon & Schuster, 1991.

Why the Tides Ebb and Flow. John Chase Bowden. Illustrated by Marc Brown. Boston: Houghton Mifflin, 1979.

The Witch's Broom. Chris Van Allsburg. Boston: Houghton Mifflin, 1992.

The World of Water. Wendy & Jack Richardson. Chicago: Children's Press, 1991.

A Year of Birds. Ashley Wolff. New York: Dodd, Mead, 1984.

Your Own Best Secret Place. Byrd Baylor. Illustrated by Peter Parnall. New York: Scribner & Sons, 1978.

APPENDIX

B

Exploring the Books of Tomie dePaola

The Art Lesson. New York: Putnam, 1989.

Akimba and the Magic Cow: A Folk Tale from Africa. Ann Rose. New York: Four Winds, 1976.

The Badger and the Magic Fan: A Japanese Folktale. Tony Johnson. New York: Putnam, 1990.

Big Anthony and the Magic Ring. San Diego: Harcourt Brace Jovanovich, 1979.

Bill and Pete. New York: Putnam, 1978.

Bonjour Mr. Satie. New York: Putnam, 1991.

The Carsick Zebra and Other Animal Riddles. David Adler. New York: Holiday, 1983.

The Cat on the Doverfel. George Dascent. New York: Putnam, 1979.

Charlie Needs a Cloak. New York: Prentice Hall, 1973.

The Christmas Pageant. New York: Winston Press, 1978.

The Clown of God. San Diego: Harcourt Brace Jovanovich, 1978.

The Comic Adventure of Old Mother Hubbard and Her Dog. San Diego: Harcourt Brace Jovanovich, 1981.

Cookie's Week. Cindy Ward. New York: Putnam, 1988.

An Early American Christmas. New York: Holiday, 1987.

The Family Christmas Tree Book. New York: Holiday, 1980.

Fin M'Coul: The Giant of Knockmany Hill. New York: Holiday, 1981.

Flicks San Diego: Harcourt Brace Jovanovich, 1979.

Francis, The Poor Man of Assisi. New York: Holiday, 1982.

The Ghost with the Halloween Hiccups. Stephen Mooser. New York: Avon, 1978.

The Good Giants and the Bad Puckwudgies. Jean Fritz. New York: Putnam, 1982.

Haircuts for the Woolseys. New York: Putnam, 1989.

Helga's Dowry. San Diego: Harcourt Brace Jovanovich, 1977.

Hey Diddle Diddle and Other Mother Goose Rhymes. New York: Putnam, 1988.

The Hunter and the Animals. New York: Holiday, 1981.

I Love You Mouse. John Graham. San Diego: Harcourt Brace Jovanovich, 1990.

Jamie O'Rourke and the Big Potato: An Irish Folktale. New York: Putnam, 1992.

Jingle the Christmas Clown. New York: Putnam, 1992.

The Kid's Cat Book. New York: Holiday, 1979.

The Knight and the Dragon. New York: Putnam, 1992.

The Lady of Guadalupe. New York: Holiday, 1980.

The Legend of Old Befana. San Diego: Harcourt Brace Jovanovich, 1980.

The Legend of the Bluebonnet: An Old Tale of Texas. New York: Putnam, 1983.

The Legend of the Indian Paintbrush. New York: Putnam, 1988.

The Legend of the Poinsettia. New York: Putnam, 1993.

Little Grunt and the Big Egg. New York: Holiday, 1990.

The Magic Porridge Pot. Paul Galdone. New York: Clarion, 1976.

Maggie and the Monster. Elizabeth Winthrop. New York: Holiday, 1988.

Mary Had a Little Lamb. Sarah, J. Hale. New York: Holiday, 1984.

Merry Christmas Strega Nona. San Diego: Harcourt Brace Jovanovich, 1986.

The Mountains of Quilt. Nancy Willard. San Diego: Harcourt Brace Jovanovich, 1987.

My First Hanukkah. New York: Putnam, 1989.

My First Passover. New York: Putnam, 1991.

The Mysterious Giant of Barletta. San Diego: Harcourt Brace Jovanovich, 1988.

Nana Upstairs, Nana Downstairs. New York: Putnam, 1973.

Nicholas Bentley Stoningpot III. Ann McGovern. Honesdale, PA; Boyds Mills, 1992.

Noah and the Ark. New York: Harper & Row, 1985.

Now One Foot, Now the Other. New York: Putnam, 1981.

Oh Such Foolishness. William Cole. New York: HarperCollins, 1991.

Oliver Button Is a Sissy. San Diego: Harcourt Brace Jovanovich, 1979

Pancakes for Breakfast. San Diego: Harcourt Brace Jovanovich, 1978.

Patrick, Saint of Ireland. New York: Holiday, 1992.

Petook: An Easter Story. New York: Holiday, 1988.

The Popcorn Book. New York: Holiday, 1978.

Queen Esther. New York: Harper & Row, 1987.

The Quilt Story. Tony Johnson. New York: Putnam, 1992.

"A Round," in *A Sky Full of Poems*. Eve Merriam. New York: Dell, 1986.

"Spaghetti," in *Where the Sidewalk Ends*. Shel Silverstein. New York: Harper & Row, 1974.

"Spaghetti, Spaghetti," in *Rainy Rainy Saturday*. Jack Prelutsky. New York: Greenwillow Books, 1980.

The Sorcerer's Apprentice. Nancy Willard. Illustrated by Leo and Diane Dillon. New York: Blue Sky/Scholastic, 1993.

Strega Nona. New York: Prentice Hall, 1975.

Strega Nona Meets Her Match. New York: Putnam, 1993.

Strega Nona's Magic Lessons. San Diego: Harcourt Brace Jovanovich, 1982.

The Family Christmas Tree Book. New York: Holiday, 1980.

Tom. New York: Putnam, 1993.

Tomie dePaola's Book of Bible Stories. New York: Putnam, 1991.

Tomie dePaola's Favorite Nursery Tales. New York: Putnam, 1986.

Tomie dePaola's Mother Goose. New York: Putnam, 1985.

Tony's Bread. New York: Putnam, 1989.

The Walking Coat. New York: Prentice Hall, 1987.

Watch out for Chicken Feet in Your Soup. New York: Prentice Hall, 1974.

What the Mailman Brought. New York: Putnam, 1987.

APPENDIX

C

*Sources for Art
Materials and
Information*

ART SUPPLIES

Arthur Brown
   58–95 Maurice Ave.
   Maspeth, NY 11378
   1-718-628-0600
   1-800-237-0619

Binney & Smith Inc.
   1100 Church Lane
   P.O. Box 451
   Easton, PA 18044-0431

Dick Blick Art Material
   1-800-723-2787 (Customer Service)

      Dick Blick West
      P.O. Box 521
      Henderson, NV 89015
      702-451-7662

      Dick Blick Central
      P.O. Box 1267
      Galesburg, IL 61401
      309-343-6181

      Dick Blick East
      P.O. Box 26
      215-965-6051

AUDIOVISUAL MATERIALS

Weston Woods
   Sound Filmstrips and Video Tapes
   Weston, CT 06883-1199
   1-800-243 5020
   In Connecticut call collect 1-226-3355

CALLIGRAPHY SOCIETIES

U.S.A.

Chicago Calligraphy Collective
   P.O. Box 11333
   Chicago, IL 60610

Society of Scribes Ltd.
   Box 933
   New York, NY 10150

Portland Society for Calligraphy
   P.O. Box 4621
   Portland, OR 97208

Society for Calligraphy
   Box 64174
   Los Angeles, CA 90064

Canada

La Sócieté des Calligraphes
   P.O. Box 704 Snowdon
   Montreal, Quéebec H3X 3X8

INTERACTIVE LASER VIDEODISCS AND SOFTWARE

The Voyager Company
   1351 Pacific Coast Highway
   Santa Monica, CA 90401

MEDIEVAL & RENAISSANCE MATERIALS

Canton Enterprises, Ltd.
   P.O. Box 442
   Elmhurst, IL 60216

MUSEUM RESOURCES

Art Institute of Chicago
   S. Michigan and E. Adams
   Chicago, IL 60603

Metropolitan Museum of Art
   Fifth Ave and 82nd St.
   New York, NY 10028

Museum of Fine Arts
   465 Huntington Ave.
   Boston, MA 02115

National Gallery of Art
   Sixth Street and Constitution Ave. N.W.
   Washington, DC 20565

J. Paul Getty Museum
   17985 Pacific Coast Highway
   Malibu CA 90265
   Mailto P.O. Box 2112
   Santa Monica, CA 90406

APPENDIX

Picturebooks for Older Students

Agee, Jon. *The Incredible Painting of Felix Clousseau*. New York: Farrar, Straus & Giroux, 1988.

Anno, Mitsumasa. *Anno's Journey*. New York: World, 1979

Bang, Molly. *Dawn*. New York: Morrow, 1983.

Bang, Molly. *The Paper Crane*. New York: Morrow, 1985.

Baskin, Leonard. *Leonard Baskin's Miniature Natural History*. Saxonville, MA: Picture Book Studio, 1993.

Bauman, Kurt. *The Hungry One*. Translated by Naomi Lewis. Illustrated by Stasys Eidrigevicius. New York: North South, 1993.

Baylor, Byrd. *I'm in Charge of Celebrations*. Illustrated by Peter Parnall. New York: Scribner's, 1986.

Briggs, Raymond. *Father Christmas Goes on Holiday*. New York: Puffin, 1977.

Briggs, Raymond. *Fungus the Bogeyman*. New York: Puffin, 1977.

Briggs, Raymond. *When the Wind Blows*. New York: Schocken, 1982.

Browne, Anthony. *Gorilla*. New York: Franklin Watts, 1983.

Browne, Anthony. *The Tunnel*. New York: Knopf, 1989.

Bunting, Eve. *Fly Away Home*. Illustrated by Ron Himler. New York: Clarion, 1991.

Bunting, Eve. *Terrible Things: An Allegory of the Holocaust*. New York: Harper & Row, 1989.

Bunting, Eve. *The Wall*. Illustrated by Ron Himler. New York: Clarion, 1990.

Cendrars, Blaise. *Shadow*. Illustrated by Marcia Brown. New York: Scribner's, 1982.

Cherry, Lyn. *A River Ran Wild*. San Diego Harcourt Brace Jovanovich, 1992.

Coerr, Eleanor. *Sadako*. Illustrated by Ed Young. New York: Putnam, 1993.

Cole, Babette. *Prince Cinders*. New York: Putnam, 1987.

Cole, Babette. *Princess Smartypants*. New York: Putnam, 1986.

Coltman, Paul. *Tog the Ribber or Granney's Tale*. Illustrated by Gillian McClure. New York: Farrar, Straus & Giroux, 1985.

Coltman, Paul. *Witch Watch*. Illustrated by Gillian McClure. New York: Farrar, Straus & Giroux, 1989.

De Cervantes, Miguel. *Don Quixote and Sancho Panza*. Adapted by Margaret Hodges. Illustrated by Stephen Marchesi. New York: Scribner's, 1993.

Demi. *Chingis Khan*. New York: Henry Holt, 1991.

dePaola, Tomie. *Bonjour, Mr. Satie*. New York: Putnam, 1991.

Fisher, Leonard Everett. *Cyclops*. New York: Holiday House, 1991.

Fisher, Leonard Everett. *Jason and the Golden Fleece*. New York: Holiday House, 1990.

Fisher, Leonard Everett. *Theseus and the Minotaur*. New York: Holiday House, 1988.

Fox, Mem. *Guess What?* San Diego: Gulliver, 1990.

French, Fiona. *Anancy and Mr. Dry-Bone*. Boston: Little, Brown, 1991.

French, Fiona. *Snow White in New York*. New York: Oxford, 1986.

Gallaz, Christophe, & Innocenti, Roberto. *Rose Blanche*. Illustrated by Roberto Innocenti. Mankato, MN: Creative Education, 1985.

Gerrard, Roy. *Sir Cedric*. New York: Farrar, Straus & Giroux, 1984.

Goodall, John. *The Story of an English Village*. New York: Atheneum, 1979.

Grimm Bros. *Rapunzel*. Retold by Barbara Rogasky. Illustrated by Trina Schart Hyman. New York: Holiday House, 1982.

Grimm Bros. *Snow White*. Retold by Paul Heins. Illustrated by Trina Schart Hyman. Boston: Little, Brown, 1974.

Hastings, Selina. *Reynard the Fox*. Illustrated by Graham Percy. New York: Tambourine, 1990.

Heide, Florence Parry, & Gilliland, Judith Heide. *The Day of Ahmed's Secret*. Illustrated by Ted Lewin. New York: Lothrop, 1990.

Hodges, M. *The Golden Deer*. Illustrated by Daniel Sans Souci. New York: Charles Scribner's Sons, 1992.

Hodges, Margaret. *The Kitchen Knight*. Illustrated by Trina Schart Hyman. New York: Holiday House, 1990.

Hodges, Margaret. *Saint George and the Dragon*. Illustrated by Trina Schart Hyman. Boston: Little, Brown, 1984.

Hodges, Margaret. *St. Jerome and the Lion*. Illustrated by Barry Moser. New York: Orchard, 1991.

Hooks, William H. *The Ballad of Belle Dorcas*. Illustrated by Brian Pinkney. New York: Knopf, 1990.

Johnson, Tony. *The Cowboy and the Black Eyed Pea*. Illustrated by Warren Ludwig. New York: Putnam, 1992.

Joyce, William. *A Day with Wilbur Robinson*. New York: Harper & Row, 1990.

Kalman, Maira. *Chicken Soup, Boots*. New York: Viking, 1993.

Kalman, Maira. *Ooh-la-la (Max in Love)*. New York: Viking, 1991.

Kalman, Maira. *Roarr Calder's Circus*. Photographs by Donatella Brun. New York: Delacorte, 1991.

Kellogg, Steven. *Paul Bunyan*. New York: Morrow, 1984.

Kellogg, Steven. *Pecos Bill*. New York: Morrow, 1984.

Kesey, Ken. *Little Tricker the Squirrel Meets Big Double the Bear*. Illustrated by Barry Moser. New York: Viking, 1990.

Khalsa, Dayal K. *Cowboy Dreams*. New York: Clarkson N. Potter, 1990.

Lattimore, Deborah Nourse. *The Dragon's Robe*. New York: Harper & Row, 1990.

Lattimore, Deborah Nourse. *The Lady with the Ship on Her Head*. San Diego: Harcourt Brace Jovanovich, 1990.

Lattimore, Deborah Nourse. *The Flame of Peace: A Tale of the Aztecs*. New York: HarperCollins, 1987.

Lattimore, Deborah Nourse. *The Sailor Who Captured the Sea: The Story of the Book of Kells*. New York: HarperCollins, 1991.

Lattimore, Deborah Nourse. *Why There Is No Arguing in Heaven: A Mayan Myth*. New York: HarperCollins, 1989.

Le Guin, Ursula K. *A Ride on Red Mare's Back*. Illustrated by Julie Downing. New York: Orchard, 1992.

Lewis, Richard. *All of You Was Singing*. Illustrated by Ed Young. New York: Athenum, 1991.

Lyon, George Ella. *Dream Place*. Illustrated by Peter Catalanotto. New York: Orchard, 1993.

Macaulay, David. *Baaa*. Boston: Houghton Mifflin, 1985.

Macaulay, David. *Black and White*. Boston: Houghton Mifflin, 1990.

Macaulay, David. *Motel of the Mysteries*. Boston: Houghton Mifflin, 1980.

Maruki, Toshi. *Hiroshima No Pika*. New York: Lothrop, 1980.

Mayer, Marianna. *Iduna and the Magic Apples*. New York: Macmillan, 1988.

McKissack, Patricia C. *Mirandy and Brother Wind*. Illustrated by Jerry Pinkney. New York: Knopf, 1988.

Merrill, Jean. *The Girl Who Loved Caterpillars*. Illustrated by Floyd Cooper. New York: Philomel, 1992.

Mikolaycak, Charles. *Orpheus*. San Diego: Harcourt Brace Jovanovich, 1992.

Musgrove, Margaret. *Ashanti to Zulu: African Traditions*. Illustrated by Leo and Diane Dillon. New York: Dial, 1976.

Noyes, Alfred. *The Highwayman*. Illustrated by Charles Keeping. New York: Oxford University Press, 1981.

Noyes, Alfred. *The Highwayman*. Illustrated by Charles Mikolaycak. New York: Lothrop, 1983.

Nygren, Tord. *The Red Thread*. New York: R & S, 1987.

O'Neill, Catharine. *Mrs. Dunphy's Dog*. New York: Viking, 1987.

Oakley, Graham. *The Diary of a Church Mouse*. New York: Atheneum, 1987.

Paterson, Katherine. *The Tale of the Mandarin Ducks*. Illustrated by Leo and Diane Dillon. New York: Lodestar, 1990.

Perrault, Charles. *Puss in Boots*. Translated by M. Arthur. Illustrated by Fred Marcellino. Farrar, Straus & Giroux, 1990.

Perrault, Charles. *Snow White*. Photographs by Sarah Moon. Mankato MN: Creative Education, 1986

Pilkey, Dav. *Dogzilla*. San Diego: Harcourt Brace Jovanovich, 1993.

Price, Leontyne. *Aida*. Illustrated by Leo and Diane Dillon. San Diego: Harcourt Brace Jovanovich, 1990.

Rylant, Cynthia. *An Angel for Solomon Singer*. Illustrated by Peter Catalanotto. New York: Orchard, 1992.

Rylant, Cynthia. *The Dreamer*. Illustrated by Barry Moser. New York: Blue Sky, 1993.

Sandburg, Carl. *Arithmetic*. Illustrated by Ted Rand. Harcourt Brace Jovanovich, 1993.

Sans Souci, Robert. *The Samuri's Daughter*. Illustrated by Stephen T. Johnson. New York: Dial, 1992.

Say, Allen. *El Chino*. Boston: Houghton Mifflin, 1990.

Scieszka, Jon. *The Frog Prince Revisited*. Illustrated by Steve Johnson. New York: Viking, 1991.

Scieszka, Jon. *The Stinky Cheese Man and Other Fairly Stupid Tales*. Illustrated by Lane Smith. New York: Viking, 1992.

Scieszka, Jon. *The True Story of the Three Little Pigs*. Illustrated by Lane Smith. New York: Viking, 1989.

Service, Robert W. *The Cremation of Sam McGee*. Illustrated by Ted Harrison. New York: Greenwillow Books, 1987.

Shulevitz, Uri. *Toddlecreek Post Office*. New York: Farrar, Straus & Giroux, 1990.

Sis, Peter. *A Small Tale from the Far Far North*. New York: Knopf, 1993.

Snyder, Diane. *The Boy of the Three-Year Nap*. Illustrated by Allen Say. Boston: Houghton Mifflin, 1988.

Stafford, William. *The Animal That Drank Up Sound*. Illustrated by Debra Frasier. San Diego: Harcourt Brace Jovanovich, 1992.

Stanley, Diane, & Vennema, Peter. *Bard of Avon: The Story of William Shakespeare*. Illustrated by Diane Stanley. New York: William Morrow, 1993.

Stanley, Diane, & Vennema, Peter. *Charles Dickens: The Man Who Had Great Expectations*. Illustrated by Diane Stanley. New York: William Morrow, 1993.

Stanley, Diane. *Fortune*. New York: William Morrow, 1990.

Steptoe, John. *Mufaro's Beautiful Daughters*. New York: Lothrop, 1987.

Stolz, Mary. *Zekmet the Stone Carver*. Illustrated by Deborah Nourse Lattimore. San Diego: Harcourt Brace Jovanovich, 1988.

Swift, Jonathon. *Gulliver's Adventures in Lilliput*. Retold by Ann Keay Beneduce. Illustrated by Gennady Spirin. New York: Putnam, 1993.

Talbott, Hudson. *Your Pet Dinosaur*. New York: William Morrow, 1992.

Turner, Ann. *Dakota Dugout*. Illustrated by Ron Himler. New York: Macmillan, 1985.

Van Allsburg, Chris. *The Mysteries of Harris Burdick*. Boston: Houghton Mifflin, 1984.

Van Allsburg, Chris. *The Sweetest Fig*. Boston: Houghton Mifflin, 1993.

Walker, Alice. *To Hell with Dying*. Illustrated by Catherine Dexter. San Diego: Harcourt Brace Jovanovich, 1988.

Wiesner, David. *Tuesday*. New York: Clarion, 1991.

Wiesner, David. *June 29, 1999*. New York: Clarion, 1992.

Wild, Margaret. *Let the Celebrations Begin*. Illustrated by Julie Vivas. New York: Orchard, 1990.

Willard, Nancy. *Pish, Posh, Said Hieronymous Bosch*. San Diego: Harcourt Brace Jovanovich, 1991.

Willis, Jeanne. *Earthlets as Explained by Professor Xargle*. Illustrated by Tony Ross. New York: Dutton, 1989.

Wisniewski, David. *Sundiata Lion King of Mali*. New York: Clarion, 1992.

GLOSSARY

Acrylics   Pigments bound with synthetic resin (vinyl). They resemble oil paint, but they are faster drying. They can also be thinned with water to give the effect of transparent watercolor.

Airbrush   A mechanical instrument for applying paint to a surface. Airbrushes are most often used in commercial art. The implement, which looks like a large pen, holds a small amount of paint and is attached to a compressor. When this is activated, the paint is sprayed on the surface in very even, subtle tones.

Analogous Colors   See Color

Assemblage   The creation of a three-dimensional picture through the assembling of a variety of materials and found objects.

Balance   The unification of visual elements in a compostion. Symetrical balance results when very similar or identical elements are arranged on both sides of a picture. Asymetrical balance is achieved when different elements equalize each other in competing for visual attention in the composition.

Batik   An Indonesian method of resist printing on textiles, batik processes are also used in African art. The design is drawn on fabric with wax and then immersed in dye. When the fabric is boiled, the wax disappears and the color remains. The process is usually repeated with several colors.

Book Binding   The signatures of a book can be bound together in two ways. In saddle stitching, each signature is sewn through the middle with the pages open. In side stitching, it is sewn along the folded edge with the pages closed.

Brayer   A rubber roller used to apply ink in printing.

Carbon Pencil   See Crayons

Caron d'Ache   See Crayons

Charcoal   See Crayons

Collage   Pictures created with a variety of materials and textures.

Color   The property of reflecting light waves of a particular strength.

  Hue   Designates a color's basic identity and indicates its place on the color wheel or in the spectrum.

Intensity   Saturation or strength of color, determined by the amount of light reflected from it. Bright or vivid colors have high intensity; dull colors have low intensity.

Shade   The result of altering a hue (color) through the addition of black or the color's complement. This addition changes both the intensity of the color and its value.

Tint   The result of altering a hue (color) through the addition of white. This addition changes both the intensity of the color and its value.

Analogous Colors   Those close to each other on the color wheel.

Complementary Colors   Colors with maximum contrast—found opposite each other on the color wheel.

Monochromatic Color Scheme   Uses tints and shades of one color.

Complementary Colors   See Colors

Conte Crayon   See Crayons

Copyright Page   See Front Matter

Crayons and Other Drawing Materials

Carbon Pencil   Pencil made with lamp black or carbon instead of graphite. Available in a variety of hardnesses from hard to soft, it does not reflect light the way graphite pencils do.

Caron d'Ache   A brand name for drawing materials. The consistency of one type of their crayon is much like oil pastel but is soluble in water or turpentine.

Charcoal   A drawing material made from charred twigs.

Conté Crayon or Pencil   A brand name for an exceptionally hard crayon made of graphite and clay, it comes in stick or pencil form.

Crayon   The term is usually applied to any stick-like drawing material. Children's crayons are made from pigment and paraffin wax.

Oil Pastels   Oily base combines the features of crayons and pastel.

Pastel   Stick of color made from powdered pigment and bound with gum.

Crosshatching   The crisscrossing of lines to create shadows or model shapes.

Double-Page Spread   The two facing pages of a book.

Dummy   A three-dimensional model of the finished book.

Endpapers   (Also called end leaves, book linings, or fly leaves.) Sheets of paper glued to the inside front and back covers.

Engraving   The process of cutting into metal or wood.

Wood Engraving   Negative areas of a design are cut away from a block of hardwood sawed across the grain, leaving raised lines and shapes for inking.

Metal Engraving   A process by which a design is cut into a smooth metal plate, usually copper, with an engraving tool, and paper is pressed into the inked furrows.

Etching   A type of chemical engraving process which uses acid. In etching, a dark, acid-resistant waxy ground is applied to a plate, usually a metal such as copper. An etching needle is used to draw into the wax, exposing the metal plate. The plate is then immersed in an acid bath (the back is protected), and the acid eats into the exposed metal surface. After the ground is removed, the plate is inked, and the print is pulled.

Etching   See Engraving

Frisket   A device that protects part of the artwork while a painting or drawing medium is applied. Some friskets are made of paper and are attached to the surface of the artwork with rubber cement. This approach is generally used with airbrush techniques. Liquid frisket can be applied with a brush and is easily removed.

Front Matter   The preliminary pages necessary to identify the book. These consist of:

Half-Title   Usually on page 1 and contains the title only (not subtitle).

Title Page   Includes full title, names of author, illustrator, translator, and publisher. The title may appear on one or two pages. When it appears on one page, it is on the right hand side, and the left hand page can have a frontispiece or be left blank.

Copyright Page   Gives copyright notice, symbol, date, and name of copyright holder. It can also include the Library of Congress information, although some designers delete this for aesthetic purposes. Some publishers occasionally place copyright information at the end of the book.

Gesso   A white coating with a plastic base is applied as an undercoat to surfaces like masonite as a ground for painting in tempera or acrylic.

Gouache   [pronounced gwash] Watercolor paint made opaque by the addition of chalk. It is sometimes marketed as poster paint. It is fast drying and denser than transparent watercolor. Gouache has an effect similar to tempera.

Gutter   The space of inner margin where two pages meet at the binding.

Illumination   The hand decoration of books in color with pictures, designs, and/or ornamental letters. The illumination of manuscripts began with Egyptian papyri and continued through the 15th century. Once books began to be mass produced on printing presses, illumination declined, although some printed books continued to be hand decorated into the 16th century.

Impasto   Thick opaque paint applied with a knife or fingers.

Intensity   See Color

Jacket   (dust cover) Sheet of paper that wraps around the book and protects the cover. In a wraparound jacket, the front picture is continued on the back. The front flap usually describes the book's contents, and the back cover gives information about the author and illustrator.

Kneaded Rubber Eraser   Malleable, soft rubber eraser used to remove pastel or pencil without harming the paper. Can also be used to remove oil washes.

Line   A mark drawn, painted, or cut across a surface.

Masonite   A painting surface that is made from pressed wood fibers. It is smooth on one side and rough on the other.

Matte   Lacking luster or shine. Also a border around a picture.

Medium   1. The specific material or tool used by the artist. 2. A liquid that, when added to paint, makes it more fluid and easier to manipulate. Mediums like damar varnish are frequently used with oil paints.

Metal Engraving   See Engraving

Monochromatic Color Scheme   See Color

Monoprint   A one-time-only print made by painting on a piece of glass or metal. A sheet of paper is pressed to the surface and rubbed.

Motif   A dominant or repeated figure in a design.

Oil Paint   Pigments bound with oils and resins.

Oil Pastels   See Crayons

Opaque   Not transparent; not letting light (or paper) shine through.

Pastel   See Crayons

Perspective   A system of creating the illusion of three-dimensional space on a flat surface. Includes atmospheric perspective, which uses color and value to achieve effects. Linear perspective includes one point (one face is parallel to the picture plane), two point (objects are at an angle to the picture plane), and three point (bird's-eye view, looking down at a scene, and worm's-eye view, looking up at a scene).

Pigment   Finely ground colored powder, which forms paint. Originally pigments were ground from earth and vegetable matter, but now they are usually chemically made.

Plasticine   A modeling substance similar to clay that is nonhardening.

Relief   Any work in which important visual elements are raised above the background surface. The term is applied to sculpture and to print making.

Resist   Technique of temporarily masking a surface area so that it repels paint, dye, or ink. In crayon resist, a design is drawn on paper with a wax crayon and then painted. The areas of wax resist the paint.

Rhythm   The feeling of movement in a composition caused by repetition or accenting of elements.

Ruling Pen   A special drawing instrument that allows the artist to create lines of uniform width. The width of its two parallel blades can be controlled with a screw. The pen is then dipped in ink and used with straight edged ruler or some other drafting tool.

Shade   See Color

Shape   The space enclosed by a line or boundary. Shape can be defined by color value or texture as well as by line.

Signature   The pages of the book (usually 16 pages) are printed on a single sheet of paper and then are folded and cut. Most picture books consist of two signatures, or 32 pages.

Spine   The edge of the book that encloses the binding and where the front and back covers are joined. A strip of material is glued along the spine and the book is attached to its binding case or cover.

Stencil   (See Frisket) A pattern cut from durable paper, usually with a waxy coating that allows the repeated application of paint to a surface to create a decorative pattern or design.

Storyboard   The two-dimensional model of a book with all the pages laid out on one piece of paper. This is one of the first steps in book preparation.

Tempera   Paint made with egg yolk or egg white as a binder, mixed with water and pigment.

Texture   The actual or visual "feel" of surface areas. In picturebooks, texture is most often simulated.

Tint   See Color

Title Page   See Front Matter

Transparent   Refers to a type of watercolor where the paper can be seen through the color.

Unity   The harmonious synthesis of visual elements in a composition.

Value   The amount of lightness or darkness in a picture or color (darker colors are lower in value). Value relationships can create a feeling of three dimensionality or of flat patterned surfaces.

Variety   The introduction of elements which add vitality and introduce tension among the elements of a composition.

Vignette   A small decorative illustration.

Wash   Application of diluted watercolor or ink thinned with water (or oil thinned with turpentine). Watercolor washes can also show the texture of the paper as pigment collects unevenly in rough textured papers.

Watercolor   Transparent paint bound with gum arabic and mixed in use with water. Usually done on white paper, which reflects light through the paint and gives it a luminous appearance.

Watercolor Paper   Watercolor papers are available in different weights and surfaces. The weight of a ream of paper (500 sheets) determines the weight attached to a single sheet. 140-pound paper and heavier is preferred by most artists for transparent watercolor. Transparent watercolor used on cold pressed or rough papers results in lovely textural effects. Hot pressed paper has a smooth surface and is usually used for gouache and other water based paints when less texture is desired.

Wood Engraving   See Engraving

SOURCES

Mayer, R. (1991). *The Harper Collins dictionary of art terms and techniques*. New York: HarperCollins.

Ocvirk, O.; Bone, R.O.; Stinson, R.E.; & Wigg, P.R. (1991). *Art fundamentals: Theory and practice*. Dubuque, IA: William Brown.

Piper, D. (Ed.). (1981). *Random House library of painting and sculpture*. New York: Random House.

Shulevitz, Uri. (1985). *Writing with pictures: How to write and illustrate children's books*. New York: Watson-Guptill.

CHILDREN'S BOOK'S REFERENCES

Aardema, Verna. *Borreguita and The Coyote*. Illustrated by Petra Mathers. New York: Knopf, 1991.

Aardema, Verna. *Bringing the Rain to Kapiti Plain*. Illustrated by Beatriz Vidal. New York: Dial, 1981.

Aardema, Verna. *Why Mosquitoes Buzz in People's Ears*. Illustrated by Leo & Diane Dillon. New York: Dial, 1975.

Adkins, Jan. *Letterbox: The Art and History of Letters*. New York: Walker, 1980.

Agee, Jon. *The Incredible Painting of Felix Clousseau*. New York: Farrar, Straus & Giroux, 1988.

Albert, Burton. *Where Does the Trail Lead?* Illustrated by Brian Pinkney. New York: Simon & Schuster, 1991.

Alexander, Lloyd. *The Fortune-Tellers*. Illustrated by Trina Schart Hyman. New York: Dutton, 1992.

Aliki. *How a Book Is Made*. New York: Thomas Y. Crowell, 1986.

Aliki. *A Medieval Feast*. New York: Thomas Y. Crowell, 1993.

Andersen, Hans Christian. *The Nightingale*. Translated by Eve Le Gallienne. Illustrated by Nancy Ekholm Burkert. New York: Harper & Row, 1965.

Anno, Mitsumasa. *Anno's Alphabet*. New York: Thomas Y. Crowell, 1975.

Anno, Mitsumasa. *Anno's Britain*. New York: Philomel, 1982.

Anno, Mitsumasa. *Anno's Counting Book*. New York: Harper & Row, 1977.

Anno, Mitsumasa. *Anno's Journey*. New York: World, 1979.

Anno, Mitsumasa. *Anno's Medieval World*. Adapted from the translation by Ursula Synge. New York: Philomel, 1980.

Arnosky, Jim. *Deer at the Brook*. New York: Lothrop, 1986.

Aylesworth, Jim. *Country Crossing*. Illustrated by Ted Rand. New York: Atheneum, 1991.

Azarian, Mary. *A Farmer's Alphabet*. New York: David Godine, 1981.

Baker, Jeannie. *Where the Forest Meets the Sea*. New York: Greenwillow Books, 1987.

Bang, Molly. *Dawn*. New York: Morrow, 1983.

Bang, Molly. *The Grey Lady and the Strawberry Snatcher*. New York: Four Winds, 1980.

Bang, Molly. *The Paper Crane*. New York: Morrow, 1985.

Baron, Nancy. *Getting Started in Calligraphy*. Sterling, 1979.

Baskin, Leonard. *Leonard Baskin's Miniature Natural History*. Saxonville, MA: Picture Book Studio, 1993.

Bauman, Kurt. *The Hungry One*. Translated by Naomi Lewis. Illustrated by Stasys Eidrigevicius. New York: North South, 1993.

Baylor, Byrd. *I'm in Charge of Celebrations*. Illustrated by Peter Parnall. New York: Scribner's, 1986.

Baylor, Byrd. *Guess Who My Favorite Person Is?* Illustrated by Robert Andrew Parker. New York: Scribner's, 1992.

Baylor, Byrd. *Your Own Best Secret Place*. Illustrated by Peter Parnell. New York: Scribner's, 1979.

Berenstain, Stan and Janice. The Berenstain Bears series. Various publishers.

Bernhard, Durga. *Alphabeasts*. New York: Holiday House, 1993.

Blackhouse, J. *The Lidisfarne Gospels*. London: Phaidon Press Ltd. 1981.

Bostick, William A. *Calligraphy for Kids*. Franklin, MN: La Stampa Calligrafa, 1991.

Bowden, Joan Chase. *Why the Tides Ebb and Flow*. Illustrated by Marc Brown. Boston: Houghton Mifflin, 1979.

Brett, Jan. *Annie and the Wild Animals*. Boston: Houghton Mifflin, 1985.

Briggs, Raymond. *Father Christmas Goes on Holiday*. New York: Puffin, 1977.

Briggs, Raymond. *Fee Fi Fo Fum*. New York: Coward McCann, 1965.

Briggs, Raymond. *Fungus the Bogeyman*. New York: Puffin 1977.

Briggs, Raymond. *The Snowman*. New York: Random House, 1978.

Briggs, Raymond. *When the Wind Blows*. New York: Schocken, 1982.

Brown, Craig. *City Sounds*. New York: Greenwillow Books, 1992.

Brown, Margaret Wise. *Goodnight Moon*. Illustrated by Clement Hurd. New York: Harper, 1947.

Brown, Margaret Wise. *The Little Fireman*. Illustrated by Esphyr Slobodkina. New York: HarperCollins, 1993 (1938/1952)

Brown, P. *The Book of Kells*. New York: Thames & Hudson, 1980.

Brown, Ruth. *The Big Sneeze*. New York: Lothrop, 1985.

Browne, Anthony. *Changes*. New York: Knopf, 1983.

Browne, Anthony. *Gorilla*. New York: Franklin Watts, 1983.

Browne, Anthony. *The Tunnel*. New York: Knopf, 1989.

Bryan Ashley *I'm Going to Sing: Black American Spirituals, Volume 2*. New York: Atheneum, 1982.

Bryant, Sarah. *The Burning Rice Fields*. Illustrated by M. Funai. New York: Holt Rinehart, 1963.

Bulloch, Ivan & James, Diane. *The Letter Book*. Photographs by Toby Maudsley. New York: Simon & Schuster, 1990.

Bunting, Eve. *Fly Away Home*. Illustrated by Ron Himler. New York: Clarion, 1991.

Bunting, Eve. *The Man Who Could Call Down Owls*. Illustrated by Charles Mikolaycak. New York: Macmillan, 1984.

Bunting, Eve. *Terrible Things: An Allegory of the Holocaust*. New York: Harper & Row, 1989.

Bunting, Eve. *The Wall*. Illustrated by Ron Himler. New York: Clarion, 1990.

Burkert, Nancy Ekholm. *Valentine and Orson*. New York: Farrar, Straus & Giroux, 1989.

Burningham, John. *Come Away from the Water Shirley*. New York: Harper & Row, 1977.

Burningham, John. *Would You Rather*. New York: HarperCollins, 1993.

Carle, Eric. *The Grouchy Ladybug*. New York: Thomas Y. Crowell, 1977.

Carle, Eric. *The Very Hungry Caterpillar*. New York: Philomel, 1969.

Carrick, Carol. *Ben and the Porcupine*. Illustrated by Donald Carrick. New York: Clarion Books, 1981.

Carrick, Carol. *Whaling Days*. Illustrated by David Frampton. New York: Clarion, 1993.

Carter, Patricia. *Illuminated Calligraphy*. Turnbridge Wells, England: Search Press, 1991.

Carter, Patricia. *Illuminated Calligraphy, Borders and Letters*. Woodstock, NY: Arthur Schwartz, 1992.

Cassedy, Sylvia & Suetake, Kunihiro. *Red Dragon Fly on My Shoulder*. Illustrated by Molly Bang. New York: HarperCollins, 1992.

Cendrars, Blaise. *Shadow*. Illustrated by Marcia Brown. New York: Scribner's, 1982.

Chaffin, Lillie D. *We Be Warm Till Springtime Comes*. Illustrated by Lloyd Bloom. New York: Macmillan, 1980.

Chambers, Anne. *The Practical Guide to Marbling Paper*. New York: Thames & Hudson, 1986.

Chapman, Gillian, & Robson, Pam. *Making Books*. Brookfield, CT: Millbrook Press, 1992.

Chaucer, Geoffrey. *Canterbury Tales*. Selected and adapted by Barbara Cohen. Illustrated by Trina Shart Hyman. New York: Lothrop, 1988.

Cherry, Lyn. *A River Ran Wild*. San Diego: Harcourt Brace Jovanovich, 1992.

Christiana, David. *Drawer in a Drawer*. New York: Farrar, Straus & Giroux, 1990.

Clifton, Lucille. *All Us Come Cross the Water*. Illustrated by John Steptoe. New York: Holt, Rinehart & Winston, 1973.

Cobb, Vicki. *Vicki Cobb's Paper Making Book and Kit*. New York: HarperCollins, 1993.

Coerr, Eleanor. *Sadako*. Illustrated by Ed Young. New York: Putnam, 1993.

Cole, Allison. *Color*. New York: Dorling Kindersley, 1993.

Cole, Allison. *Perspective*. New York: Dorling Kindersley, 1993.

Cole, Babette. *Prince Cinders*. New York: Putnam, 1987.

Cole, Babette. *Princess Smartypants*. New York: Putnam, 1986.

Coltman, Paul. *Tog the Ribber or Granney's Tale*. Illustrated by Gillian McClure. New York: Farrar, Straus & Giroux, 1985.

Coltman, Paul. *Witch Watch*. Illustrated by Gillian McClure. New York: Farrar, Straus & Giroux, 1989.

Cooney, Barbara. *Hattie and the Wild Waves*. New York: Viking, 1990.

Cooney, Barbara. *Island Boy*. New York: Viking, 1988.

Cooney, Barbara. *Miss Rumphius*. New York: Viking, 1982.

Cooper, Susan. *The Selkie Girl*. Illustrated by Warwick Hutton. New York: McElderry, 1986.

Crews, Donald. *Flying*. New York: Greenwillow Books, 1986.

Crews, Donald. *Freight Train*. New York: Greenwillow Books, 1978.

Crews, Donald. *Harbor*. New York: Greenwillow Books, 1982.

Crews, Donald. *Light*. New York: Greenwillow Books, 1981.

Crews, Donald. *Rain*. New York: Greenwillow Books, 1978.

Crews, Donald. *Shortcut*. New York: Greenwillow Books, 1993.

Crews, Donald. *Truck*. New York: Greenwillow Books, 1980.

Curry, Ann. *The Book of Brendan*. New York: Holiday House, 1989.

de Angeli, Marguerite. *The Door in the Wall*. New York: Doubleday, 1949.

De Cervantes, Miguel. *Don Quixote and Sancho Panza*. Adapted by Margaret Hodges. Illustrated by Stephen Marchesi. New York: Scribner's, 1993.

dePaola, Tomie. *The Art Lesson*. New York: Putnam, 1989.

dePaola, Tomie. *Bonjour, Mr. Satie*. New York: Putnam, 1991.

dePaola, Tomie. *The Clown of God*. San Diego, CA: Harcourt, 1978.

dePaola, Tomie. *Fin M'Coul: The Giant of Knockmany Hill*. New York: Holiday House, 1981.

dePaola, Tomie. *Nana Upstairs, Nana Downstairs*. New York: Putnam, 1973.

dePaola, Tomie. *Now One Foot, Now the Other*. New York: Putnam, 1981.

dePaola, Tomie. *Strega Nona Meets Her Match*. New York: Putnam, 1993.

de Trevino, Elizabeth Borton. *I, Juan de Pareja*. New York: Farrar, Straus & Giroux, 1965.

Demi. *Chingis Khan*. New York: Henry Holt, 1991.

Demi. *The Empty Pot*. New York: Holt, Rinehart & Winston, 1990.

Dodds, Dayle Ann. *Wheel Away!* Illustrated by Thatcher Hurd. New York: HarperCollins, 1989.

Domanska, Janina. *Din Dan Don It's Christmas*. New York: Greenwillow Books, 1975.

Domanska, Janina. *I Saw a Ship a-Sailing*. New York: Macmillan, 1971.

Domanska, Janina. *If All the Seas Were One Sea*. New York: Macmillan, 1971.

Domanska, Janina. *What Do You See?* New York: Collier Macmillan, 1974.

Dorros, Arthur. *Abuela*. Illustrated by Elisa Kleven. New York: Dutton, 1991.

Dorros, Arthur. *Tonight Is Carnivale*. Illustrated by Club de Madres Virgin del Carmen. New York: Dutton, 1991.

Drescher, Henrik. *Simon's Book*. New York: Lothrop, Lee & Shepard, 1983.

Drogin, Marc. *Medieval Calligraphy: Its History and Technique*. New York: Dover Publications, 1980.

Duff, Maggie. *Rum, Pum, Pum*. New York: Macmillan, 1978.

Duffy, Dee Dee. *Barnyard Tracks*. Illustrated by Janet Marshall. Honesdale, PA: Boyds Mills, 1992.

Early, Margaret. *Sleeping Beauty*. New York: Harry Abrams, 1993.

Edwards, Margaret. *Alef-Bet: A Hebrew Alphabet*. New York: Lothrop, 1992.

Ehlert, Lois. *Color Zoo*. New York: Lippincott, 1990.

Ehlert, Lois. *Eating the Alphabet*. San Diego: Harcourt Brace Jovanovich, 1989.

Ehlert, Lois. *Feathers for Lunch*. San Diego: Harcourt Brace Jovanovich, 1990.

Ehlert, Lois. *Nuts to You*. San Diego: Harcourt Brace Jovanovich, 1993.

Ehlert, Lois. *Planting a Rainbow*. San Diego: Harcourt Brace Jovanovich, 1988.

Ehlert, Lois. *Red Leaf, Yellow Leaf*. San Diego: Harcourt Brace Jovanovich, 1992.

Ehlert, Lois. *Color Farm*. New York: Lippincott, 1990.

Falwell, Cathryn. *Shape Space*. New York: Clarion, 1992.

Falwell, Cathryn. *Clowning Around*. New York: Orchard, 1991.

Fennimore, Flora. *The Art of the Handmade Book*. Chicago: Chicago Review Press, 1992.

Fink, Joanne C. *Speedball Textbook, 22nd edition*. Philadelphia, PA: Hunt Manufacturers, 1991.

Fisher, Leonard Everett. *ABC Exhibit*. New York: Macmillan, 1991.

Fisher, Leonard Everett. *Alphabet Art: Thirteen ABC's from Around the World*. New York: Four Winds, 1978.

Fisher, Leonard Everett. *Cyclops*. New York: Holiday House, 1991.

Fisher, Leonard Everett. *Gutenberg*. New York: Macmillan, 1993.

Fisher, Leonard Everett. *Jason and the Golden Fleece*. New York: Holiday House, 1990.

Fisher, Leonard Everett. (1986) *Look Around: A Book About Shapes*. New York: Viking, 1986.

Fisher, Leonard Everett. *The Paper Makers*. New York: Godine, 1986.

Fisher, Leonard Everett. *Theseus and the Minotaur*. New York: Holiday House, 1988.

Fleming, Denise. *In a Small, Small Pond*. New York: Holt, 1993.

Fleming, Denise. *In the Tall, Tall Grass*. New York: Holt, 1991.

Fleming, Denise. *Papermaking Fun*. New York: Henry Holt, 1994.

Fox, Mem. *Guess What?* Illustrated by Vivienne Goodman. San Diego: Gulliver, 1990.

Frank, John. *Odds 'n' Ends Alvy*. Illustrated by G. Brian Karas. New York: Four Winds, 1993.

Frayling, Christopher, Frayling, Helen, & Van der Meer, Ron. *The Art Pack*. New York: Knopf, 1992.

Freedman, Russell. *Immigrant Kids*. New York: Dutton, 1980.

French, Fiona. *Anancy and Mr. Dry-Bone*. Boston: Little, Brown, 1991.

French, Fiona. *Snow White in New York*. New York: Oxford, 1986.

Fritz, Jean. *The Man Who Loved Books*. Illustrated by Trina Schart Hyman. New York: Putnam, 1981.

Froman, Robert. *Seeing Things: A Book of Poems*. Lettering by Ray Barber. New York: HarperCollins, 1974.

Galdone, Paul. *Hansel and Gretel*. New York: McGraw-Hill, 1976.

Galdone, Paul. *The Three Bears*. New York: Clarion, 1985.

Gallaz, Christophe, & Innocenti, Roberto. *Rose Blanche,* Illustrated by Roberto Innocenti. Mankato, MN: Creative Education, 1985.

Geisert, Arthur. *Oink Oink*. Boston: Houghton Mifflin, 1993.

Gerrard, Roy. *Sir Cedric*. New York: Farrar, Straus & Giroux, 1984.

Gerson, Mary-Joan. *Why the Sky Is Far Away*. Illustrated by Carla Golembe. Boston: Little, Brown, 1992.

Gerstein, Mordicai. *The Mountains of Tibet*. New York: Harper & Row, 1987.

Gobal, Paul. *Iktomi and the Boulder: A Plains Indian Story*. New York: Orchard, 1988.

Goble, Paul. *The Girl Who Loved Wild Horses*. New York: Bradbury, 1978.

Goble, Paul. *The Lost Children: The Boys Who Were Neglected*. New York: Bradbury, 1993.

Goodall, John. *The Story of an English Village*. New York: Atheneum, 1979.

Graham, David. *Color Calligraphy*. Turnbridge Wells, England: Search Press, 1991.

Green, Norma. *The Hole in the Dyke*. Illustrated by Eric Carle. New York: Thomas Y. Crowell, 1975.

Greenfeld, Howard. *Books: From Writer to Reader*. New York: Crown, 1976.

Greenfield, Eloise. *Africa Dreams*. Illustrated by Carole Byard. New York: John Day, 1977.

Greenfield, Eloise. *Grandpa's Face*. Illustrated by Floyd Cooper. New York: Philomel, 1988.

Greenfield, Eloise. *She Come Bringing Me That Little Baby Girl*. Illustrated by John Steptoe. New York: Lothrop Lee & Shepard, 1974.

Grifalconi, Ann. *Flyaway Girl*. Boston: Little, Brown, 1992.

Grifalconi, Ann. *The Village of Round and Square Houses*. Boston: Little, Brown, 1986.

Grillis, Peter. *The Calligraphy Book*. New York: Scholastic, 1990.

Grimm Bros. *The Bremen Town Musicians*. Illustrated by Donna Diamond. New York: Delacorte, 1981.

Grimm Bros. *The Bremen Town Musicians*. Illustrated by Ilse Plume. New York: Doubleday, 1980.

Grimm Bros. *The Bremen Town Musicians*. Translated by Elizabeth Shub. Illustrated by Janina Domanska. New York: Greenwillow Books, 1980.

Grimm Bros. *Cinderella*. Illustrated by Nonnie Hogrogian. New York: Greenwillow Books, 1981.

Grimm Bros. *Hansel and Gretel*. Translated by Elizabeth Crawford. Illustrated by Lisbeth Zwerger. New York: Morrow, 1979.

Grimm Bros. *Hansel and Gretel*. Illustrated by Anthony Browne. New York: Knopf, 1988.

Grimm Bros. *Hansel and Gretel*. Retold by Rika Lesser. Illustrated by Paul Zelinsky. New York: Dodd Mead, 1984.

Grimm Bros. *Little Red Riding Hood*. Retold and illustrated by Trina Schart Hyman. Holiday House, 1983.

Grimm Bros. *Rapunzel*. Retold by Barbara Rogasky. Illustrated by Trina Schart Hyman. New York: Holiday House, 1982.

Grimm Bros. *Rumplestiltskin*. Illustrated by Paul Zelinsky. New York: Dutton, 1986.

Grimm Bros. *Snow White*. Retold by Paul Heins. Illustrated by Trina Schart Hyman. Boston: Little, Brown, 1974.

Grimm Bros. *Snow White and the Seven Dwarfs*. Translated by R. Jarrell. Illustrated by Nancy Burkert. New York: Farrar, Straus & Giroux, 1972.

Grover, Max. *The Accidental Zucchini: An Unexpected Alphabet*. San Diego: Browndeer/Harcourt Brace, 1993.

Gwynne, Fred. *Pondlarker*. New York: Simon & Schuster, 1990.

Hackwell, John W. *Signs Letters Words, Archeology Discovers Writing*. New York: Scribner's, 1987.

Haley, Gail. *Jack Jouett's Ride*. New York: Vking, 1973

Haley, Gail. *A Story, a Story*. New York: Atheneum, 1970.

Hall, Donald. *Ox-Cart Man*. Illustrated by Barbara Cooney. New York: Viking, 1979.

Hastings, Selina. *Reynard the Fox*. Illustrated by Graham Percy. New York: Tambourine, 1990.

Hastings, Selena. *Sir Gawain and the Green Knight*. Illustrated by Juan Wijngaard. New York: Lothrop, 1981.

Hastings, Selena. *Sir Gawain and the Loathly Lady*. Illustrated by Juan Wijngaard. New York: Lothrop, 1985.

Heide, Florence Parry, & Gilliland, Judith Heide. *The Day of Ahmed's Secret*. Illustrated by Ted Lewin. New York: Lothrop, 1990.

Hendershot, Judith. *In Coal Country*. Illustrated by Thomas Allen. New York: Knopf, 1987.

Henkes, Kevin. *Julius, The Baby of the World*. New York: Greenwillow Books, 1991.

Hill, Donna. *Ms. Glee Was Waiting*. Illustrated by Diane Dawson. New York: Atheneum, 1978.

Hill, Eric. *Where's Spot?* New York: Putnam, 1980.

Hines, Anna Grossnickle. *Rumble Thumble Boom*. New York: Greenwillow Books, 1992.

Hoban, Tana *26 Letters and 99 Cents*. New York: Greenwillow Books, 1987.

Hoban, Tana. *A, B, See!* New York: Greenwillow Books, 1982.

Hoban, Tana. *Dots, Spots, Speckles, and Stripes*. New York: Greenwillow Books, 1987.

Hoban, Tana. *I Read Signs*. New York: Greenwillow Books, 1983.

Hoban, Tana. *Is It Red? Is It Yellow? Is It Blue?* New York: Greenwillow Books, 1978.

Hoban, Tana. *Is It Rough? Is It Smooth? Is It Shiny?* New York: Greenwillow Books, 1984.

Hoban, Tana. *Of Colors and Things*. New York: Greenwillow Books, 1989.

Hoban, Tana. *Shapes, Shapes, Shapes*. New York: Greenwillow Books, 1986.

Hodges, Margaret. *The Kitchen Knight*. Illustrated by Trina Schart Hyman. New York: Holiday House, 1990.

Hodges, Margaret. *The Golden Deer*. Illustrated by Daniel Sans Souci. New York: Scribner's, 1992.

Hodges, Margaret. *The Little Humpbacked Horse*. Illustrated by Chris Conover. New York: Farrar, Straus & Giroux, 1980.

Hodges, Margaret. *Saint George and the Dragon*. Illustrated by Trina Schart Hyman. Boston: Little, Brown, 1984.

Hodges, Margaret. *St. Jerome and the Lion*. Illustrated by Barry Moser. New York: Orchard, 1991.

Hodges, Margaret. *The Wave*. Illustrated by Blair Lent. Boston: Houghton Mifflin, 1964.

Hooks, William H. *The Ballad of Belle Dorcas*. Illustrated by Brian Pinkney. New York: Knopf, 1990.

Hopkins, Lee Bennett, Compiler. *My Mane Catches the Wind*. Illustrated by Sam Savitt. New York: Harcourt Brace Jovanovich, 1979.

Hunt, Jonathon. *Illuminations*. New York: Bradbury, 1989.

Hudson, Wade. *Pass It On: African American Poetry for Children*. Illustrated by Floyd Cooper. New York: Schlastic, 1993.

Hyman, Trina Schart. *Sleeping Beauty*. New York: Little, Brown, 1983.

Irvine, Joan. *How to Make Pop-Ups*. New York: Greenwillow Books, 1991.

Irvine, Joan. *How to Make Super Pop-ups*. New York: Greenwillow Books, 1993.

Jenkins, Jessica. *Thinking About Colors*. New York: Dutton, 1992.

Johnson, Paul. *A Book of One's Own*. Portsmouth, NH: Heinemann, 1991.

Johnson, Paul. *Literacy Through the Book Arts*. Portsmouth, NH: Heinemann, 1993.

Johnson, Tony. *The Cowboy and the Black Eyed Pea*. Illustrated by Warren Ludwig. New York: Putnam, 1992.

Jonas, Ann. *Aardvarks, Disembark!* New York: Greenwillow Books, 1990.

Jonas, Ann. *Color Dance*. New York: Greenwillow, 1989

Jonas, Ann. *Round Trip*. New York: Greenwillow Books, 1983.

Jonas, Ann. *The Trek*. New York: Greenwillow Books, 1985.

Jorgensen, Gail. *Crocodile Beat*. Illustrated by Patricia C. Mullins. New York: Bradbury, 1989.

Joyce, William. *A Day with Wilbur Robinson*. New York: Harper & Row, 1990.

Juenesse, Gallinard, & Pascale de Bourgoing. *Colors*. Illustrated by P. M. Valet and Sylvaine Perols. New York: Scholastic, 1993.

Kalman, Maira. *Chicken Soup, Boots*. New York: Viking, 1993.

Kalman, Maira. *Ooh-la-la (Max in Love)*. New York: Viking, 1991.

Kalman, Maira. *Roarr Calder's Circus*. Photographs by Donatella Brun. New York: Delacorte, 1991.

Keats, Ezra Jack. *A Letter to Amy*. New York: Harper, 1968.

Keats, Ezra Jack. *The Snowy Day*. New York: Viking, 1962.

Keeping, Charles. *Joseph's Yard*. New York: Oxford University Press, 1969.

Keeping, Charles. *Willie's Fire-Engine*. New York: Oxford University Press, 1980.

Kehoe, Michael. *A Book Takes Root: The Making of a Picture Book*. Minneapolis, MN: Carolrhoda, 1993.

Kellogg, Steven. *Paul Bunyan*. New York: Morrow, 1984.

Kellogg, Steven. *Pecos Bill*. New York: Morrow, 1984.

Kennedy, Richard. *Song of the Horse*. Illustrated by Marcia Sewall. New York: Dutton, 1981.

Kent, Jack. *The Fat Cat: A Danish Folktale*. New York: Parents Magazine Press, 1971.

Kesey, Ken. *Little Tricker the Squirrel Meets Big Double the Bear*. Illustrated by Barry Moser. New York: Viking, 1990.

Khalsa, Dayal K. *Cowboy Dreams*. New York: Clarkson N. Potter, 1990.

Kimmel, Eric. *Hershel and the Hanukkah Goblins*. Illustrated by Trina Schart Hyman. New York: Holiday House, 1989.

Kimmel, Margaret M. *Magic in the Mist*. Illustrated by Trina Schart Hyman. New York: Macmillan, 1975.

Kirstein, Lincoln. *Puss in Boots*. Illustrated by Alain Vaës. Boston: Little, Brown, 1992.

Kleven, Elisa. *The Lion and the Little Red Bird*. New York: Dutton, 1992.

Konigsburg, E.L. *From the Mixed-Up Files of Mrs. Basil E. Frankweiler*. New York: Atheneum, 1967.

Krasilovsky, Phyllis. *The Cow Who Fell in the Canal*. Illustrated by Peter Spier. New York: Doubleday, 1957.

Kumin, Maxine. *The Microscope*. Illustrated by Arnold Lobel. New York: Harper & Row, 1984.

Kuskin, Karla. *Roar and More*. New York: HarperCollins, 1990.

Larrick, Nancy. *Cats Are Cats*. Illustrated by Ed Young. New York: Philomel, 1988.

Lasker, Joe. *Merrily Ever After*. New York: Macmillan, 1976.

Lattimore, Deborah Nourse. *The Dragon's Robe*. New York: Harper, 1990.

Lattimore, Deborah Nourse. *The Flame of Peace: A Tale of the Aztecs*. New York: HarperCollins, 1987.

Lattimore, Deborah Nourse. *The Lady with the Ship on Her Head*. San Diego: Harcourt Brace Jovanovich, 1990.

Lattimore, Deborah Nourse. *The Prince and the Golden Axe: A Minoan Tale*. New York: HarperCollins, 1988.

Lattimore, Deborah Nourse. *Punga, Goddess of Ugly*. San Diego: Harcourt Brace Jovanovich, 1993.

Lattimore, Deborah Nourse. *The Sailor Who Captured the Sea: The Story of the Book of Kells*. New York: HarperCollins, 1991.

Lattimore, Deborah Nourse. *Why There Is No Arguing in Heaven: A Mayan Myth*. New York: HarperCollins, 1989.

Lattimore, Deborah Nourse. *The Winged Cat: A Tale of Ancient Egypt*. New York: HarperCollins, 1992.

Lawson, Julie. *The Dragon's Pearl*. Illustrated by Paul Morin. Boston: Houghton Mifflin, 1993.

Le Guin, Ursula K. *A Ride on Red Mare's Back*. Illustrated by Julie Downing. New York: Orchard, 1992.

Lear, Edward. *The Owl and the Pussycat*. Illustrated by Jan Brett. New York: Putnam, 1991.

Lessac, Frané. *My Little Island*. New York: Lippincott, 1984.

Levinson, Riki. *Watch the Stars Come Out*. Illustrated by Diane Goode. New York: Dutton, 1985.

Lewis, Richard. *All of You Was Singing*. Illustrated by Ed Young. New York: Athenum, 1991.

Lillie, Patricia. *When the Rooster Crowed*. Illustrated by Nancy Winslow Parker. New York: Greenwillow Books, 1991.

Lindbergh, Reeve. *Johnny Appleseed*. Illustrated by Kathy Jakobsen. Boston: Little, Brown, 1990.

Lionni, Leo. *Little Blue and Little Yellow*. New York: Astor, 1959.

Lionni, Leo. *Matthew's Dream*. New York: Knopf, 1991.

Livingston, Myra Cohn. *Sky Songs*. Illustrated by Leonard Everett Fisher. New York: Holiday, 1984.

Lobel, Anita. *Allison's Alphabet*. New York: Greenwillow Books, 1990.

Lobel, Arnold. *On Market Street*. Illustrated by Anita Lobel. New York: Greenwillow Books, 1981.

Locker, Thomas. *Where the River Begins*. New York: Dial, 1984.

Louie, Ai-Ling. *Yeh-Shen: A Cinderella Story From China*. Illustrated by Ed Young. New York: Philomel, 1982.

Lyon, Geroge Ella. *Dream Place*. Illustrated by Peter Catalanotto. New York: Orchard, 1993.

Lyons, Mary. *Stitching Stars: The Story Quilts of Harriet Powers*. New York: Scribners, 1993.

Macaulay, David. *Baaa*. Boston: Houghton Mifflin, 1985.

Macaulay, David. *Black and White*. Boston: Houghton Mifflin, 1990.

Macaulay, David. *Castle*. Boston: Houghton Mifflin, 1977.

Macaulay, David. *Cathedral: The Story of Its Construction*. Boston: Houghton Mifflin, 1973.

Macaulay, David. *Motel of the Mysteries*. Boston: Houghton Mifflin, 1980.

MacClintock, Dorcas. *Horses As I See Them*. Illustrated by Ugo Mochi. New York: Scribner's, 1980.

MacDonald, Suse. *Alphabatics*. New York: Bradbury, 1986.

MacDonald, Suse, & Oakes, Bill. *Once Upon Another*. New York: Dial, 1990.

MacGill-Callahan, Sheila. *The Children of Lir*. Illustrated by Gennady Spirin. New York: Dial, 1993.

Mahy, Margaret. *17 Kings and 43 Elephants*. Illustrated by Patricia MacCarthy. New York: Dial, 1987.

Manniche, Lise. *The Prince Who Knew His Fate*. New York: Philomel, 1981.

Martin, Ann M. *The Babysitter's Club*. New York: Scholastic, 1987.

Martin, Bill Jr., & Archambault, John. *Chicka Chicka Boom Boom*. Illustrated by Lois Ehlert. New York: Simon & Schuster, 1989.

Maruki, Toshi. *Hiroshima No Pika*. New York: Lothrop, 1980.

Matsutani, M. *The Crane Maiden*. Illustrated by C. Iwasaki. New York: Parents Magazine Press, 1968.

Mayer, Marianna. *Iduna and the Magic Apples*. New York: MacMillan, 1988.

Mayer, Mercer. *Everyone Knows What a Dragon Looks Like*. New York: Four Winds, 1976.

McKissack, Patricia C. *Mirandy and Brother Wind*. Illustrated by Jerry Pinkney. New York: Knopf, 1988.

McVitty, Walter. *Ali Baba and the Forty Thieves*. Illustrated by Margaret Early. New York: Harry Abrams, 1988.

Melmed, Laura Krauss. *The First Song Ever Sung*. Illustrated by Ed Young. New York: Lothrop, 1993.

Merrill, Jean. *The Girl Who Loved Caterpillars*. Illustrated by Floyd Cooper. New York: Philomel, 1992.

Micklethwait, Lucy. *I Spy: An Alphabet in Art*. New York: Greenwillow Books, 1992.

Mikolaycak, Charles. *Orpheus*. San Diego: Harcourt Brace Jovanovich, 1992.

Mills, Patricia. *Until the Cows Come Home*. New York: North South, 1993.

Most, Bernard. *The Cow That Went Oink*. San Diego: Harcourt Brace Jovanovich, 1990.

Musgrove, Margaret. *Ashanti to Zulu: African Traditions* Illustrated by Leo and Diane Dillon. New York: Dial, 1976.

Narahashi, Keiko. *I Have a Friend*. New York: McElderry, 1987.

Neumeier, Marty, & Glaser, Byron. *Action Alphabet*. New York: Greenwillow Books, 1985.

Noyes, Alfred. *The Highwayman*. Illustrated by Charles Keeping. New York: Oxford University Press, 1981.

Noyes, Alfred. *The Highwayman*. Illustrated by Charles Mikolaycak. New York: Lothrop, 1983.

Nygren, Tord. *The Red Thread*. New York: R&S, 1987.

O'Neill, Catharine. *Mrs. Dunphy's Dog*. New York: Viking, 1987.

Oakley, Graham. *The Diary of a Church Mouse*. New York: Atheneum, 1987.

Ormerod, Jan, & Lloyd, David. *The Frog Prince*. Illustrated by Jan Ormerod. New York: Lothrop, 1990.

Parker, Nancy Winslow & Wright, Joan Richards. *Frogs, Toads, Lizards, and Salamanders*. New York: Greenwillow Books, 1990.

Paterson, Katherine. *The Tale of the Mandarin Ducks*. Illustrated by Leo and Diane Dillon. New York: Lodestar, 1990.

Perrault, Charles. *Cinderella*. Illustrated by Marcia Brown. New York: Scribner's, 1954.

Perrault, Charles. *Little Red Riding Hood*. Photographs by Sarah Moon. Mankato, MN: Creative Education, 1986.

Perrault, Charles. *Puss in Boots*. Translated by M. Arthur. Illustrated by Fred Marcellino. New York: Farrar, Straus & Giroux, 1990.

Perrault, Charles. *Sleeping Beauty*. Illustrated by Trina Schart Hyman. Boston: Little, Brown, 1974.

Perrault, Charles. *Snow White*. Photographs by Sarah Moon. Mankato, MN: Creative Education, 1986.

Picard, Barbara Leonie. *One Is One*. New York: Holt, 1966.

Pilkey, Dav. *Dogzilla*. San Diego, CA: Harcourt Brace Jovanovich, 1993.

Pilkey, Dav. *When Cats Dream*. New York: Orchard, 1992.

Polacco, Patricia. *The Keeping Quilt*. New York: Simon & Schuster, 1988.

Polacco, Patricia. *Mrs. Katz and Tush*. New York: Bantam, 1992.

Polacco, Patricia. *Thunder Cake*. New York: Putnam, 1990.

Polushkin, Maria. *Mother, Mother, I Want Another*. Illustrated by Diane Dawson. New York: Crown, 1978.

Price, Leontyne. *Aida*. Illustrated by Leo and Diane Dillon. San Diego: Harcourt Brace Jovanovich, 1990.

Provensen, Alice, & Provensen, Martin. *A Peaceable Kingdom: the Shaker ABECEDARIUS*. New York: Viking, 1978.

Pyle, Howard. *King Stork*. Illustrated by Trina Schart Hyman. Boston: Little, Brown, 1986.

Ransome, Arthur. *The Fool of the World and the Flying Ship*. Illustrated by Uri Shulevitz. New York: Farrar, Strauss & Giroux, 1968.

Reid, Barbara. *Two by Two*. New York: Scholastic, 1993.

Ringold, Faith. *Tar Beach*. New York: Crown, 1991.

Robbins, Ruth. *Baboushka and the Three Kings*. Illustrated by Nicholas Sidjakov. Berkeley, CA: Parnassus Press, 1960.

Roehrig, Catharine. *Fun With Hieroglyphs* (boxed kit). New York: Viking/Metropolitan Museum of Art, 1990.

Roop, Peter, & Roop, Connie. *Ahyoka And the Talking Leaves*. Illustrated by Y. Miyake. New York: Lothrop, 1992.

Rosetti, Christina. *Color*. Illustrated by M. Teichman. New York: HarperCollins, 1992.

Rossini, Stephanie. *Egyptian Hieroglyphics: How to Read and Write Them*. New York: Dover, 1989.

Rubin, Cynthia. *ABC Americana*. New York: Greenwillow Books, 1981.

Russo Marisabina. *A Visit to Oma*. New York: Greenwillow Books, 1991.

Russo, Marisabina. *Waiting for Hannah*. New York: Greenwillow Books, 1989.

Rylant, Cynthia. *An Angel for Solomon Singer*. Illustrated by Peter Catalanotto. New York: Orchard, 1992.

Rylant, Cynthia. *The Dreamer*. Illustrated by Barry Moser. New York: Blue Sky, 1993.

Rylant, Cynthia. *The Relatives Came*. Illustrated by Stephen Gammell. New York: Bradbury, 1985.

Rylant, Cynthia. *When I Was Young in the Mountains*. Illustrated by Diane Goode, New York: Dutton, 1982.

Sandburg, Carl. *Arithmetic*. Illustrated by Ted Rand. San Diego: Harcourt Brace Jovanovich, 1993.

Sans Souci, Robert D. *Sukey and the Mermaid*. Illustrated by Brian Pinkney. New York: Four Winds, 1992

Sans Souci, Robert. *The Samuri's Daughter*. Illustrated by Stephen T. Johnson. New York: Dial, 1992.

Say, Allen. *El Chino*. Boston: Houghton Mifflin, 1990.

Say, Allen. *Grandfather's Journey*. Boston: Houghton Mifflin, 1993.

Schotter, Roni. *Captain Snap and the Children of Vinegar Lane*. Illustrated by Marcia Sewall. New York: Orchard, 1989.

Scieszka, Jon. *The Frog Prince Continued*. Illustrated by Steve Johnson. New York: Viking, 1991.

Scieszka, Jon. *The Stinky Cheese Man and Other Fairly Stupid Tales*. Illustrated by Lane Smith. New York: Viking, 1992.

Scieszka, Jon. *The True Story of the Three Little Pigs*. Illustrated by Lane Smith. New York: Viking, 1989.

Scott, Ann Herbert. *Cowboy Country*. Illustrated by Ted Lewin. New York: Clarion, 1993.

Scott, Sally. *The Magic Horse*. New York: Greenwillow Books, 1985.

Sendak, Maurice. *Outside Over There*. New York: Harper & Row, 1981.

Sendak, Maurice. *We Are All in the Dumps with Jack and Guy: Two Nursery Rhymes with Pictures*. New York: HarperCollins, 1993.

Serfozo, Mary. *Who Said Red*? Illustrated by Keiko Narahashi. New York: McElderry, 1988.

Service, Robert W. *The Cremation of Sam McGee*. Illustrated by Ted Harrison. New York: Greenwillow Books, 1987.

Sewall, Marcia. *The Pilgrims of Plimoth*. New York: Atheneum, 1986.

Shannon, George. *Climbing Kansas Mountains*. Illustrated by Thomas Allen. New York: Bradbury, 1993.

Shulevitz, Uri. *Dawn*. New York: Farrar, Straus & Giroux, 1974.

Shulevitz, Uri. *Oh What A Noise*. New York: Macmillan, 1971.

Shulevitz, Uri. *Rain Rain Rivers*. New York: Farrar, Straus & Giroux, 1969.

Shulevitz, Uri. *Toddlecreek Post Office*. New York: Farrar, Straus & Giroux, 1990.

Sis, Peter. *Komodo*. New York: Greenwillow Books, 1993.

Sis, Peter, *A Small Tale from the Far Far North*. New York: Knopf, 1993.

Sneve, Virgina Driving Hawk. *Dancing Teepees*. Illustrated by Stephen Gammell. New York: Holiday House, 1989.

Snyder, Diane. *The Boy of the Three-Year Nap*. Illustrated by Allen Say. Boston: Houghton Mifflin, 1988.

Spellman, Linda. *Castles, Codes, Calligraphy*. Santa Barbara, CA: Learning Works, 1984.

Stafford, William. *The Animal That Drank Up Sound*. Illustrated by Debra Frasier. San Diego: Harcourt Brace Jovanovich 1992.

Stanley, Diane. *Fortune*. New York: William Morrow, 1990.

Stanley, Diane & Vennema, Peter. *Bard of Avon: The Story of William Shakespeare*. Illustrated by Diane Stanley. New York: William Morrow, 1993.

Stanley, Diane, & Vennema, Peter. *Charles Dickens: The Man Who Had Great Expectations*. Illustrated by Diane Stanley. New York: William Morrow, 1993.

Stevenson, James. *Higher on the Door*. New York: Greenwillow Books, 1987.

Steptoe, John. *Daddy Is a Monster . . . Sometimes*. New York: J. B. Lippincott, 1980.

Steptoe, John. *Mufaro's Beautiful Daughters*. New York: Lothrop, 1987.

Steptoe, John. *Stevie*. New York: Harper, 1969.

Steptoe, John. *The Story of Jumping Mouse*. New York: Lothrop, Lee & Shepard, 1984.

Steptoe, John. *Train Ride*. New York: Harper & Row, 1971.

Stolz, Mary. *Pangur Ban*. New York: Harper, 1988.

Stolz, Mary. *Zekmet the Stone Carver*. Illustrated by Deborah Nourse Lattimore. San Diego: Harcourt Brace Jovanovich, 1988.

Sullivan, Charles. *Alphabet Animals*. New York: Rizzoli, 1991.

Sutcliff, Rosemary. *The Witch's Brat*. New York: Walck, 1970.

Swift, Jonathon. *Gulliver's Adventures in Lilliput*. Retold by Ann Keay Beneduce. Illustrated by Gennady Spirin. New York: Putnam, 1993.

Talbott, Hudson. *Your Pet Dinosaur*. New York: William Morrow, 1992.

Taylor, Harriet Peck. *Coyote Places the Stars*. New York: Bradbury, 1993.

Tejima, Keizaburo. *Swan Sky*. New York: Philomel, 1988.

Tiller, Ruth. *Cinnamon, Mint and Mothballs: A Visit to Grandmother's House*. Illustrated by Aki Sogabe. San Diego: Browndeer/Harcourt, 1993.

Tresselt, Alvin. *Hide and Seek Fog*. Illustrated by Roger Duvoisin. New York: Lothrop, 1965.

Turkel, Brinton. *Deep in the Forest*. New York: Dutton, 1976.

Turner, Ann. *Dakota Dugout*. Illustrated by Ron Himler. New York: Macmillan, 1985.

Van Allsburg, Chris. *The Garden of Abdul Gasazi*. Boston: Houghton Mifflin, 1980.

Van Allsburg, Chris. *Jumanji*. Boston: Houghton Mifflin, 1981.

Van Allsburg, Chris. *The Mysteries of Harris Burdick*. Boston: Houghton Mifflin, 1984.

Van Allsburg, Chris. *The Polar Express*. Boston: Houghton Mifflin, 1985.

Van Allsburg, Chris. *The Stranger*. Boston: Houghton Mifflin, 1986.

Van Allsburg, Chris. *The Sweetest Fig*. Boston: Houghton Mifflin, 1993.

Van Allsburg, Chris. *Two Bad Ants*. Boston: Houghton Mifflin, 1988.

Van Allsburg, Chris. *The Wreck of the Zephyr*. Boston: Houghton Mifflin, 1983.

Van Allsburg, Chris. *The Z was Zapped: A Play in Twenty-Six Acts*. Boston: Houghton Mifflin, 1987.

Van Laan, Nancy. *Buffalo Dance*. Illustrated by Beatriz Vidal. Boston: Little, Brown, 1993.

Van Ness, Tryntje. *The Gift of Changing Woman*. Illustrated by Apache Artists. New York: Holt, 1993

Vivas, Julie. *The Nativity*. San Diego, CA: Gulliver Books, 1986.

Waddell, Martin. *Farmer Duck*. Illustrated by Helen Oxenbury. Cambridge, MA: Candelwick, 1992.

Walker, Alice. *To Hell with Dying*. Illustrated by Catherine Dexter. San Diego: Harcourt Brace Jovanovich, 1988.

Walsh, Ellen S. *Mouse Paint*. San Diego: Harcourt Brace Jovanovich, 1988.

Walsh, Jill Paton. *The Green Book*. Illustrated by Lloyd Bloom. New York: Farrar, Straus & Giroux, 1982.

Wangerin, Walter, Jr. *The Book of the Dun Cow*. New York: HarperCollins, 1978.

Weiss, Harvey. *How to Make Your Own Books*. New York: Thomas Y. Crowell, 1974.

Wells, Ruth. *A to Zen: A Book of Japanese Culture*. Illustrated by Yoshi. Saxonville, MA: Picture Book Studio, 1992.

Westray, Kathleen. *A Color Sampler*. New York: Ticknor & Fields, 1993.

Whybrow, Ian. *Quacky Quack-Quack*! Illustrated by Russell Ayto. New York: Four Winds, 1991.

Wiesner, David. *June 29, 1999*. New York: Clarion, 1992.

Wiesner, David. *Tuesday*. New York: Clarion, 1991.

Wild, Margaret. *Let the Celebrations Begin*. Illustrated by Julie Vivas. New York: Orchard, 1990.

Willard, Nancy. *Pish, Posh, Said Hieronymous Bosch*. San Diego: Harcourt Brace Jovanovich, 1991.

Williams, Sue. *I Went Walking*. Illustrated by Julie Vivas. San Diego: Harcourt Brace Jovanovich, 1990.

Willis, Jeanne. *Earthlets as Explained by Professor Xargle*. Illustrated by Tony Ross. New York: Dutton, 1989.

Wilson, Diana Hardy. *The Encyclopedia of Calligraphy Techniques*. Philadelphia, PA: Running Press, 1990.

Wilson, Eva. *Celtic and Early Medieval Designs from Britain for Artists and Craftspeople*. New York: Dover Publications, 1987.

Wisniewski, David. *Sundiata Lion King of Mali*. New York: Clarion, 1992.

Wolff, Ashley. *A Year of Birds*. New York: Dodd, Mead, 1984.

Wood, Audrey. *The Napping House*. Illustrated by Don Wood. San Diego: Harcourt Brace Jovanovich, 1984.

Yagawa, Sumiko. *The Crane Wife*. Translated by Katherine Paterson. Illustrated by Suekichi Akaba. New York: William Morrow, 1981.

Yenawine, Phillip. *Colors*. New York: Delacorte, 1991.

Yenawine, Phillip *Lines*. New York: Delacorte, 1991.

Yenawine, Phillip *Shapes*. New York: Delacorte, 1991.

Yolen, Jane. *The Emperor and the Kite*. Illustrated by Ed Young. New York: Philomel, 1988.

Yolen, Jane. *Greyling*. Illustrated by David Ray. New York: Philomel, 1991.

Yolen, Jane. *Greyling*. Illustrated by William Stobbs. New York: World Publishing Co., 1968.

Yolen, Jane. *Owl Moon*. Illustrated by John Schoenherr. New York: Philomel, 1987.

Young, Caroline. *Calligraphy from Beginner to Expert*. Illustrated by Chris Lyon & Paul Sullivan. Calligraphy by Susan Hufton. Tulsa, OK: EDC Publishing, 1990.

Zacharias, Thomas & Zacharias, Wanda. *But Where Is the Green Parrot*? New York: Delacorte, 1968.

Ziner, Feenie. *Cricket Boy*. Illustrated by Ed Young. New York: Doubleday, 1977.

Zolotow, Charlotte. *Mr. Rabbit and the Lovely Present*. Illustrated by Maurice Sendak. New York: Harper & Row, 1962.

Zolotow, Charlotte. *Say It*. Illustrated by James Stevenson. New York: Greenwillow Books, 1980.

REFERENCES

Alderson, B. (1986). *Sing a song of sixpence: The English picture book tradition and Randolph Caldecott*. Cambridge England: Cambridge University Press.

Anderson, R. C., Reynolds, R. E., Schallert, D. L., & Goetz, T. E. (1977). Frameworks for comprehending discourse. *American Educational Research Journal, 14*, 367–381.

Applebee, A. N. (1978). *The child's concept of story*. Chicago: University of Chicago Press.

Aries, P. (1962). *Centuries of childhood: A social history of family life*. (R. Baldick, Trans.). New York: Knopf.

Association of Library Services to Children. (1991). *The Newbery and Caldecott Awards: A guide to medal and honor books*. Chicago: American Library Association.

Association for Library Service to Children. (1980). *Caldecott Award committee manual*. Chicago: American Library Association

Avrin, L. (1991). *Scribes, script and books: The book arts from antiquity to the Renaissance*. Chicago: American Library Association.

Bader, B. (1976). *American picturebooks: From Noah's ark to the beast within*. New York: Macmillan.

Bang, M. (1991). *Picture this: Perception and composition*. Boston, MA: Bullfinch Press.

Beach, R. (1993). *A teacher's introduction to reader response theories*. Urbana, IL: National Council of Teachers of English.

Benedict, S., & Carlisle L. (1992). *Beyond words: Picture books for older readers and writers*. Portsmouth, NH: Heinemann.

Bettleheim, B. (1975). *The uses of enchantment* New York: Random House.

Bland, D. (1958). *A history of book illustration: The illuminated manuscript and the printed book*. New York: World Publishing Co.

Bradley, D. H. (1991). John Steptoe: Retrospective of an imagemaker. *The New Advocate, 4*(1), 11–23.

Brandt, R. (1988). On discipline-based art education: A conversation with Elliott Eisner. *Educational Leadership, 45*(4), 6–9.

Butler, D. (1980). *Cushla and her books*. Boston MA: The Hornbook.

Caldwell, H. & Moore, B. H. (1991). The art of writing: Drawing as preparation for narrative writing in the primary grades. *Studies in Art Education, 32*(4), 207–219.

Calkins, L. (1994). *The Art of Teaching Writing*. Portsmouth, NH: Heinemann.

Campbell, J. (1986). *The masks of God: Primitive mythology*. New York: Viking Penguin.

Cazden, C. (1966). *Some implications of research on language development for preschool education*. Paper presented to Social Research Council Conference on Preschool Education. ED 011 329.

Cianciolo, P. J. (1990). *Picture books for children* (3rd. ed.). Chicago: American Library Association.

Cocking, R. R., and Sigel, I. E. (1979). The concept of decalage as it applies to representational thinking. In N. Smith & M. Franklin (Eds.), *Symbolic functionalism in childhood* (pp. 67–86). Hillsdale, NJ: Erlbaum.

Coles, P., Sigman, M., & Chessel, K. (1977). Scanning strategies of children and adults. In G. Butterworth (Ed.), *The child's representation of the world*. New York: Plenum Press.

Commire, A. (Ed.). (1990). *Something about the author*, V. 59. Detroit, MI: Gale Research Inc.

Considine, D. (1987). Visual literacy and the curriculum: More to it than meets the eye. *Language Arts, 64*, 634–640.

Cooney, B. (1988). Remarks made at a symposium, "Ways of Saying, Ways of Knowing: Art for all Ages." The New England Reading Association Annual Conference, Portland, ME.

Cummings, P. (1992). *Talking with artists*. New York: Bradbury.

Debes, J. L. (1970). The loom of visual literacy—An overview. In C. M. Williams & J. L. Debes (Eds.), *Proceedings of the First National Conference on Visual Literacy* (pp. 1–15). New York: Pitman.

dePaola, Tomie. *Panel discussion on visual literacy*. International Reading Association Annual Conference, San Antonio, TX, 1993.

Dyson, A. H. (1989). *Multiple worlds of child writers: Friends learning to write*. New York: Teachers College Press.

Fransecky, R. B., & Ferguson, R. (1973, April). New ways of seeing: The Milford visual communication project. *Audio-Visual Instruction*, 45.

Gambrell, L. & Sokolski, C. (1983). Picture potency, use Caldecott Award books to develop children's language. *The Reading Teacher, 36*(9), 868–871.

Gardner, H. (1982). *Art, mind, and brain: A cognitive approach to creativity*. New York: Basic Books.

Gardner, H. (1988). Towards more effective arts education. *Journal of Aesthetic Education, 22*(1), 157–167.

Gaur, A. (1992). *A history of writing*. New York: Cross River Press.

Genova, J. (1979). The significance of style. *Journal of Aesthetics and Art Criticism, 37*(3), 315–324.

Gerard, E. (1990). *Children's Literature Review*, V. 20. Detroit, MI: Gale Research Inc.

Golden, J. (1990). *The narrative symbol in children's literature: Explorations of the construction of text*. New York: Mouton de Gruyter.

Goldstone, B. P. (1989). Visual interpretation of children's books. *The Reading Teacher, 42*(8), 592–595.

Gombrich, E. H. (1982). *The image and the eye: Further studies in the psychology of pictorial representation*. Ithaca, NY: Cornell University Press.

Goodman, N. (1976). *The languages of art*. Indianapolis: Hackett Publications.

Graves, D. (1975). An examination of the writing processes of seven-year-old children. *Research in the Teaching of English, 9*, 227–241.

Greene, M. (1978). *Landscapes of learning*. New York: Teachers College Press.

Groff, P. (1973). The picturebook paradox. *PTA Magazine, 67*, 26–29.

Groff, P. (1974). Children's literature versus wordless books. *Top of the News, 30*, 294–303.

Hall, S. (1990). *Using picture story books to teach literary devices*. Phoenix, AZ: Oryx.

Halliday, M. A. K. (1975). *Learning how to mean: Explorations in the development of language*. London: Longman Group Ltd.

Hankla, S. (1982). Letter to the editor. *The Horn Book, 58*, 347.

Harker, J. O. (1988). Contrasting the content of two story reading lessons: A propositional analysis. In J. Green and J. Harker (Eds.), *Multiple perspective analysis of classroom discourse*. Norwood, NJ: Ablex.

Harthan, J. (1981). *The history of the illustrated book: The western tradition*. New York: Thames and Hudson.

Hearn, M. P. (1979). The ubiquitous Trina Schart Hyman. *American Artist, 43*, 36–43+.

Heath, S. B. (1983). *Ways with words: Language, life, and work in communities and classrooms.* Cambridge, England: Cambridge University Press.

Hellman, G. (1977). Symbol systems and artistic styles. *Journal of Aesthetics and Art Criticism, 35*(3), 279–292.

Hepler, S. & Hickman, J. (1982). "The book was okay. I love you: Social aspects of response to literature. *Theory Into Practice*, XXI, 278–283.

Hepler, Susan I. (1979). Profile: Tomie de Paola, a gift to children. *Language Arts, 56*(3), 296–301.

Hickman, J. (1979). *Responses to literature in the school environment: Grades K–5.* Unpublished doctoral dissertation, The Ohio State University, Columbus, OH.

Hickman, J. (1981). A new perspective on response to literature. *Research in the Teaching of English, 15*, 343–354.

Hochberg, J., & Brooks, V. (1962). Pictorial recogniton as an unlearned ability: A study of one child's performance. *American Journal of Psychology, 75*, 624–628.

Hubbard, R. (1989). *Authors of pictures, draughtsmen of words.* Portsmouth, NH: Heinemann.

Huck, C., Hepler, S., & Hickman, J. (1993). *Children's literature in the elementary school* (5th ed.). San Diego: Harcourt Brace Jovanovich.

Hughes, R. (1988, October 31). Evoking the spirit ancestors. *Time*, pp. 79–80.

Hyman, T. S. (1981). *Self portrait: Trina Schart Hyman.* Reading, MA: Addison-Wesley.

Hyman, T. S. (1984). *Panel discussion.* The Artist as Storyteller Symposium sponsored by the National Endowment for the Humanities, Chicago, IL.

Hyman, Trina Schart. (1993). Zen and the art of children's book illustration. In B. Hearne (Ed.), *The Zena Sutherland Lecture: 1983–1992* (pp. 183–205). New York: Clarion Books.

I am a painter, not yet an artist. (1969, 29 August). *Life, 67*(9), 53–59.

Iser, W. (1978). *The act of reading: A theory of aesthetic response.* Baltimore, MD: Johns Hopkins University Press.

Jahoda, G., Deregowski, J. B., Ampene, E., & Williams, N. (1977). Pictorial recognition as an unlearned ability: A replication with children from pictorially deprived environments.

In G. Butterworth (Ed.), *The child's representation of the world* (pp. 203–213). New York: Plenum Press.

Janson, H. W. (1991). *History of art.* Englewood Cliffs, NJ: Prentice-Hall.

Kaelin, E. F. (1989). *An aesthetics for art educators.* New York: Teachers College Press.

Kiefer, B. (1982). *The response of primary children to picture books.* Unpublished doctoral dissertation, The Ohio State University, Columbus, Ohio.

Kiefer, B. (1988). Picture books as contexts for literary, aesthetic and real world understandings. *Language Arts, 65*, 260–271.

Kiefer, B. (1993a). Children's responses to illustrations: A developmental perspective. In K. Holland (Ed.). *Journeying: Children responding to literature* (pp. 267–283). Portsmouth, NH: Heinemann.

Kiefer, B. (1993b). Visual criticism and children's literature. In B. Hearne & R. Sutton, (Eds.), *Evaluating children's books: A critical look: Aesthetic, social and political aspects of analyzing and using children's books* (pp. 73–91). Urbana, IL: Graduate School of Library and Information Services.

Kimmel, Eric. (1982). Children's literature without the children. *Children's Literature in Education, 13*(1), 38–43.

Kingman, L. (Ed.). (1965). *Newbery and Caldecott Medal books, 1956–1965.* Boston: Horn Book.

Kingman, L. (Ed.). (1975). *Newbery and Caldecott Medal books, 1966–1975.* Boston: Horn Book.

Koenke, K. (1987, May). Pictures in reading materials: What do we know about them? *The Reading Teacher*, 902–905.

Lacy, L. E. (1986). *Art and design in children's books: An analysis of Caldecott Award winning illustrations.* Chicago: American Library Association.

Landes, S. (1985). Picture books as literature. *Children's Literature Association Quarterly, 10*(2), 51–54.

Langer, S. K. (1942). *Philosophy in a new key.* Cambridge, MA.: Harvard University Press.

Langer, S. K. (1953). *Feeling and form.* New York: Scribner's.

Levin, J. (1981). On functions of pictures in prose. In F. Pirozzolo & M. Wittrock (Eds.), *Neuropsychological and cognitive processes in reading* (pp. 203–227). New York: Academic Press.

Mandler, J. M., & Robinson, C. A. (1978). Developmental changes in picture recognition. *Journal of Experimental Child Psychology, 26,* 122–136.

Manzo, A. & Legenza, A. (1975). A method of assessing the language stimulation value of pictures. *Language Arts, 52,* 1085–1089.

Marantz, K. (1977). The picturebook as art object: A call for balanced reviewing. *The Wilson Library Bulletin,* 148–151.

Martin, H. (1931). *Children's preferences in book illustrations.* Cleveland, OH: Western Reserve University Bulletin.

MacCann, D., & Richard, O. (1973). *The child's first books.* New York: H. W. Wilson.

Miller, B. M. (1957). *Caldecott Medal books: 1938–1957.* Boston: Horn Book.

Miller, W. A. (1936). The picture choices of primary grade children. *Elementary School Journal, 37,* 273–282.

Moebius, W. (1986). Introduction to picturebook codes. *Word & Image, 2*(2), 141–152.

Murphy, S. (1992). Visual learning strategies. *Book Links, 1,* 15–21.

Ninio, A., & Bruner, J. (1978). The achievement and antecedents of labelling. *Journal of Child Language, 51*(1), 1–15.

Nodelman, P. (1988). *Words about pictures: The narrative art of children's books.* Athens, GA: The University of Georgia Press.

Norton, D. (1991). *Through the eyes of a child: An introduction to children's literature* (3rd ed.). New York: Merrill/Macmillan.

Novitz, D. (1976). Conventions and the growth of pictorial style. *British Journal of Aesthetics, 16*(4), 324–337.

Ocvirk, O. C., Bone, R. O., Stinson, R. E, & Wigg, P. R. (1991). *Art fundamentals: Theory and practice* (6th ed.). Dubuque, IA: Brown & Benchmark.

Olmert, M. (1992). *The Smithsonian book of books.* Washington, DC: Smithsonian Institution.

Opie, I., & Opie, P. (1951). *The Oxford dictionary of nursery rhymes.* Oxford: Oxford University Press.

Peltola, B. J. (1988) Choosing the Caldecott Medal winners. *Journal of Youth Services to Libraries, 1*(2), 155.

Piper, D. (1981). *The Random House Library of Painting and Sculpture, Volume 1: Understanding art: Themes, techniques and methods.* New York: Random House.

Pitz, H. (1975). *Howard Pyle.* New York: Clarkson Potter.

Purves, A., & Beach, R. (1972). *Literature and the reader: Research in response to literature, reading interests, and the teaching of literature.* Urbana, IL: National Council of Teachers of English.

Purvis, J. R. (May 1973). Visual literacy: An emerging concept. *Educational Leadership, 50,* 714–716.

Rohwer, W. D. & Harris W. J. (1975). Media effects on prose learning in two populations of children. *Journal of Educational Psychology, 67,* 651–657.

Rosenblatt, L. (1976). *Literature as exploration* (3rd ed.). New York: Noble and Noble.

Rosenblatt, L. (1978). *The reader, the text and the poem: The transactional theory of the literary work.* Carbondale, IL: Southern Illinois University Press.

Rudisill, M. (1952). Children's preferences for color versus other qualities in illustrations. *Elementary School Journal, 52,* 444–451.

Sadler, G. (1992). *Teaching children's literature: Issues, pedagogy, resources.* New York: Modern Language Association of America.

Samuels, S. J. (1970). Effects of pictures on learning to read, comprehension and attitudes. *Review of Educational Research, 40,* 397–408.

Scarfe, L. (1975). *A history of children's books and juvenile graphic art.* New York: Visual Publications.

Schallert, D. L. (1980). The role of illustrations in reading comprehension. In R. Spiro, B. C. Bruce, & W. F. Brewer, (Eds.), *Theoretical issues in reading comprehension: Perspectives from cognitive psychology, linguistics, artficial intelligence, and education* (pp. 503–525). Hillsdale, NJ: Erlbaum.

Sendak, Maurice. (1993, July). Panel discussion on *We are all in the dumps with Jack and Guy.* New York.

Shulevitz, U. (1985). *Writing with pictures: How to write and illustrate children's books.* New York: Watson Guptill.

Sigel, I. (1978). The development of pictorial comprehension. In B. S. Randhawa & W. E. Coffman (Eds.), *Visual learning, thinking and communication* (pp. 93–111) New York: Academic Press.

Smerdon, G. (1976). Children's preferences in illustration. *Children's Literature in Education, 20,* 97–131.

Steptoe, J. (1988). Acceptance speech for The Boston Globe-Horn Book Award for Illustration for Illustration for *Mufaro's Beautiful Daughters*. *The Horn Book, LXIV*, 1, p. 25–28.

Storey, D. (1985). Reading comprehension, visual literacy and picture book illustrations. *Reading Horizons, 25*, 54–59.

Sulzby, E. (1985). Children's emergent reading of favorite storybooks: A developmental study. *Reading Research Quarterly, 20*, 458–481.

Teale, W. H. (1984). Reading to young children: Its significance for literacy development. In H. Goelman, A. A. Oberg, & F. Smith (Eds.), *Awakening to literacy* (pp. 110–121). Exeter, NH: Heinemann.

Tierny, R. J., & Cunningham, James W. (1984). Research on teaching reading comprehension. In D. Pearson (Ed.), *Handbook on reading research* (pp. 605–655). New York: Longman.

Ward, L. (1978). The book artist: Ideas and techniques. In L. Kingman (Ed.), *The illustrator's notebook* (pp. 80–83). Boston: The Horn Book.

Wells, G. (1986). *The meaning makers: Children learning language and using language to learn*. Portsmouth, NH: Heinemann.

Weiss, M. J. (1982). Children's preferences for format factors in books. *The Reading Teacher, 35*, 400–407.

Weitzman, K. (1947). *Illustrations in roll and codex*, Princeton, NJ: Princeton University Press.

White, D. E. (1983). Profile: Trina Schart Hyman. *Language Arts, 60*, 782–792.

Wolfflin, H. (1950). *Principles of art history*. (Translated by M. Hottinger). New York: Dorer Publications.

Yaden, D., Smolkin, L., & Conlon, A. (1989). Preschoolers' questions about pictures, print convention, and story text during reading aloud at home. *Reading Research Quarterly, XXIV*, 188–213.

INDEX